State and Local Government

2007–2008

Edited by Kevin B. Smith
University of Nebraska–Lincoln

CQ PRESS

A Division of Congressional Quarterly Inc., Washington, D.C.

CQ Press
1255 22nd Street, NW, Suite 400
Washington, DC 20037

Phone: 202-729-1900; toll-free, 1-866-4CQ-PRESS (1-866-427-7737)

Web: www.cqpress.com

Cover design by Auburn Associates, Inc., Baltimore, Maryland
Composition by Circle Graphics, Columbia, Maryland

∞ The paper used in this publication exceeds the requirements of the American National Standard for Information Sciences—Permanence of Paper for Printed Library Materials, ANSI Z39.48-1992.

Printed and bound in the United States of America

11   10   09   08   07   1   2   3   4   5

ISBN: 978-0-87289-471-6
ISSN: 0888-8590

Contents

Preface

This latest edition of *State and Local Government,* like the previous editions, seeks to provide an annual sounding on the health, direction, and performance of states and localities. And as in previous editions, if there is any central theme running throughout the readings, it is change. Perhaps the most obvious change at the state and local level since the previous volume is a shift in partisan fortunes, with Democrats scoring important electoral gains, especially at the state level. Yet the most important change has less to do with the party labels of the officeholders than it does with the content of the policies they are formulating and adopting. States and localities continue to innovate and adapt in their traditional arenas of responsibility: education, health and welfare, and criminal justice. More interesting are the innovations in nontraditional policy areas. States, for example, are forging independent energy policies; adopting regulations to combat global warming; and, along with their local counterparts, addressing such traditional federal government issues as illegal immigration. All these issues, traditional and not-so-traditional, are covered in the readings that follow.

Change, albeit of a more incremental variety, also characterizes the content of this latest volume. As in the past, the readings are all new to this edition, and they are organized by key institutions, processes, and policy areas. Most of the essays draw from the same trusted sources that will be familiar to long-term readers: *Governing, State Legislatures, State News,* and *Campaigns and Elections.* This year, however, there are also selections from the academic journal *Publius* and from the professional organization National Center for State Courts. The three articles tend to be somewhat longer than the readings traditionally included, but they offer a rich source for in-depth analyses and assessments of cutting-edge issues that hopefully broaden and deepen the coverage and perspectives we include in *State and Local Government.*

Regardless of the particular source, the readings continue to demonstrate not just the importance of states and localities to an astonishing variety of important issues, but also the importance of states and localities to the daily lives of citizens. Government at the subnational level continues to face vexing problems. Some of these challenges can be dealt with more easily and effectively than others. Yet the overall picture remains one of flexibility and adaptability—a continuing willingness to experiment that is a hallmark of the American federal system. As the

readings that follow amply demonstrate, state and local governments remain a vital and vibrant part of the political, social, and economic life of all citizens.

Thanks are owed to a number of people for making this volume possible. I am indebted to Charisse Kiino, Dwain Smith, Lorna Notsch, Allyson Rudolph, and the rest of the good folks at CQ Press for their editorial skill and hard work on this edition. A special thanks is also owed to Jana Hudakova, who served as my graduate assistant as this volume was being put together and provided invaluable assistance in helping me cast a wide net (as well as helping me sift through what we caught). We hope that you find what follows informative and thought-provoking.

Federalism and Intergovernmental Relations

Hurricane Katrina, the 2005 storm that devastated New Orleans and other Gulf Coast communities from Texas to Mississippi, provided a harsh lesson on how intergovernmental relations should *not* work. Specifically, effective responses to disasters, and effective public policies period, require local, state, and federal governments to coordinate and cooperate more and to snipe, bicker, and pass the buck less. All involved with Katrina agreed the daunting, multi-year task of reconstruction would benefit if such lessons were learned by all levels of government.

So ... two years later, how's it going?

Well, New Orleans mayor Ray Nagin has slammed the Bush administration for lacking the interest and political will to fully back reconstruction efforts and has hinted that race and class are behind the foot dragging. The Bush administration has slammed back, claiming it is doing its best under tough circumstances and hinting that Nagin should maybe pay a little more attention to putting his own glass house in order before commenting on the order, or lack thereof, in others' houses.[1]

Some have sympathy with Nagin's frustration. President George W. Bush didn't mention the post-Katrina challenge at all in his 2007 State of the Union address, for example, an omission that struck many as odd given previous promises to make reconstruction a central domestic policy focus. But it's not simply the feds dragging their feet that is hampering the reconstruction of New Orleans. Mayor Nagin won reelection in 2006 on promises to develop a 100-day plan to rebuild the city. The election has come and gone, but no plan has been issued from City Hall. The mayor has consistently called for the release of federal and state reconstruction funds, but has done less

1

to satisfy the accountability requirements needed to win that release. Nagin's shoot-from-the-hip commentary also has soured relations with people at other levels of government who might otherwise be predisposed to help. For example, he referred to the World Trade Center site—ground zero for the 9/11 terrorist attacks—as just a "hole in the ground." This raised hackles in New York and Washington, D.C., and sent Louisiana governor Kathleen Blanco rushing to issue a statement thanking New Yorkers for their generous contributions to the recovery efforts.

Blanco's administration also has found itself the target of criticism for incompetence, delay, and poor coordination in its efforts in the aftermath of Hurricane Katrina. The federal government is using the state as the mechanism to disburse millions in aid, and a number of critical recovery efforts have been bottlenecked at the state level by chronic understaffing, poor planning, and poor coordination with relevant federal and local agencies.[2]

It seems some lessons, even those learned the hard way, can be tough to make stick. The post-Katrina good intentions to improve intergovernmental relations that were expressed by pretty much everyone seemed genuine enough. That they dissolved into another round of difficulties among local, state, and federal governments shows just how tough it can be to make and implement effective public policies in a federal system. Perhaps the real wonder is not that federalism sometimes doesn't work well, but that it works at all. Certainly relations between state, federal, and, to a lesser extent, local governments are a history of give and take; the wax and wane of who gets the upper hand on particular public policies; and above all, conflict. In this sense, Hurricane Katrina and its aftermath is just a particularly painful chapter in a very long book.

What Hurricane Katrina and its aftermath have given us is not really a fundamental rethinking of how local, state, and federal governments work together; at least not yet. But they have given us a high-profile window into how the federal system actually operates, and as the readings in this section highlight, perhaps a sense of how it might change in the future. Right now, federalism in the United States seems to stand at something of an awkward juncture. In recent years New Federalism, the broad movement to devolve power from the federal government back to the states, gradually has lost steam,

mostly because states' rights and powers have dropped in the list of policy priorities pursued by the White House and Congress. In its place we have seen the rise of what has been termed ad hoc federalism, or the idea that the federal government supports or opposes state and local autonomy based on political and fiscal convenience, rather than on the basis of a core philosophy of governance. Generally speaking, the federal government has been taking a larger role in a wide variety of issue areas—everything from disaster response to insurance regulation to public education. As Katrina showed, however, this larger role has not always translated into effective—or even accountable—governance.

These days the states seem to be less interested in letting Washington set intergovernmental relations in whatever manner suits the feds best. A few years ago, the big news was the federal government muscling into policy areas that were traditionally the provinces of localities and states (education, with the No Child Left Behind law, being the big example). Today, we are seeing states increasingly willing to forge independent paths in policy areas that are traditionally seen as the federal government's policy turf. Examples of these issues include immigration, global warming, and the development of alternative fuels.[3] It's not clear where these cross-pressured policy trends—the federal government moving into state policy domains, states moving into federal government domains—are leading in terms the evolution of intergovernmental relations. Except for one thing: as always, there will be conflict and change.

NEW FEDERALISM BECOMES AD HOC FEDERALISM

Federalism is the central organizational characteristic of the American political system. In federal systems, national and regional governments share powers and are considered independent equals.[4] In other words, states are independent, sovereign governments. They must obey the mandates of the U.S. Constitution, but with that caveat, they are free to do as they wish. State governments primarily get their power from their own citizens in the form of their own state constitutions. At least in theory, they are not dependent on the federal government for power, nor do they have any obligation to obey federal requests that are not mandated by the Constitution.

In practice, the federal system established by the U.S. Constitution leaves the federal and state governments to figure out for themselves who does what, and who foots the bill for doing it.[5] The federal and state governments initially tried to keep to themselves, pursuing a doctrine of dual federalism, or the idea that federal and state governments have separate and distinct jurisdictions and responsibilities. Dual federalism was dead by World War II, however, a victim of the need to exert centralized economic and social power to fight two world wars and deal with the Great Depression.

These needs, and the general acknowledgement that state and federal governments share overlapping interests in a wide range of policy areas, gave rise to cooperative federalism. The core of cooperative federalism is the idea that both levels of government must work together to address social and economic problems. The basic division of labor that emerged under cooperative federalism was for the federal government to identify the problem, establish a basic outline of how to respond to the problem, and then turn over the responsibility of implementing the response to state and local governments—along with some or all of the money to fund the solutions.

Cooperative federalism defined and described the basic relationship between state governments and the federal government for much of the twentieth century. This arrangement, though, always had critics who feared that the transfer of money at the heart of the relationship allowed the federal government to assert primacy over the states. The basic argument was that by becoming a central source of money for programs run by the states, the federal government would become a living embodiment of the golden rule: he who has the gold gets to make the rules.

This concern turned out to have merit.. The federal government began putting strings on its grants to state and localities, requiring them to pass and enforce certain laws or meet certain requirements as a condition of receiving the money. States didn't like this much, but were faced with an uncomfortable choice. They could refuse to go along—as they were allowed to as sovereign governments—but then they lost the money. Things got really bad when the federal government began passing unfunded mandates in the 1970s and 1980s, essentially ordering the states to establish programs and policies while providing either a fraction of their cost or no financial support at all.

Cooperative federalism spawned a backlash that coalesced into a sustained political agenda termed New Federalism, which took as its explicit goals the reversal of the flow of power from the states to the federal government and the cutting of the federal government's fiscal responsibilities to the states. President Ronald Reagan openly embraced New Federalism in the 1980s, cutting and consolidating grant programs. President Bill Clinton, like Reagan a former governor, also supported key New Federalism initiatives in the 1990s. These included radically transforming welfare policy by turning over much of the responsibility to the states and supporting passage of the Unfunded Mandate Reform Act, which was designed to stop the federal government from passing obligations on to the states without funding them.

When George W. Bush became president in 2001, it seemed as if New Federalism was about to hit a threshold moment. Bush was also a former governor, and his conservative political philosophy seemed naturally sympathetic to the notion of pushing power down from the federal government and toward states and localities. Very early during his tenure as president, however, powerful forces aligned to slow, and even reverse, the trend of decentralization that had emerged during the previous two decades. A recession, the terrorist attacks of September 11, 2001, and drawn-out guerilla conflicts in Afghanistan and Iraq created pressures on the federal government to once again take the central role. Political scientists and historians have long noted that power tends to flow toward the states during times of peace and prosperity and back toward the federal government during times of war and economic stress (this is sometimes called the cyclical theory of federalism). The reason for power accumulating at the federal level during such times is simple: the federal government is simply better positioned to coordinate and implement responses to problems whose causes and consequences are beyond the borders of the states.

Yet the fading of New Federalism is not just a product of unforeseen national and international events. The Bush administration has pushed for federal primacy across a wide range of policy areas, many of which are considered the jurisdiction of state and local governments. Key domestic initiatives of the Bush administration have strengthened the federal government's hand at the expense of the states. The No Child Left Behind (NCLB) Act, for example, requires states and localities to set up expensive new programs that are not fully funded by the federal laws that require them.

NCLB is an example of the ad hoc nature of federal-state partnerships that has evolved under the Bush administration. Underlying cooperative federalism was a core philosophy of governance, a systematic notion of how federalism should work: the federal government will identify the problems, provide the resources (along with some constraints), and states and localities will actually address the problems. New Federalism had a different notion of how federalism should work, but one that was still relatively systematic: the federal government should allow the states to take more policymaking discretion and less money. Ad hoc federalism seems to lack any such consistency. In this vacuum of a guiding idea of what federalism is all about, states increasingly seem to be willing to impose their own ideas of good governance and good policy, even if these conflict with federal perspectives.

This chapter contains a series of essays that highlight state-federal relations as they seem to be approaching a shift of direction. It is too early to tell exactly what this direction will be, or how far down a particular path it will go. There does seem to be a general notion, though, that ad hoc federalism is not satisfactory from many perspectives and is ripe for change.

The first essay, by Valsin Marmillion, is an analysis of the breakdown in federal, state, and local relations that compounded the devastating effects of Hurricane Katrina and its aftermath. An underlying theme here is that failure by any one level of government can have disastrous consequences. The second essay, by William Pound, explores the central role of state governments in the federal system. Key to Pound's thesis is that states are forging their own policy paths, and making effective policies even in areas that normally would be thought of as the responsibility of the federal government. Pound also argues that when the federal government has faith in the states—when it actually follows through on its New Federalism intentions—the policy results can be pretty remarkable.

Carl Tubbesing and Vic Miller's article takes a look at the current state of fiscal relations between the states and the federal government. These relations, to put it mildly, continue to be contentious. The federal government has done little to curb its appetite for pressing unfunded mandates onto the states. Yet while such unfunded mandates have long been a point of contention, the federal government recently has formulated a new set of tools to impose federal priorities onto the states that robs the states of much of their ability to innovate.

The final article, by Richard Cole and John Kincaid, examines public opinion toward different levels of government and intergovernmental relations. Although public attitudes toward local, state, and federal governments have changed over the years, as have opinions on what their respective policy roles should be, Cole and Kincaid's research shows that citizens generally prefer governance done at the state and local level. The most important conclusion the authors draw is that public support for the federal government has been trending down, whereas support for localities and states has trended upward. This suggests that if the federal political system of the United States is responsive to its citizens, then whatever emerges to take the place of ad hoc federalism will include a bigger role for states and localities.

Notes

1. Mike Doring, "Obama Criticizes Pace of Katrina Rebuilding," *Chicago Tribune,* January 30, 2007. www.popmatters.com/pm/news/article/10641 /obama-criticizes-pace-of-katrina-reuilding.htm.

2. Jeffrey Meitrodt, "Understaffed and Overwhelmed," *New Orleans Times-Picayune,* January 28, 2007. www .nola.com/news/t-p/frontpage/index.ssf?/base/news-7 /1169970765301220.xml&coll = 1.

3. Kevin Smith, "Policy Challenges," in *State and Local Government, 2005–2006* (Washington, D.C.: CQ Press, 2006), 225–226.

4. Kevin B. Smith, Alan Greenblatt, and John Buntin, *Governing States and Localities* (Washington, D.C.: CQ Press, 2004), 26.

5. The U.S. Constitution does lay down a basic set of responsibilities for federal and state governments. See Lee Epstein and Thomas G. Walker, *Constitutional Law for a Changing America: Institutional Powers and Constraints,* 5th ed. (Washington, D.C.: CQ Press, 2004), 323.

1

Democracy Disaster

Valsin A. Marmillion

In the wake of a disaster like Hurricane Katrina, failure by one level of government leads to failure by other levels of government.

Americans like their headlines juicy. So the topics of representative democracy or federalism rarely make the cut for interesting news. While Katrina was the biggest story in years with an angle riveting for a political scientist or historian, it was all but untold in the context of federalism. In one event you had the agony and ecstasy, miracles and tragedies, political intrigue and suspicions, with life hanging in the balance—all in the glare of a world press picking through the debris. This was not your typical story about federalism.

At first, many people wanted to tell the story of Katrina as a tale of two cities, New Orleans and New York after 9/11, New Orleans and San Francisco after the great fire. But this is a tale of two contexts— personal and statistical—that demonstrates how clearly linked government and federalism are to life, death and survival in 21st century America.

Hidden under the rubble a year later is a sad tale of failure and collapse, not just of a city, but of our system of democratic federalism. FEMA, the federal agency empowered to act in a disaster, imploded, its future uncertain. The governor of a state asks the White House to "give us everything you've got," and the feds later say that the request lacked specificity. And the self-described "lone-wolf" mayor of New Orleans comes face-to-face with realities of governance that he never faced as a former business executive. One universal failure would rise above the rest: the collapse of cooperation and communication that could support E Pluribus Unum, one cooperative answer to a complicated disaster. USA TODAY laid out the riveting personal context in a Nov. 11, 2005 article by Jill Lawrence, *"Behind an iconic photo, one family's tale of grief."*

from *State Legislatures*
July/August 2006

It explored the mishaps and missteps that destroyed Lillian and Edgar Hollingsworth's lives.

> When she saw the picture in the newspaper, she couldn't speak. There was her front porch, bare of the hanging spider plants she had taken down for the storm. And there in the arms of a soldier lay her husband, emaciated and unconscious, hooked up to oxygen and fluids. It was 17 days after she had kissed him goodbye, 16 days after Hurricane Katrina made landfall, 15 days after the floodwaters rose to fill the bowl that is New Orleans. "I just held the paper and looked at it for a while. I was hoping they had rescued him."

The photograph Lillian refers to was taken by Bruce Chambers of *The Orange County* (Calif.) *Register.* It became a symbol of all that went terribly wrong in the wake of Katrina.

> Lillian and Edgar Hollingsworth lived a modest version of the American Dream. She was a secretary, and he worked at an A&P warehouse.... Like many city residents, the Hollingsworths did not drive much outside town.... On Sunday morning, Aug. 28, she went to the airport to get the [rental] van, only to be told there were no vehicles available. Families across New Orleans were scrambling to come up with plans. The Hollingsworths decided to take refuge with relatives who had second floors ... but Edgar refused to go.
>
> "I'll be just as safe here as I would at [son] Wesley's house," Edgar said. "The storm's not going to hit. It's going to go around, the way all the others did."

Unlike a large American corporation with thousands of well-trained managers to deploy in an emergency, Louisiana had only a small cadre of senior staff in the governor's office to manage the worst disaster in American history. Having just revised evacuation plans following a scare from Hurricane Ivan, the state reworked its population movement strategy, called "contra flow," and nervously waited news of hurricanes plowing the warm Gulf waters.

Louisiana officials had warned for years that the state was extremely vulnerable and it was only a matter of time before "the big one" would hit. In fact, just five days before Katrina landed, Governor Kathleen Blanco led an entourage of local, state and federal leaders on a tour from New Orleans to the most hurricane-prone regions of the state to build citizen unity for efforts to halt coastal erosion. The consequences for not acting were too dire to imagine—for Louisiana and the nation.

At the opening of hurricane season on June 1, 2005, the Save America's WETLAND campaign created a dramatization of flooding in New Orleans' French Quarter, hanging 18-foot sections of blue tarp from balconies to demonstrate what the streets would look like if flood waters rose to the height scientists predicted after a direct hurricane hit on the city. Kids in orange life preservers mimicked the way New Orleans could be lost if the federal government failed to protect the city. It was a prophetic display,

> [Lillian] told her neighbors across the street that Edgar was staying behind, but she made few other preparations. She didn't take any valuables with her. She packed a change of clothing and assumed she'd be back in a day or two. She gave her husband a kiss and left. At that moment the Hollingsworths joined a group that eventually numbered in the tens of thousand: families divided by Katrina.
>
> The next day the storm came and the water rose. Wesley, his mother and his girlfriend stayed dry in Wesley's second floor apartment, even as water lapped at the rooflines of single-story houses across the street. But they didn't feel safe. "We were just lucky for the time being. But we didn't know when our luck was going to run out," Wesley says.
>
> From the moment the storm ended, they started trying to make contact with Edgar. But they couldn't get back to the house and the phones were all out.
>
> Rescuers came by in boats and said they'd return, but they never did. On Thursday, a neighbor floated by on a flatboat and said he'd be back for them. He kept his promise. Late Thursday afternoon, the party arrived at a staging area at Interstate 10 and Causeway Boulevard. They expected to find buses ready to take them to shelter. Instead they found thousands of people and no buses. The Hollingsworths waited all night and through most of the next day in the heat and chaos. They finally boarded a bus so crowded that Lillian had to sit on the floor until a young woman offered her seat. They did not know where they were headed.

Katrina hit, and Americans viewed the unfolding saga. Every major news organization set up shop at hotels in New Orleans. The U.S. Geological Survey reported some appalling news. The protective chain of Chandelier Islands was ripped asunder. Louisiana had been losing approximately 24 square miles of land a year to erosion. But when Katrina hit, it lost nearly 200 square miles of land in two days.

Katrina Statistics

The story of Katrina was staggering statistically, as well as personally.

By November 2005:

- 467 Small Business Bridge Loan applications totaling $8.8 million were approved by Louisiana Economic Development.
- 519,469 households received more than $389 million in Disaster Food Stamp Benefits.
- 2,350 Louisiana Swift commuters had been transported—on free buses—to and from New Orleans for jobs, job searches and recovery efforts.
- 2,223 citizens displaced because of Hurricanes Katrina and Rita remained in shelters from the original 62,000.
- 129,349 people from the original 1.4 million who lost electricity remained without power.
- 4,900 mobile home trailers had been placed with Louisiana businesses for temporary employee housing.
- $292.7 million in unemployment and disaster assistance was distributed to displaced citizens from the Labor Department.

New Orleans and Lake Charles were hit hard, and smaller communities along the coast that were in the storm's eye, were completely destroyed.

The unthinkable had happened.

The Hollingsworths called the Red Cross to try to locate Edgar. They called an emergency number announced on the radio station. They called a number crawling along the TV screen. But they didn't hear back from anyone.

Volumes could be penned to explain what went wrong in the midst of this tragedy. The media pounced on the notion of "if" not "how" to rebuild one of America's unique major cities. Questions about governance in the wake of the two storms—who did what, when, how, by what authority—had few answers. And blame was directed everywhere. One thing was clear: The system had broken down at every level of government and the nation was ill prepared for natural disasters of this magnitude.

On Tuesday, Sept. 13, Captain Bruce Gaffney led a National Guard unit from San Diego through the

Hollingsworths' neighborhood. It reeked of mold and sewage. The wrought-iron security gate at the [Hollingsworths'] front door was locked, but the door was cracked open a few inches. Sergeant Jeremy Ridgeway spotted part of a leg and called to Lt. Frederick Fell, the platoon leader. "You could see his heart beating through his chest, he was so emaciated," says Peter Czuleger, 55, an emergency room doctor with the Orange County team. "One of the Guardsmen said, 'He looks like he has AIDS.' I said no, this is what someone looks like who has not had food or water for 10 days."

Louisiana called on civic leaders to help direct recovery efforts through new foundations and commissions. "Katrina fatigue" was highlighted in the national press. Hurricane survivors suffered from anxiety disorders. Layers of government were acting without some of the local and state elected officials having a say. There was a period when orders were coming from all levels of government and the democratic process took a back seat. The storms gave rise to a national dialogue about whether our system of federalism is effective. As they did to the roof of the Louisiana Superdome, the storms peeled back the veneer of a nation with festering problems. Federalism and democracy were in conflict as people scrambled to find fixes.

Lillian stared in shock at the picture of her husband on the front page of The [Baton Rouge] Advocate. They called the newspaper and got the California photographer's name and phone number. He told them where Edgar had been taken. They rented a car the next day, drove the 120 miles to New Orleans and sat with him for 20 minutes before he died.

People across the world gave generously to aid the victims of Katrina. National foundations and think tanks poured into Louisiana, offering expertise and advice about everything from urban planning to dietary needs of evacuees. Local and state officials were overwhelmed with the onslaught, just as they had been with the tragedy. Airports were filled with thousands of people, many clad with specially designed storm-related organizational logos. Animal rescuers mingled with mental heath providers, school teachers with EMTs. Criticism rang out that offers for help were not being processed, and that great ideas were not accepted. In reality, the vessel was not big enough to take it all in, to process highbrow ideas and the on-the-ground offers of help. At first, there was a sense that the federal government would broaden the capacity of state and local officials, but again, the rhetoric rarely matched the need, complexity and challenges of the events unfolding daily.

> "Everyone failed the people," Gaffney says. "The soldiers and the poor people had to bear the brunt of everybody else's failures."

Reality for Louisiana has changed. Without visitors, the New Orleans region loses an average of $15.2 million per day in direct tourism income. The Lake Charles region loses an average of $1.5 million per day. Before Katrina, 10.1 million visitors came to New Orleans in 2004 and spent $5.5 billion. More than 75,000 people were directly employed in the travel industry in the New Orleans metropolitan area in 2004. Louisiana lost more than $ 1 billion in direct tourism revenue by the end of 2005 because of Katrina's devastation.

> There's nowhere to walk near her apartment, in a desolate part of town. Lillian yearns for her grandsons. They've lived next door to her all their lives. Now they are in Dallas, where a bus took them after the storm. Her family pictures—her husband in better days, the baby pictures and school pictures of her son and his sons—are stained with water and mud.

Just one day before New Orleans would elect its mayor, the headlines rang out clearly that the impact of a natural disaster and the limitations of federalism continued to shake the systems of government and the lives of American citizens living in Louisiana.

2

Strong States, Strong Nation

William T. Pound

From *State Legislatures*, July/August 2006

State governments are forging their own policy paths, no longer waiting for the federal government to take the lead.

The premise of NCSL's 2006 Annual Meeting is that as the states are strong, so is the nation. This has never been so true as it is today.

Not all federal systems balance responsibility and power as we do in the United States—in fact, most do not. Although much tension and stress exist in the state-federal relationship, it remains vital after nearly 230 years. The states are more vigorous, innovative and important to the daily lives of Americans than at any previous time despite trends in various areas toward greater federal preemption of authority and mandating action. In recent years, most innovation in domestic policy has taken place at the state and local levels.

If we do not have strong states, many national programs would be ineffective, because states in many cases deliver them. Without strong and innovative states, the "laboratories of democracy" as described by Justice Louis Brandeis, would not be able to experiment and develop policy initiatives on a smaller and more manageable level. We would lose the freedom and diversity that characterize the United States. While regional differences are harder to find today, they do exist. One-size-fits-all should be a limited prescription for policymaking in this country.

Strong states create a strong nation and provide many outlets for pressure, tension and innovation within our governmental system. Legislators from other countries tell us they are often surprised by the vigor of our states and by the independent financial resources available to them. Even the European Union—with its emphasis on unity and melding nations—is seeing the desire for regional autonomy expressed in countries such as Italy, Germany and the United Kingdom.

In recent years, the states have led the country in many policy areas. Maine, Massachusetts and Vermont have created laws to make health insurance available and affordable to most of their citizens. Arkansas, Florida, Hawaii, Iowa, Montana, New Mexico, Oklahoma, Tennessee, Kentucky and West Virginia all have laws that seek to reduce the ranks of the uninsured. States started pharmaceutical assistance programs when there was no federal program. Now in the aftermath of Medicare Part D. they are still in the business, changing their programs to provide additional support or find ways to help more people.

Strong states create a strong nation and provide many outlets for pressure, tension and innovation within our governmental system.

States are tackling environmental challenges, on their own and in regional coalitions, setting tough standards to reduce greenhouse gas emissions and timelines to meet them. Maine's 2003 law aims to reduce greenhouse gas emissions to 1990 levels by 2010 and to 10 percent below 1990 levels by 2020. Connecticut, Maine, Massachusetts, New Jersey, New York, Oregon, Rhode Island, Vermont and Washington are following California's lead and will phase in tough emissions regulations that require automakers to reduce tailpipe gases by an average of 29 percent starting with the 2009 model year.

It's the states that are pushing green energy, establishing standards that require a certain percentage of power to come from renewable sources. Twenty-one states and the District of Columbia have some type of standard in place ranging from 1.1 percent in Arizona by 2012 to 25 percent in New York by 2013.

It is also state lawmakers who are pressing for effective ways to handle the millions of units of e-scrap we throw out each year. Legislation aimed at managing e-waste was introduced or considered in 25 states this session. Strong programs are being implemented in California, Maine and Maryland.

Lawmakers are embracing new technologies to better investigate crimes, identify criminals and protect the public. States are building and sharing DNA databases and deploying global positioning technology to keep track of people who might be dangerous to the community.

States are on the cutting edge of telecom policy, too. Texas passed the nation's first law to create a statewide video franchising system last year. It streamlined a system that was run by local governments and means telephone companies or other entities can quickly get into what used to be called the "cable TV" business. The new law gave consumers more choice and reportedly brought cable prices down by as much as 30 percent in some places. California, Indiana, Kansas, Michigan, New Jersey, Pennsylvania, South Carolina and Virginia are considering similar legislation. And so is the federal government.

Also making the rounds in Congress are bills based on state innovations for preventing identity theft—such as allowing citizens to put freezes on their credit reports and requiring companies to notify consumers of security breaches.

And these aren't the first time state innovations have made their way into federal law. The No Child Left Behind Act is built on 30 years of state experimentation. As early as 1980, states started measuring what students were actually learning. By the time the federal act was put in place in 2001, nearly every state had already developed its own method for gauging student achievement. Another example is the 1996 State Children's Health Insurance Program (SCHIP), which is based on work in Florida, New York and Pennsylvania. They were first in pushing health care coverage for poor, uninsured children.

Today, while Washington. D.C., lawmakers are gridlocked on immigration legislation, the states have taken matters into their own hands. State legislators introduced close to 500 immigration bills this session, and they passed 48 of them. Some bills sought to give unauthorized immigrants more rights and others aimed to crack down on people in the country illegally. They focus on access to in-state college tuition, voter registration procedures, human trafficking concerns, and access to public benefits and health care. Georgia's omnibus bill enters new territory by requiring public employers and subcontractors to participate in a work authorization program to ensure that new hires are in the country legally.

The nation's welfare program is stronger because of state-federal cooperation. The 1996 shift from an entitlement program to the current Temporary Assistance for Needy Families block grant system showed that the feds had faith in the states. This flexibility has made it one of the most successful state-federal partnerships.

States have also engaged in joint efforts to resolve common problems without federal action or interference. The Streamlined Sales Tax effort, which went into effect last October, is a prime example. Joint action by state legislators, executives and the private sector has created a voluntary collection system for sales taxes on electronic commerce. Thirteen states are currently full participating members of the Streamlined Collection Agreement with 28 additional states having taken initial action to join. Not only do the states collect revenues they are owed but had difficulty collecting, businesses also benefit from a greatly simplified system of tax administration.

Coordination of state emergency management efforts has come about through an interstate compact involving all 50 states, Puerto Rico, the Virgin Islands and the District of Columbia. The multi-state response to hurricanes Katrina and Rita was facilitated by this voluntary state coordination effort.

For the states to remain strong they need to be unified to resist the increasing tendency by the federal government to preempt or mandate state action to carry out national programs and reach national goals, both for political and practical reasons. The growing trend to do this poses a great threat to state authority. The states often have superior administrative systems, and the national government lacks the means or the will to finance its own programs. Implementation of the Real ID Act over the next few years provides a real challenge to cooperative federal-state action. The federal government has chosen to utilize a licensing system developed and managed by the states to achieve a national goal—an authenticated identification card. There will be significant record checking and retention requirements on the states. The cost of this system will be considerable and—as of now—largely borne by the states.

Additional challenges to state legislatures include the increasing use of direct democracy—the initiative process—to make state policy often with inconsistent or contradictory results. State revenue systems will also be challenged to provide the resources to meet demands to respond to the problems of a more complex, populous and diverse America. Health care and education—both financing and quality—are prime examples of such challenges.

If America is to remain strong, then it is vital this experimentation continues. In the same spirit that caused state legislators to create NCSL, we continue to lobby Congress and the administration to let the voice of states be heard. We firmly believe that the spirit of America resides with the states and that the future of our country depends on states' ability to lead the discussion on public policy issues.

3

Our Fractured Fiscal System

Carl Tubbesing and Vic Miller

The federal government is still interested in getting the states to implement its policy priorities. It just is less interested in paying for them.

B one stress fractures are unbearably painful. Ask any basketball player who has tried to play with one. Stress on a weakened bridge truss is dangerous. Ask any civil engineer who has done the computer modeling. And the stress that has built up in fiscal relations between the states and federal government is painful to the states and dangerous to the long-term health of the federal system. Ask any appropriations chair trying to balance a state's budget.

For two decades, unfunded federal mandates have symbolized the growing fracture in state-federal fiscal relations. Most legislators can readily name the current offenders—the Individuals with Disabilities Education Act, No Child Left Behind, the Help America Vote Act and homeland security. And they are girding for the possibility of the next huge one, the Real ID act. The National Conference of State Legislatures estimates that the federal government has shifted $100 billion in costs to states over the past four fiscal years—not including the $11 billion that Real ID could cost states over the next five years.

Those numbers are staggering, but they barely begin to describe the range and magnitude of fiscal stress that has come to characterize the country's federal system. To get a sharper picture, we need to enter the green eyeshade world of grants-in-aid, block grants, categorical grants, entitlements, clawbacks and trust funds. We need to explore the fundamental effects that changes in this seemingly arcane world have on the role of the states in the federal system. Let's start with a *Cliff's Notes* history of 200 years worth of state-federal fiscal relations.

For most of the country's first 200 years, the federal government was fiscally weak. It didn't tax much, except in wartime, financed itself through customs revenues and land sales, and shared

From *State Legislatures,*
April 2007

little, if any, of the few revenues it mustered with the states. This changed with the Great Depression of the 1930s. The national government used the income tax and deficit spending to stimulate the economy and fund the New Deal. Much of the program was administered by the states, funded by money supplied by the national government. By the end of World War II, the federal government, which had been in a fiscal slumber for almost two centuries, suddenly was dominant. In 1948, its revenues tripled those of all state and local governments combined. This dominance eased through the 1950s and 1960s. During the 1970s, 1980s and 1990s, federal revenues were approximately double those of state and local governments.

The national government's fiscal problem today: It is spending more than it is taking in. Federal revenues and spending as percentages of gross domestic product—in other words, as shares of the economy—illustrate this. The decade began with federal revenues peaking at about 21 percent of the economy, but they currently are in the 16 percent to 18 percent range. By contrast, in the same period, federal spending has grown from 18 percent to 20 percent of the economy. David Walker, the comptroller general of the United States, the Concord Coalition and other groups are conducting forums throughout the country to raise the alarm about the short- and long-term effects of this federal deficit. It is a very grim picture. (For more, go to www.concordcoalition .org/events/fiscal-wake-up/index.html.) The effect of recent federal revenue and spending practices has constituted a radical alteration in fiscal relations among the national government and the states. These practices fall into three categories. Federal grants-in-aid to states have become more restrictive and specific. The national government is making increasingly greater use of state money. And, the incidence and amount of unfunded federal mandates have increased exponentially. Together, the changes mean that federal grants to states now direct state spending rather than support it and that the national government now uses state and local government revenues for its purposes rather than providing grants to support theirs.

FROM NO STRINGS TO STRINGS

The federal government makes money available to state and local governments through different kinds of grants-in-aid. Grants vary greatly, but they share the objective of making a service available to the public—building a highway, providing vaccines, offering job training, teaching disabled students, and so on. They can be arranged along a continuum. At one end of the continuum are federal funds that have come to states with few, if any, strings attached. At the other end are those that come with very specific requirements on state governments' use of the money.

At the "no strings" end are general purpose grants. Epitomized by President Richard Nixon's general revenue sharing program of the 1970s, general purpose grants come with few, if any, limitations on how they are to be spent. They have been used primarily to stimulate the economy and to ensure that state governments—especially those with weak economies—can provide services during economic downturns. Because state governments must balance their budgets, their response to a weak economy—cutting services and raising taxes—has the effect of prolonging or deepening a downturn. Unimpeded by a balanced budget requirement, the federal government uses general purpose grants to help states and the country pull out of the downturn. The most recent example came in fiscal years 2003 and 2004 when state legislators, working with a bi-partisan group of five U.S. senators, secured $20 billion to ease states through the recession in the early part of this decade.

Next to general purpose grants on the continuum are block grants. Block grants are targeted to a service or a range of services—welfare or maternal and child health, for example—and, in theory at least, provide states considerable flexibility in how to spend the money. Moving further along, are two kinds of categorical grants, both of which come with plenty of strings. They differ in how the funds are distributed. Formula categorical grants, such as Low Income Home Energy Assistance, are distributed among the states by formula. Discretionary categorical grants earmark money for a specific purpose or give a federal agency broad latitude in allocating the funds.

The continuum ends with two kinds of grants that require state governments to spend money in order to access the federal money: entitlement programs, such as Medicaid, and transportation trust fund grants, such as the highway fund. They require states to match the federal money or maintain a certain level of fiscal effort—or both.

The four-decade history of grants-in-aid indicates a clear movement from no strings to lots of strings. With the exception of the 2003 fiscal relief funds, general purpose grants have mostly disappeared. Last year's renewal of the welfare (TANF) law shows how vulnerable block grants are to being encumbered by federal conditions—how easily flexibility turns to rigidity. And, driven largely by growth in the Medicaid program, legislatures find themselves using more and more state money to support federal entitlement spending.

WHAT'S WRONG WITH THIS PICTURE?

Medicare Part D, the new Medicare prescription drug benefit that took effect January 2006, achieved considerable notoriety among consumers, pharmacists, and drug and insurance companies. It managed another kind of notoriety for how it was financed—by forcing a contribution from the states that can only be described as a direct federal tax on state governments—single-handedly establishing a new category at the end of our continuum.

As Congress and the administration negotiated over a Medicare prescription drug benefit during 2003, several things became clear. One, the benefit would be very, very expensive. Two, there would be no "normal" tax increases to finance it. And, three, the negotiators would have to be very creative to find other ways to pay for it. One of the latter is the "clawback"—a monthly payment from the states to the federal government that initially funded about 20 percent of the benefit—in other words, a tax on state governments. Over the first five years of Part D coverage, it is estimated that states will have to pay almost $50 billion to the federal government from their general funds, the largest single flow of funds from states to the federal government in support of a totally federal program.

Congressional transportation earmarks are another way the federal government mandates state priorities. The lat-est surface transportation law—SAFETEA-LU—contains $22.1 billion in earmarked highway projects and another $2.1 billion in earmarked mass transit projects. These earmarks come from the dwindling highway trust fund. They substitute federal government priorities for those of state legislatures and transportation departments.

THE CONSEQUENCES

Substituting federal priorities for state priorities is not new. That is, after all, what federal unfunded mandates do. With No Child Left Behind, the federal government imposed numerous testing, reporting and intervention requirements while paying only a fraction of their costs. The Help America Vote Act told states how to run elections, then left them holding a $725 million bag. The Individuals with Disabilities Education Act, the longest-running federal unfunded mandate, promised that the federal government would pay the excess cost of educating a special education student. But the best it's ever done was about half of what was promised. And, unless Congress soon has a collective epiphany of conscience, state legislatures will have to find at least $11 billion to fund Real ID, the federal vision of a secure driver's license system.

What is relatively new is the federal government's use of other tools that cause states to spend money. The potential effect of all of this—the unfunded mandates, underfunding, clawbacks, earmarks and their fiscal cousins—is to sap states of their vitality. State innovation—one of the great strengths of the country's federal system—doesn't always require money. But the more the federal government commandeers state revenues for its purposes, the less there is for state legislatures to pursue their own priorities and to be responsive to the unique cultures and demands of their constituents.

Public Opinion on U.S. Federal and Intergovernmental Issues in 2006: Continuity and Change

4

Richard L. Cole and John Kincaid

Attitudes about and toward government change over the years. Yet citizens consistently feel more comfortable with, and more trusting of, state and local governments.

A 2006 trend survey found that Americans most often select local government as giving them the most for their money, followed by the federal and state governments. African Americans are most supportive of the federal government as giving them the most for their money; Hispanics are most supportive of local government. As in many previous years, the local property tax was viewed as the worst tax, followed by the federal income tax, state sales tax, and state income tax. Americans displayed reduced trust and confidence in the federal government; however, trust in all three spheres of government—federal, state, and local—dropped between 2004 and 2006, possibly reflective of the poor response of all governments to Hurricane Katrina. Analysis of surveys since 1972 reveals that there has been a long-term decline in the public's support for the federal government and a corresponding increase in support of state and especially local governments.

This study reports the results of the authors' 2006 survey of public attitudes toward federal, state, and local tax values and tax fairness, as well as trust and confidence in the governments of the American federal system. Prior to its termination in October 1996, the U.S. Advisory Commission on Intergovernmental Relations (ACIR) reported annually on public opinions about a variety of important intergovernmental issues such as federal, state, and local taxing and spending policies; perceptions of the governments best able to perform certain functions; trust and confidence in the federal, state, and local governments; and intergovernmental distributions of power.[1] Since 1999, the authors have commissioned and reported annually on national surveys of Americans replicating questions asked by the ACIR. In this way, we have extended the ACIR time-series data to 2006 and are able to report

From *Publius: The Journal of Federalism*, May 2006.

on public attitudes in these areas up to the present (Cole and Kincaid 2000; Kincaid and Cole 2001, 2005; Cole et al. 2002, 2004; Kincaid et al. 2003).

These surveys are important for their theoretical significance and for what they suggest about the impacts of major social, political, and economic events on the public's attitudes toward various federalism issues. From a theoretical perspective, numerous scholars have argued that federalism means more than just certain constitutional arrangements by which government powers are distributed. The essence of federalism, argued William Livingston, "lies not in the institutional or constitutional structure but in [the attitudes of] society itself" (Livingston 1952). Daniel J. Elazar put it directly when he said, federalism is "a way of thinking" (Elazar 1987). Livingston, Elazar, and others[2] speak of the kinds of public attitudes, beliefs, and opinions that they view as conducive to the creation, support, and maintenance of a federal polity. Our surveys, and those of the ACIR, help tap into federalist attitudes and opinions long discussed by scholars, and they give us at least one measure of how these attitudes apply and how they change in the context of America's federal system.

In terms of social and political impacts, these longitudinal surveys provide a partial indication of the impact that major events have on the public's attitudes toward federalism-relevant issues over time. During the three decades for which data are available, the United States has experienced significant economic upturns and downturns, a presidential resignation, threats of presidential impeachment, terrorist attacks, military engagements, many U.S. Supreme Court decisions favoring one sphere of government over another, major natural disasters, and significant shifts in taxing and spending patterns. The survey data help us to theorize about the extent to which events such as these affect the public's attitudes toward issues of federalism.

Our 2006 survey asked the following questions: "From which level of government do you feel you get the most for your money?" "Overall, how much trust and confidence do you have in the federal government to do a good job in carrying out its responsibilities?" "Overall, how much trust and confidence do you have in your state government to do a good job in carrying out its responsibilities?" "Overall, how much trust and confidence do you have in your local government to do a good job in carrying out its responsibilities?" and "Which do

you think is the worst tax, that is the least fair?" This year, as in the past, we commissioned OmniTel, a national telephone surveying firm, to conduct the polling. The survey of 1,000 adult Americans (ages eighteen and over) was completed in January 2006.[3]

GOVERNMENT GIVING THE MOST FOR THE MONEY

Table 1 displays responses to the most-for-your-money question. It also compares the 2006 responses with those from all previous surveys.

Table 1 shows that surveys conducted from the late 1970s up until the late 1990s revealed a general decline in public support for the federal government coupled with a corresponding increase in support for state and local governments—a trend finding consistent with other research using different questions (Hibbing and Theiss-Morse 2001). Throughout the 1990s, the highest level of public support was shown for local governments whereas support for the federal government declined to the lowest levels recorded during the thirty-four survey years.

This trend was broken in 2002, though, when there was a noticeable upturn in favorable attitudes toward the federal government and a corresponding decline in support for state and local governments. In fact, the federal government, which had received the lowest proportion of public support on this question in both the 1999 and 1993 surveys, bounced back in 2002 to score the highest of the three orders of government. We have argued elsewhere that these results can most probably be attributed to the rally-around-the-flag effect of the terrorist attacks of September 11, 2001. Other surveys also reported significant upturns in public support for the federal government following those attacks (Stille 2001; Mackenzie and Labiner 2002; Kincaid et al. 2003). Table 1 shows further that the heightened support for the federal government persisted at least through 2004 when an even slightly larger proportion of the sample that year than in 2002 (33 percent compared with 32 percent) said that the federal government gave them the most for their money.

Even so, it should be noted that the high ratings received by the federal government in 2002 and 2004 were still lower than the ratings it usually received in the 1970s (e.g., 39 percent in 1972 and 38 percent in 1975). Thus, the post-2001 surge was not sufficient to boost the federal government to levels recorded during much of

Table 1 From Which Level of Government Do You Feel You Get the Most for Your Money?

Year	Federal (%)	State (%)	Local (%)	Don't Know/ No answer (%)
2006	29	20	31	20
2004	33	21	36	10
2002	32	24	25	19
1999	23	29	31	17
1993	23	20	38	20
1991	26	22	31	22
1989	33	23	29	15
1988	28	27	29	16
1987	28	22	29	21
1986	32	22	33	13
1985	32	22	31	15
1984	24	27	35	14
1983	31	20	31	19
1982	35	20	28	17
1981	30	25	33	14
1980	33	22	26	19
1979	29	22	33	16
1978	35	20	26	19
1977	36	20	25	18
1976	36	20	25	19
1975	38	20	25	17
1974	29	24	28	19
1973	35	18	25	22
1972	39	18	26	17

Sources: Authors' 2006, 2004, 2002, and 1999 surveys, and U.S. ACIR (1972–1993 passim).
Note: In this and all subsequent tables and statistical analysis, data are analyzed in "weighted" form according to a procedure accounting for age, sex, education, race, and region.

the 1970s—the decade of Watergate, Arab oil-embargo crisis, stagflation, and President Jimmy Carter's famous "malaise" diagnosis of the country.

The 2006 survey suggests that the public's attitudes toward the various governments may be returning to more "normal" historical (i.e., 1979–1999) levels. That is, the proportion of respondents saying in 2006 that the federal government gives them the most for their money declined to 29 percent, and again this year, as in 2004, the largest proportion said that their local govern-

ments give them the most for their money. Perhaps, then, the public's post-2001 support of the federal government peaked in 2004.

Several other interesting features of the public's opinions on this matter are revealed in Table 1. First, the public's confidence in the value delivered by local governments is not shared equally by its confidence in state governments. The proportion saying that state governments give them the most for their money has continued to slip from a relative high in 1999 (when 29 percent of respondents said they got the most for their money from state governments) to 2006 when only 20 percent so responded. The generally low levels of support for the states over the years are consistent with the tax-and-expenditure revolts and term-limits movements that have plagued states in recent decades. These results also suggest that the general public may not understand, appreciate, or support what the academic literature has termed "the resurgence of the states" and what many contemporary liberals see as progressive policy activism and innovation in the states in the face of a conservative federal government (Kincaid 2006). Indeed, shortly after our survey recorded this low level of support for states, congressional Democrats took the unusual step of having a governor, Timothy M. Kaine of Virginia, respond to President George W. Bush's 2006 State of the Union address, apparently in the belief that the performance of President Bush and the federal government would pale in comparison to the greater performance values offered citizens by the states and state officials. Kaine's theme, and refrain throughout his address, was "there is a better way," namely, policies and practices pioneered by the states. Yet, our trend finding is consistent with other research showing that public support for state governments has very little to do with the capacity and responsiveness of state governments and much more to do with other factors, especially distrust of the federal government, ideology, and partisanship (Hetherington and Nugent 2001).

Second, it can be seen in table 1 that support for all three spheres of government slipped from the 2004 survey to the present—4 percentage points for the federal government, 1 percentage point for state governments, and 5 percentage points for local governments. Whether this general slippage heralds the onset of a new trend, or perhaps represents only a temporary negative reaction to the poor response of all governments to Hurricane

Katrina in August 2005, is impossible to say, in part because small percentage fluctuations are to be expected across annual surveys.

Third, the survey recorded a high level (20 percent) of "don't know" and "no answer" responses in 2006, although this is not unusual. Over the years, this question has regularly recorded high levels in this category, the highest being 22 percent in 1991 and 1973. On average, a high or low level of "don't know" and "no answer" responses has no impact on rankings for the federal government. However, on average, when the "don't know" and "no answer" percentage exceeds 18, the percentage ranking for state governments drops from 23 to 21. In turn, when the percentage of "don't know" and "no answer" responses exceeds 18, the ranking for local governments drops from 31 to 28. These findings are consistent with research suggesting that public support for state and local governments is strongly influenced by support for the federal government and by general levels of political trust(Uslaner 2001). In a year in which a sizable number of respondents are uncertain, therefore, many of those unwilling to choose the federal government do not then resolve or put aside their uncertainty by choosing state or local government.

TREND ANALYSIS

Another way to analyze responses to the most-for-your-money question, and also to visualize the possible impact of some historic social, political, and economic events on these responses, is to compare the proportions selecting the federal government compared to the proportion selecting state and local governments combined. This analysis is presented in figure 1.

Here, one can see a general long-term decline in support for the federal government and a corresponding increase in support for state and local governments together. In 1972, at the start of the trend analysis, support for the federal government (at 39 percent) and for state and local governments (at 44 percent combined) was very close. Today, support for the federal government has declined to under 30 percent while support for state and local governments combined has been consistently at or above 50 percent. Major events appear to have had some impact on this trend. A noticeable decline in support for the federal government and a corresponding increase in support for state and local governments is shown during

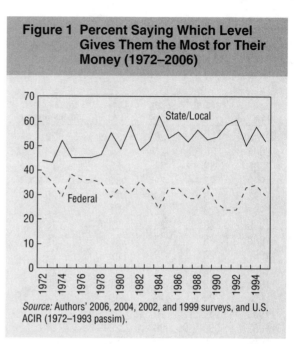

Figure 1 Percent Saying Which Level Gives Them the Most for Their Money (1972–2006)

Source: Authors' 2006, 2004, 2002, and 1999 surveys, and U.S. ACIR (1972–1993 passim).

and following both the Watergate years and oil crisis (1972–1974), the 1982–1984 period of Ronald Reagan's presidency, and the 1993 and 1999 survey years.

The dip in support for the federal government by the end of Reagan's first term in office may have reflected Reagan's own stated suspicion of the federal government and corresponding support for state and local governments, as well as the rhetorically pro–state and local policies pursued during the early years of the Reagan presidency.[4] In its 1984 report, the ACIR accounted for this dip in federal support and increase in state-local support as follows:

> In a period of high and continuing federal deficits, part of the sharp decline in public support for the national government might be attributed to recent publicity highlighting wasteful spending, such as that reported by the Grace Commission. Increased public support for local and state governments indicates that the Reagan Administration may be achieving some of its "New Federalism" goals—instead of citizens turning to Washington to solve their problems, they are more likely to turn to their state and local governments.

However, data are not available to reach a definitive explanation.

Likewise, the absence of annual data for the 1990s makes it impossible to speculate plausibly about the reduced federal support and increased state-local support seen for 1993 and 1999 other than seeing those levels as part of the long-term overall decline of support for the federal government since the 1970s. In turn, as noted earlier, a fairly substantial increase in support for the federal government is shown in the years immediately following the terrorist attacks of 2001—a level of support that now seems to be slipping.

While it is interesting to note the apparent impact of events on this most-for-your-money question, the major conclusion to be drawn from figure 1 is the general decline in the public's support for the federal government compared with its increased support for state and

local governments, especially local governments, over a period that extends now for three decades.

DEMOGRAPHIC ANALYSIS

Table 2 shows responses to the most-for-your-money question accounting for various demographic and political variables.

African American respondents were considerably more likely than white respondents to say that the federal government gives them the most for their money and considerably less likely to say that their local government gives them the most for their money. At the same

Table 2 Demographic Characteristics of Most-For-Your-Money Respondents, 2006

Characteristics	Federal (%)	State (%)	Local (%)	Sig.[a]	CC[b]
Gender					
Female	30.7[c]	29.7	39.7	ns	
Male	33.1	24.3	42.6		
Race					
Black	54.1	17.9	26.4	.000	.160
White	32.7	27.1	40.1		
Ethnicity					
Hispanic	36.1	15.5	48.5	.031	.093
Non-Hispanic	35.5	26.9	37.6		
Education					
Less than high school	44.8	31.3	23.9	.025	.147
High school graduate	34.3	28.9	36.8		
Some college	30.0	26.5	43.5		
Graduated college	26.2	24.3	49.5		
Postgraduate school	30.0	26.4	43.6		
Party identification					
Democrat	30.8	26.5	42.7	ns	
Independent	28.5	28.5	43.0		
Republican	36.6	24.7	38.7		
Region					
Northeast	31.1	23.6	45.3	.028	.131
Midwest	25.4	26.8	47.8		
South	38.4	27.9	33.7		
West	31.5	29.0	39.5		

Notes:
[a]Level of significance reported is based on the chi-square value.
[b]Contingency coefficient.
[c]Percentage calculations exclude "don't know" and "no answer" respondents.

time, they were the least likely to report that their state government gives them the most for their money. Black support clearly lies with the federal government—a finding consistent with our previous years' findings and with other research (Cole et al. 2004). Hispanic respondents were more likely to say that their local government gives them the most for their money and less likely to say that their state government gives them the most than were non-Hispanics. In short, state governments fare least well among blacks and Hispanics.

Less-educated respondents were somewhat more likely to say that the federal government gives them the most for their money and less likely to say that local governments give them the most than were more educated respondents. Respondents from the South (which includes the federal district and Maryland and Virginia)

were more likely to select the federal government as the one giving them the most for their money than were respondents from other regions, and respondents from the Northeast, Midwest, and the West were more likely to select their local government as the one giving them the most for their money. These findings are largely consistent with findings from previous years.

THE WORST OR LEAST FAIR TAX

Table 3 looks at responses to the question "Which do you think is the worst tax—that is, the least fair?"

The information presented in table 3, when compared with results shown in table 1 and figure 1, presents somewhat of a paradox. While data in tables 1 and figure 1 show a general decline over the years in support

Table 3 Which Do You Think is the Worst Tax—That Is, The Least Fair?

Year	Federal Income Tax (%)	State Income Tax (%)	State Sales Tax (%)	Local Property Tax (%)	Don't Know/ No Answer (%)
2006	25	10	15	41	9
2004	27	8	17	41	6
1999	37	11	16	28	8
1993	36	10	16	26	14
1991	26	12	19	30	14
1989	27	10	18	32	13
1988	33	10	18	28	11
1987	30	12	21	24	13
1986	37	8	17	28	10
1985	38	10	16	24	12
1984	36	10	15	29	10
1983	35	11	13	26	15
1982	36	11	14	30	9
1981	36	9	14	33	9
1980	36	10	19	25	10
1979	37	8	15	27	13
1978	30	11	18	32	10
1977	28	NA	17	33	11
1976	NA	11	NA	NA	NA
1975	28	10	23	29	10
1974	30	10	20	28	10
1973	30	13	20	31	11
1972	19	10	13	45	11

Source: 1972–1993 data, ACIR (1993); 1999, 2004, and 2006 data, authors' surveys.

for the federal government and a general increase in support for state and local governments, table 3 in some ways shows the reverse. That is, over time—and especially in recent years—the proportion of respondents selecting the federal income tax as the least fair has diminished considerably, while the proportion selecting the local property tax as least fair has increased significantly. Looking at the 2006 results, as an example, only about a quarter of respondents said they find the federal income tax to be least fair (compared to 37 percent who so responded in 1999), while 41 percent of respondents reported the local property tax to be the least fair (compared with 28 percent so responding in 1999).

Clearly, some significant changes in the public's views of the fairness of the various taxes have occurred in a short period. Undoubtedly, these attitudinal shifts relate to the changing tax burdens imposed by these various sources of revenue. While Congress, at the urging of President Bush, enacted income tax reductions in 2001 and 2003, local property taxes have risen an average of 6 percent nationally in recent years (Bradley 2005). A number of states with an income tax also increased rates in recent years, although dissatisfaction with this tax rose only slightly over 2004. A reasonable hypothesis is that the public's attitudes toward these taxes reflect these tax changes. Otherwise, dissatisfaction with the state sales tax actually declined slightly from 17 percent in 2004 to 15 percent in 2006.

On average over the twenty-two survey years, the federal income tax has been selected the worst by 31.7 percent of respondents, the local property tax by 30.5 percent, the state sales tax by 17.0 percent, and the state income tax by 10.2 percent. Ratings of the state income tax and sales tax have fluctuated within a much smaller range than the ranges for the federal income tax and local property tax.

DEMOGRAPHIC ANALYSIS

As table 4 indicates, very little significant variation in responses to the worst tax question exists along various demographic and political lines. The only variable reflecting statistically significant differences is ethnicity. By a fairly wide margin, non-Hispanics viewed the federal income tax as the worst tax more often than did Hispanic respondents, and Hispanic respondents were considerably more likely than non-Hispanics to report the

state sales tax as being the worst tax. Remarkably, no other relationships were found to be statistically significant, thus suggesting that the impacts of these taxes are felt fairly uniformly across various groups of Americans.

These findings deviate slightly from our previous findings. In 2004, for example, the variable most strongly related to the worst tax question was region. Respondents from the Northeast were considerably more likely to view the property tax as the worst than were respondents from any other part of the country, especially the South (by a margin of 53–35 percent). While the 2006 survey shows that roughly 48 percent of those from the Northeast still believe the local property tax to be the worst, the differences in regional responses have narrowed considerably and were not statistically significant in 2006.

TRUST AND CONFIDENCE IN VARIOUS GOVERNMENTS

Responses to the trust-and-confidence-in-governments questions are shown in tables 5 through 7. Information in those tables compares results of the 2006 survey with those of previous years.

Information presented in tables 5–7 is reasonably consistent with the results discussed above, especially when considering the most-for-your-money question (table 1). Table 5 shows that the public's level of trust in the federal government declined considerably from 1987, when this question was first asked, to 1999, but that it increased markedly following the terrorist attacks of 2001. In 2002 and again in 2004, fully two-thirds of respondents said they had a "great deal" or a "fair amount" of trust in the federal government. The 2006 results, however, suggest that trust in the federal government is again on the decline. This year, just 54 percent of respondents said they have a "great deal" or "fair amount" of trust in the federal government, and a higher percent (14 percent) than previously said they have "no trust at all" in the federal government—the highest negative recorded in our time series. These results probably reflect public dissatisfaction with the war in Iraq, the performance of Congress, and the job performance of President Bush. On average over the six survey years, 59 percent of respondents expressed a "great deal" or "fair amount" of trust in the federal government within a range of 42–68 percent.

Table 4 Demographic Characteristics of "Worst Tax" Respondents, 2006

Characteristics	Federal Income Tax (%)	State Income Tax (%)	State Sales Tax (%)	Local Property Tax (%)	Sig.[a]	CC[b]
Gender						
Female	30.1[c]	9.2	14.4	46.2	ns	
Male	28.8	11.4	15.8	44.0		
Race						
Black	25.5	9.4	17.9	47.2	ns	
White	29.7	11.0	15.0	44.4		
Ethnicity						
Hispanic	19.7	11.1	26.5	42.7	.01	.111
Non-Hispanic	28.9	10.4	15.2	45.5		
Education						
Less than high school	27.9	10.3	17.6	44.1	ns	
High school	30.1	10.1	15.4	44.4		
Some college	30.2	10.1	13.6	46.2		
Graduated college	31.4	10.2	10.2	48.2		
Postgraduate	26.3	10.2	22.9	40.7		
Part identification						
Democrat	27.2	10.1	16.3	46.3	ns	
Independent	31.2	11.3	16.8	40.8		
Republican	30.6	10.0	12.5	46.9		
Region						
Northeast	24.6	10.2	17.1	48.1	ns	
Midwest	29.7	7.6	14.1	48.6		
South	31.3	11.3	15.1	42.3		
West	31.2	12.4	14.5	41.9		

Notes:
[a]Level of significance reported is based on the chi-square value.
[b]Contingency coefficient.
[c]Percentage calculations exclude "don't know" and "no answer" respondents.

By comparison, the proportions saying they have a "great deal" or "fair amount" of trust in state and local governments have not changed a great deal over the 1987–2006 period. However, for both state and local governments, the proportions recording this high level of trust declined between 2004 and 2006 (from 69 percent to 65 percent for state governments and from 74 percent to 69 percent for local governments). The last time the federal, state, and local governments all experienced a decline in trust was between 1987 and 1992. Then, between 1992 and 1999, all three experienced an increase in trust. However, contrary to some research suggesting that trust in all three governments moves together, because it is generally driven by trust in the federal government, between 1999 and 2002 an increase in trust for the federal government was accompanied by a decrease in trust for state and local governments, while between 2002 and 2004, a decrease in support for the federal government was coupled with increased support for state and local governments.

On average over 1987–2006, 65 percent of respondents recorded a "great deal" or "fair amount" of trust in their state governments (within a range of 51–73 percent) and 69 percent reported this level of trust in their local governments (within a range of 60–74 percent). Thus, over time, trust and confidence in state and local governments have remained fairly consistent and comparatively high, while trust for the federal government has been lower and slightly more volatile.

DEMOGRAPHIC ANALYSIS

As shown in table 8, some variations in responses to the trust-in-government questions are evident, especially when considering trust in the federal government.

White respondents were considerably more likely to report high levels of trust in the federal government than were black respondents, although black respondents, as will be recalled from table 2, were more likely to say they get the most for their money from the federal government. These results are not necessarily contradictory if one considers that federal civil rights protections and social welfare programs have been tremendously beneficial for

Table 5 Trust and Confidence in Governments: Federal

Trust Level	2006 (%)	2004 (%)	2002 (%)	1999 (%)	1992 (%)	1987 (%)
Great deal	11	15	16	9	4	9
Fair amount	43	51	52	47	38	59
Not very much	30	23	21	30	41	24
None at all	14	9	9	12	13	4
Don't know/no answer	2	2	2	2	4	4

Sources: Authors' 2006, 2004, 2002, and 1999 surveys, and U.S. ACIR (1987, 1992).

Table 6 Trust and Confidence in Governments: State

Trust Level	2006 (%)	2004 (%)	2002 (%)	1999 (%)	1992 (%)	1987 (%)
Great deal	11	13	10	10	5	11
Fair amount	54	56	55	57	46	62
Not very much	26	22	23	23	36	19
None at all	9	8	9	7	8	4
Don't know/no answer	—	2	3	3	5	4

Sources: Authors' 2006, 2004, 2002, and 1999 surveys, and U.S. ACIR (1987, 1992).

Table 7 Trust and Confidence in Governments: Local

Trust Level	2006 (%)	2004 (%)	2002 (%)	1999 (%)	1992 (%)	1987 (%)
Great deal	15	22	14	14	6	16
Fair amount	54	52	53	55	54	57
Not very much	18	16	20	20	26	16
None at all	10	8	10	8	9	7
Don't know/no answer	3	2	3	3	5	4

Sources: Authors' 2006, 2004, 2002, and 1999 surveys, and U.S. ACIR (1987, 1992).

Table 8 Demographic Characteristics of Respondents Reporting Trust in Governments, 2006

Characteristics	Federal		State		Local	
	GD/FA (%)	NVM/None	GD/FA (%)	NVM/None	GD/FA (%)	NVM/None
Gender						
Female	53.5	46.5	66.2	33.8	71.8	28.2
Male	54.7	45.3	62.1	37.9	72.8	27.2
Race						
Black	41.5	58.5*	57.4	42.6	68.5	31.5
White	54.6	45.4	64.0	36.0	72.8	27.2
Ethnicity						
Hispanic	64.6	35.4**	70.1	29.9	67.7	32.3
Non-Hispanic	53.7	46.3	64.3	35.7	71.2	28.8
Education						
Less than high school	54.5	45.5	63.3	36.7	66.2	33.8**
High school graduate	56.1	43.9	63.4	36.6	67.5	32.5
Some college	53.7	46.3	65.6	34.4	71.5	28.5
Graduated college	53.1	46.9	64.9	35.1	78.7	21.3
Postgraduate	49.6	50.4	61.5	38.5	78.2	21.8
Party Identification						
Democrat	37.4	62.6***	62.5	37.5**	72.3	27.7
Independent	48.5	51.5	61.0	39.0	70.9	29.1
Republican	78.2	21.8	71.1	28.9	75.9	24.1
Region						
Northeast	54.3	45.7	60.7	39.3	71.6	28.4
Midwest	51.6	48.4	62.7	37.3	76.3	23.7
South	54.5	45.5	65.5	34.5	69.1	30.9
West	56.7	43.3	67.8	32.2	72.4	27.6

Notes: In this table, response categories "great deal" and "fair amount" have been collapsed into the response heading "GD/FA," and response categories "not very much" and "none at all" have been collapsed into the response heading, "NVM/None."
*Significant (chi-square) at the .05 level.
**Significant (chi-square) at the .01 level.
***Significant (chi-square) at the .001 level, or lower.

African Americans, thus producing a high most-for-your-money response. At the same time, their low level of trust in the federal government might reflect a fear that Republicans, who control the Congress and the White House, might not vigorously enforce and maintain those benefits.

Hispanic respondents were considerably more likely to report high levels of trust in the federal government than were non-Hispanics, and Republicans were considerably more likely to report high levels of trust in the federal government than were Democrats or independents. Republi-

cans also reported significantly higher levels of trust in their state governments than did Democrats or independents, and respondents with higher levels of education generally reported higher levels of trust in their local government than did those with lower levels of education. Many of these findings correspond with findings from previous years. In 2004, for example, Republicans reported significantly higher levels of trust in both the federal and state governments than did Democrats or independents, and education was found that year also to be related to trust in local government in the same direction as in 2006.

CONCLUSION

The 2006 survey results conform to many long-term trends in public attitudes toward various issues in federalism and intergovernmental relations reported in our previous studies, while also revealing some interesting recent, perhaps short-term, deviations from those trends. Probably the most significant long-term trend is the decline in the public's support of the federal government and corresponding increase in support of state and especially local governments. Beginning with almost equal levels of support in the early 1970s, a gap of 22 percentage points in 2006 separated the public's views of which governments (federal or state-local) give them the most for their money. Although the surveys show that a reversal of this trend followed the terrorist attacks of 2001, the 2006 results suggest that this reversal was temporary. Support for the federal government seems to continue to decline; support for state and local governments seems to be relatively stable, if not increasing.

Another long-term trend confirmed in 2006 is the reasonably consistent and low proportion of respondents selecting the state income tax or the state sales tax as the worst tax. In many cases, as well, the demographic and political variables found to be significantly related to these issues in 2006 are the same as those that were significant in past surveys. Race seems consistently related to the most-for-your-money question, with African American respondents showing considerably higher support for the federal government on this question than did white respondents. White respondents believed they get more for their money from state and local governments.

Partisanship is typically related to the trust-in-governments and most-for-your-money questions. When a Democrat is president, Democratic respondents tend to rate the federal government higher; when a Republican is president (as in 2006), Republicans tend to rate the federal government higher. Region is also frequently related to these questions. Respondents from the South tend to view the federal government as providing the most for their money although fewer regional differences emerge in the governmental trust question in 2006.

The 2006 survey also reveals some deviations from these long-term trends. Although the 2006 survey showed a return to declining levels of support for the federal government, it also disclosed a decline in support for all governments—federal, state, and local. Typically, declines in support for the federal government have been accompanied by corresponding increases in support for state and local governments on the most-for-your-money question (see figure 1). This year, though, support for all governments declined, and a large proportion of respondents said "don't know." Likewise, trust in all three spheres of government declined between 2004 and 2006.

We also see in the 2006 results (as well as the 2004 results) noticeable declines in the percentage of respondents believing that the federal income tax is the worst tax, and significant increases in the percentage believing that the local property tax is the worst. Whether these shifts represent permanent change in public attitudes toward these taxes remains to be seen. Another deviation is that prior to 2006, our surveys showed considerable regional variations in responses to this question. Respondents from the Northeast tended to identify the local property tax as the worst; respondents from other regions—particularly the South—were more likely to identify other taxes as the worst. This year, the highest proportions of respondents from all regions identified the local property tax as the worst, and regional differences were not statistically significant.

In summary, the 2006 survey confirms many long-term trends, while also revealing some interesting deviations from these trends. Whether these deviations represent long-term attitude shifts or temporary departures from "normal" patterns of response remains to be seen.

Notes

1. These reports, entitled *Changing public attitudes on governments and taxes,* were issued from 1972 through 1994 by the U.S. ACIR, Washington, DC.

2. For example see, Ivo D. Duchacek, *Comparative federalism: The territorial dimension of politics* (New York: University Press of America, 1987) and David Schleicher and Brendon Swedlow, eds., *Federalism and political culture* (New Brunswick, NJ: Transaction Publishers, 1998).

3. The survey was conducted in January 13–15, 2006. It consisted of telephone interviews of a sample of 1,000 adult men and women in approximately equal numbers, all 18 years of age or over. The survey is based on a random-digit dialing probability sample of all telephone households in the continental United States, ensuring that households with both listed and

unlisted phones are represented in their proper proportions. All households selected were subject to an original and at least four follow-up attempts to complete an interview. The margin of error for a sample of this size is approximately plus or minus 3 percent, at the 95 percent level of confidence.

4. As Reagan announced in his first inaugural address, "It is time to check and reverse the growth of government which shows signs of having grown beyond the consent of the governed. It is my intent to curb the size and influence of the Federal government and to demand recognition of the distinction between the powers granted to the Federal government and those reserved to the states." See Ronald Reagan, Inaugural Address of President Ronald Reagan, January 20, 1981. Weekly Compilation of Presidential Documents 17 (4) (Washington, DC: Office of the Federal Register, General Services Administration, 1981): 1–5.

References

Bradley, D. 2005. *Property taxes in perspective.* Center on Budget and Policy Priorities. Washington, DC, March 17, 2005. www.cbpp.org.

Cole, R., and J. Kincaid. 2000. Public opinion and American federalism. *Publius: The Journal of Federalism* 30:189–201.

Cole, R., J. Kincaid, and A. Parkin. 2002. Public opinion on federalism in the United States and Canada in 2002: The aftermath of terrorism. *Publius: The Journal of Federalism* 32:123–147.

Cole, R., J. Kincaid, and A. Rodriguez. 2004. Public opinion on federalism and federal political culture in Canada, Mexico, and the United States, 2004. *Publius: The Journal of Federalism* 34:201–221.

Elazar, D. 1987. *Exploring federalism.* Tuscaloosa: University of Alabama Press.

Hetherington, M., and J. Nugent. 2001. Explaining support for devolution: The role of political trust. In *What Is it about Government that Americans Dislike?* ed. John R. Hibbing and Elizabeth Theiss-Morse. Cambridge: Cambridge University Press.

Hibbing, J., and E. Theiss-Morse. 2001. *What Is it about Government that Americans Dislike?* Cambridge: Cambridge University Press.

Kincaid, J. 2006. State-federal relations: Federal dollars down, federal power up. In *The Book of the States.* Lexington, KY: Council of State Governments.

Kincaid, J., and R. Cole. 2001. Changing public attitudes on power and taxation in the American federal system. *Publius: The Journal of Federalism* 31:205–214.

Kincaid, J., A. Parkin, R. Cole, and A. Rodriguez. 2003. Public opinion on federalism in Canada, Mexico, and the United States in 2003. *Publius: The Journal of Federalism* 33:145–162.

Kincaid, J., and R. Cole. 2005. Public opinion on issues of U.S. federalism in 2005: End of the post-2001 pro-federal surge? *Publius: The Journal of Federalism* 35:169–185.

Livingston, W. 1952. A note on the nature of federalism. *Political Science Quarterly* 67:81–95.

Mackenzie, G., and J. Labiner. *2002. Opportunity lost: The rise and fall of trust and confidence in government after September 11.* Center for Public Service. Washington, DC: The Brookings Institution.

Stille, A. 2001. Suddenly, Americans trust Uncle Sam. *New York Times,* November 3.

U.S. Advisory Commission on Intergovernmental Relations (ACIR). 1972–1993. *Changing public attitudes on governments and taxes.* Washington, DC: ACIR.

Uslaner, E. 2001. Is Washington really the problem? In *What Is it about Government that Americans Dislike?* ed. John R. Hibbing and Elizabeth Theiss-Morse. Cambridge: Cambridge University Press.

II

Elections and Political Environment

D emocracy, according to one of its keenest and most cynical chroniclers, is based on the notion that average citizens know what they want and deserve to get it good and hard.[1] Recent elections and trends in political participation in state and local politics seem to turn this notion on its head. Voters appear to believe they've gotten it good and hard, and from this experience, they know what they *don't* want. What they do want is not quite so clear.

Among the things voters clearly do not want is the permanent Republican majority much speculated on after the 2004 presidential election. Indeed, Republicans have been having a very tough time in state and local elections of late. In 2007 Democrats gained control of a majority of the nation's state legislatures for the first time since 1994. These newly empowered legislative majorities had plenty of company in governors' mansions. There were twenty-eight Democratic governors in 2007. Again, that's the best showing Democrats have had since 1994.

This string of electoral good fortune for Democrats, however, may be based less on widespread support for the party and its policies than on widespread dissatisfaction with Republicans. Some of that dissatisfaction is undoubtedly tied to broader trends in national politics, especially the public's souring on the war in Iraq and the nosedive in President George W. Bush's approval ratings. Still more of it has been caused by state-level Republicans sinking into quicksand.

Perhaps the best example of this is Ohio. Prior to 2006, state government in Ohio was dominated by the GOP, with Republicans controlling all statewide offices and holding majorities in both houses of the state legislature. Leading up to the 2006 elections, however, Republicans staggered from one piece of bad news to another: Gov. Bob Taft pleaded guilty to a series of ethics violations. Secretary of state Ken Blackwell was criticized heavily for serving as co-chair of President Bush's 2004 Ohio campaign committee. Blackwell's job presumably had made him the neutral overseer of the state's elections; this neutrality was brought into question by his high-profile role in Bush's reelection campaign. Conflict of interest criticisms intensified when Blackwell made a series of controversial decisions in his official capacity that many saw as benefiting Bush. Blackwell was the GOP nominee to replace Taft in the 2006 election, and outcries of electoral favoritism dogged his gubernatorial campaign.

The beneficiary of the tattered reputations of Republican officialdom was the Democratic gubernatorial nominee, Ted Strickland. Strickland won the election with roughly 60 percent of the vote, becoming the first Democratic governor of Ohio in nearly two decades.[2] Democratic inroads into the state's political offices were considered particularly noteworthy not just because of the historical dominance of those offices by Republicans, but also because Ohio is viewed as a "bellwether" state; many look to developments there as a preview of what might happen in the 2008 presidential elections.

Voters have not just been saying no thanks to Republican candidates these days, they've also been less supportive of issues and policies tied to the broader conservative trends dominant in American politics in recent electoral memory. For example, term limits and tax cuts, long popular issues for successful ballot initiatives, have performed pretty poorly of late. This trend was noticeable in 2005, when ballot initiatives aimed at increasing government taxes and revenues not only were pretty successful, they also gained the backing of some high-profile conservative Republicans.[3] This continued into 2006, as measures proposing to cut the size or authority of government failed more than they succeeded.

So after roughly a decade of mostly positive news for Republican candidates and conservative policies, in 2007 we clearly saw a changing political environment. Although election outcomes and participation trends show that the shift is away from Republicans, it is hard to tell whether voters are in process of consciously shifting more support to Democratic candidates and liberal issues or if Democrats are on the upswing mainly because they are not Republicans.

PARTICIPATION AND OUTCOMES: RECENT TRENDS

The essays in this section chronicle the recent electoral successes of the Democrats (or, perhaps more accurately, the electoral setbacks of Republicans), as well as recent trends in ballot initiatives. The essay by Tim Storey and Nicole Casal Moore provides an in-depth look at Democratic successes and Republican failures in state elections. In 2006 and 2007, the Democratic Party was clearly on the rise. As the story details, however, there was no core issue or electoral mandate behind these successes. Democrats argue they succeeded because they ran on locally important issues. Other political analysts disagree; they think Democrats won mostly because they were not Republicans.

Sometimes a candidate's party is irrelevant. Roughly half the states allow some form of direct democracy, in which citizens get to make policy decisions themselves rather than electing representatives to make those decisions on their behalf. The most common method is the ballot initiative, which puts proposed laws to a popular vote. Ballot initiatives are one way to measure which way the political winds are blowing because they index where voters stand on high-profile social and political issues. The essay by Jennie Drage Bowser reports that support for conservative issues is on a downswing, whereas enthusiasm for their liberal counterparts is moving in the opposite direction. Voters seem less enamored of tax cuts and term limits than in the past and appear more favorably predisposed toward such liberal positions as instituting smoking bans, supporting bonds to pay for public projects, and even restoring voting rights to felons. Also noteworthy in this story is the fact that initiatives in general, regardless of their particular ideological champions, are having a harder time getting approved by voters. The vast majority of ballot initiatives are failing to attract approval at the polls.

The essay by John Straayer gives some insight into exactly why the bloom may be off the direct democracy rose. His is a cautionary tale on the unintended consequences of ballot initiatives. Colorado's Amendment 41 was approved through the initiative process, and was intended to restrict lobbyists and special interests from giving gifts to public officials. The measure, however, was so complicated, convoluted, and poorly understood that its full ramifications only became apparent to citizens after they had officially made it part of the state constitution. Among other things, the children of public employees now find themselves ineligible for some scholarships, and it is not clear if the governor can legally recruit legislators for cabinet positions.

The final two essays deal with two high-profile aspects of political participation that are independent of any particular election. The first, by Kat Zambon, deals with the literal machinery of voting. Over the past few years, many states have pushed to replace their low-tech paper ballot systems with sophisticated electronic voting machines. These electronic machines have some clear advantages; for example, they make it easier for those with disabilities to vote. However, these same machines have raised some disturbing questions about their vulnerability to various forms of election mischief. The shift to high-tech voting machines turns out to have a set of tradeoffs for which there are no easy answers.

The final essay by Jan Goehring and Stephanie Walton focuses on the perennial concern of getting younger citizens to participate politically. Younger adults are among the least likely to vote, contact a public official, write a letter to the editor, or engage in other forms of political participation. America's Legislators Back to School Program is trying to do something about this apathetic take on government. This story details how this program is successfully motivating younger people to take a more active role in politics.

Notes

1. H. L. Mencken, *A Mencken Chrestomathy* (New York: Vintage), 1982.

2. William Hershey, "Strickland Becomes First Dem Gov Since '91," *Dayton Daily News,* November 8, 2006. www.daytondailynews.com/n/content/oh/story/news/local/2006/11/08/ddn110806gov.html.

3. Kevin B. Smith, "Elections and Political Environment," *State and Local Government* (Washington, DC: CQ Press), 2007, 19–20.

5

Democrats Deliver a Power Punch

Tim Storey and Nicole Casal Moore

Elections shake up politics at the state level. For the first time since 1994, Democrats control a majority of state legislatures.

A powerful left hook took down hundreds of Republican state legislators across the country this election. For the first time in more than a decade, Democrats control more legislative chambers and more state governments than the GOP.

In Congress, governors' mansions and state legislatures alike, voters opted for change, and more often than not, that meant Democrat.

"So much of it was a statement of disappointment in Republican leadership rather than an embrace of the Democratic alternative," says Republican pollster Frank Luntz. "The election was a referendum on the national GOP." As they have done in nearly every mid-term election for decades, voters aimed their wrath at partisans of the president's party. Exit polls showed that the Iraq war and ethics scandals worked against Republicans at every level of government.

Why does Luntz believe Americans largely voted against Republicans by default? He was in the Republican knock-out in 1994, when the GOP gained 472 seats and 20 chambers in state legislatures, in addition to control of Congress and 10 governors' offices. Back then, Newt Gingrich's Contract with America was specific, Luntz says. This year, he says, the Democrats "didn't run on anything." Not true, says Michael Davies, executive director of the Democratic Legislative Campaign Committee. Democrats ran on something. It just wasn't the same in every district.

"These were really local races and I think the Democrats ran on very strong local messages." Davies says. "How do we restore confidence in our state? How do we fix education? How do we deal with energy in a way that makes sense to our state? What the Republicans

From *State Legislatures,*
December 2006

30

didn't have this time that they've held in other elections is the national trump card at the last minute. When they turned on the national brand, it wasn't there."

THE NEW NUMBERS

Power shifted to Democrats in 10 of the 11 state legislative chambers that changed hands Nov. 7, according to unofficial figures with recounts pending in seemingly every state. Democratic pick-ups came in the Iowa House and Senate, the Indiana House, the Minnesota House, the Michigan House, the Montana House, the New Hampshire House and Senate, the Oregon House and the Wisconsin Senate.

The GOP did gain enough seats to tie the senate chamber in Oklahoma, but the Democrats remain in power. In the Oklahoma Senate, the lieutenant governor casts deciding votes, and she is a Democrat.

As of Nov. 14, Democrats control both legislative chambers in 24 states, Republicans in 16. In nine states, control is split. Nebraska's unicameral legislature is nonpartisan and the Pennsylvania House is undecided. Going into the election, Democrats controlled both chambers in 19 states. Republicans in 20, and 10 states were split. Democrats went from 47 chambers to 56; the GOP from 49 to 41. Two chambers were tied before the election and one chamber is tied after the voting.

In six states, Democrats won the governorship from Republicans; Arkansas, Colorado, Maryland, Massachusetts, New York and Ohio, giving them 28 governors' mansions to the Republican's 22—more than they've held since 1994.

Democratic pollster Peter Hart had predicted his party would be "exceptionally strong" in the states, in both the legislative and executive branch. He was not surprised by the results.

"I thought we would do well along the Mississippi and we did. The Democrats won five of six governors' races there," Hart says. "That sort of underscores the spine of America."

Democrats hold control in more states than the GOP for the first time since 1994. When the governor's party is combined with legislative control, 16 states are blue; 10 are red and 23 have divided government. Before the election, Democrats had both chambers of the legislature as well as the governor's office in just eight states; Republicans in 12 states and 29 states were divided.

State changes mirror the federal elections, where Democrats won control of the U.S. House and the U.S. Senate. Congressional gains also reflect the election of 1994. Pundits frequently invoked that election as this one approached. It was a midterm election, when the party of the president historically has lost a significant number of state legislative seats.

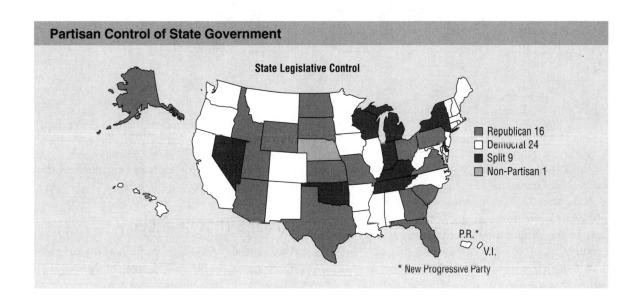

Partisan Control of State Government

State Legislative Control

Republican 16
Democrat 24
Split 9
Non-Partisan 1

P.R. *
V.I.

* New Progressive Party

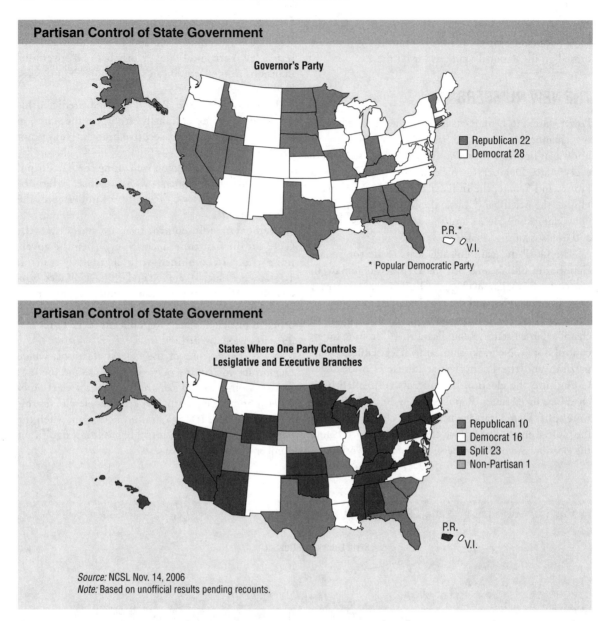

Partisan Control of State Government

Governor's Party

Republican 22
Democrat 28

P.R.*
V.I.

* Popular Democratic Party

Partisan Control of State Government

States Where One Party Controls
Lesiglative and Executive Branches

Republican 10
Democrat 16
Split 23
Non-Partisan 1

P.R.
V.I.

Source: NCSL Nov. 14, 2006
Note: Based on unofficial results pending recounts.

In 1994, President Bill Clinton's attempt at universal health care had failed. The country was in recession. In *State Legislatures* magazine, then-Republican National Committee Chairman Haley Barbour called it "the largest midterm election majority sweep of the century."

Although this is only the third election cycle of this relatively new century, that could be said about 2006 as well. Since 2000, the parties have controlled, within three, the same number of legislatures.

CHAMBERS THAT CHANGED

At least 12 chambers will be under new management when sessions start next month. Some of these changes were surprises. Experts saw others coming.

Marching Off to Congress

The 110th Congress will feature not only new party control but more than five dozen new faces. Nearly half of them bring state legislative experience to the halls of Congress. The November elections proved once again that public policymaking experience gained at the state level can be a steppingstone to the nation's capital. When Congress convenes in January, half of the total House and Senate membership will have come from state legislative ranks. This is the same percentage that has prevailed for the past decade.

Twenty-nine of the 64 members of the freshmen class are state legislative veterans. Two of them, Maryland Senator-elect Ben Cardin and Tennessee Representative-elect Steve Cohen served on NCSL's Executive Committee. Nine come with state legislative leadership credentials. Four of the nine new senators have served in their respective state legislatures. All are Democrats. They are Cardin, Sherrod Brown of Ohio, Claire McCaskill of Missouri and Montana's Senate President Jon Tester. Cardin once served as the speaker of the Maryland House.

In the House, newcomers with state legislative credentials include Republicans Michelle Bachmann of Minnesota, Gus Bilirakis of Florida, David Davis from Tennessee, Mary Fallin from Oklahoma, Dean Heller from Nevada, Jim Jordan of Ohio, Doug Lamborn of Colorado, Kevin McCarthy from California, Peter Roskam of Illinois, Bill Sali of Idaho, Adrian Smith of Nebraska and Tim Walberg from Michigan.

Thirteen of the new members are Democrats including Cohen, Keith Ellison of Minnesota, Gabrielle Giffords of Arizona, Baron Hill from Indiana, Mazie Hirono from Hawaii, Ron Klein from Florida, Harry Mitchell of Arizona, Chris Murphy of Connecticut, Ed Perlmutter from Colorado, Albio Sires of New Jersey, Betty Sutton of Ohio, Peter Welch from Vermont and Charlie Wilson from Ohio.

Lamborn, Perlmutter and Welch have all held the title of president pro tem. Representative-elect Sires was New Jersey's Assembly speaker for four years. McCarthy and Klein filled the minority leader slot in their respective chambers, and Wilson had a four-year run as an assistant minority leader.

A bevy of state-federal issues will confront this group immediately. Legislative changes to the Real ID Act, immigration reform, reauthorization of the No Child Left Behind Act and State Children's Health Insurance Program, telecommunications reform, collection of state sales and use taxes from remote sellers, Medicaid, air quality and numerous fiscal issues are on tap. These members with legislative experience frequently become supporters for NCSL's advocacy efforts and defenders against preemption and unfunded federal mandates.

At press time, nine more House races were undecided and most involved incumbents and challengers with state legislative backgrounds.

—Michael Bird, NCSL

The Montana House, the Indiana House and the Wisconsin Senate are chambers that often pivot. In the 35 elections since 1938, which marks the beginning of NCSL records, the Montana legislative chambers have changed a record 28 times. The Montana House was tied going into the election, but now the Democrats have one more seat than the Republicans, and the nation's first Constitution Party legislator will round out the body.

The Indiana House had a 52-48 Republican majority before the election; now it's 51-49 for the Democrats. It's the 15th time that chamber has changed hands in the past 35 elections. Another perennial candidate for change is the Wisconsin Senate where Democrats picked up four seats to give them a narrow majority.

Term limits hit Democrats in the Oklahoma Senate hard this year. Republicans took advantage, and picked up two seats to earn a tie.

In Oregon, no Democratic incumbents lost as they seized control of the House—even coming close to upsetting the speaker in her own district.

Democrats had strong footing in Iowa. The Senate was tied for the last two years, but Democrats picked up four seats, giving them an eight-seat lead. In the Iowa House, Democrats needed only one seat to take control, but grabbed nine.

In the Minnesota House, Republicans had a two-seat majority and knew they were up against the ropes. But they didn't envision the Democrats would pick up 18 seats for a 36-strong lead.

The sweeping Democratic gains in the Michigan House surprised some observers, who considered the state's district lines quite Republican-friendly. The blue team was down by nine going into the contest. But it weathered the uphill battle to claim six new seats and retain three vacancies for a six-person advantage.

The biggest swing happened in the New Hampshire House, which, at 400 members, is the largest chamber in the nation. On Election Day, the GOP ruled, with a 92-seat lead. After ballots were tallied, Democrats had picked up 92 seats, giving them a 78-seat advantage and a majority of seats for the first time since the Civil War. Gains in the Senate were no less monumental. There the Democrats picked up five seats in the small 24 seat body.

"I'd be lying if I told you I wasn't astounded by the New Hampshire House," says Davies, of the Democratic Legislative Campaign Committee. He was also surprised by the size of the new majorities in the Minnesota and Michigan houses. He was pleased by gains in the Pennsylvania House, where Democrats picked up 10 seats to bring them within one seat of the Republicans. And with several races within a small margin and pending recounts at press time, it's possible that the Pennsylvania House could still go to the Democrats.

"You don't usually see shifts that big," Davies says.

"Big" was relative this year.

"It was a big night in Oklahoma. I didn't look at what happened elsewhere," quips Alex Johnson, executive director of the Republican Legislative Campaign Committee.

"This was a year we sought to minimize our losses and we were successful in a few places, Ohio being one of them," Johnson says. "They had a terrible anti-Republican problem and yet we're still in power [in the legislature]. We tried in other places. It didn't work as well. Our guys were swimming upstream everywhere, let there be no doubt."

He cites exit polls that said 65 percent of Americans made their voting decisions based on national issues. "When you get numbers like that, it's hard for our guys to compete locally."

SOUTHERN EXPOSURE

Compared to other regions, Democratic gains in the South were relatively small, but had historic significance.

The Democrats gained 19 seats in the South this year, marking the first time they haven't suffered a net loss of southern legislative seats since 1982.

Since the high point of the "solid South" in 1958, when Democrats held 95 percent of the seats there, the party's fortunes have been declining in the region, punctuated by occasional small recoveries like this one. Today, Democrats hold 54 percent of southern legislative seats and Republicans have 46 percent.

WHAT IT ALL MEANS

Turnout this year was average for a midterm election, at around 39 percent of eligible voters, says Michael McDonald, who studies American voting behavior at George Mason University.

He says the results are proof enough that Democratic voters were more energized than Republicans, and came out in higher numbers. But he pointed to exit polls showing independents were a key voting bloc and around two-thirds of them went for Democrats. "It was a very important piece of the puzzle," says McDonald.

McDonald speculates that in Congress and state legislatures a large number of moderate Republicans lost their seats. That's what happened to the Democrats in 1994, he says.

"Now, the party could move more to the right. They could decide that being more conservative is going to help them more in upcoming elections than trying to take moderate positions."

Or it could go the other way. McDonald said President Bush's reaction to the results, and the resignation of Secretary of Defense Donald Rumsfeld, could signal a new direction.

"Maybe the era of nasty partisan politics is over," he says.

The Democrats have their own work cut out for them, McDonald says. "They won a lot of seats, but the curse is they have a more divisive caucus. The challenge for Democrats now is, How do they govern?"

6

Election Day Lawmaking

Jennie Drage Bowser

Is enthusiasm for direct democracy waning? Voters seem less excited about ballot initiatives, especially those with a conservative tilt.

Americans approved a mix of conservative and liberal measures on Election Day and sent some surprising signals on tax relief, same-sex marriage, abortion restrictions and tobacco taxes.

Voters took firm stands on taxes, minimum wage, marijuana legalization, abortion restrictions, immigration restrictions, eminent domain and smoking restrictions. They were reluctant to approve measures to reduce government power but receptive to conservative-leaning measures. Liberal-leaning measures received mixed results.

Americans acted on 204 measures on Tuesday and took a more cautious approach to the 76 placed by the initiative process, the second highest in the last eight election cycles. Only a little more than a third of those initiatives were approved, compared with 48 percent of initiatives approved between 1990 and 2004.

LIMITING GOVERNMENT

Almost all of the initiatives that sought to limit the power of government failed. These included:

- The broader, more controversial property rights measures called regulatory takings (the narrower, more straightforward eminent domain measures are not included in this group).
- Term limits.
- Efforts to expand the initiative process.
- Limits on the judiciary.
- Tax and spending limitations (aka TABOR).
- Major tax and revenue cuts.

From *State Legislatures*, December 2006.

Of the 17 measures in this vein, just one passed—a combined regulatory takings/eminent domain initiative in Arizona. Similar measures in California and Idaho failed, as well as a simple regulatory takings initiative in Washington.

Legislative term limits failed to pass in Oregon, which will almost certainly drive a nail in the coffin of the term limits movement. Measures to rein in the judiciary failed in three states, including South Dakota's sweeping "judicial accountability" measure. This would have let a panel of volunteers draft rules for how judges, juries, prosecutors and certain local officials must make decisions. The panel would also be empowered to decide who followed the rules, and to punish those who didn't with fines, jail time, and the loss of public pension and insurance benefits.

Also failing to pass were three state tax and expenditure limit proposals patterned after Colorado's Taxpayers Bill of Rights (TABOR) amendment.

Why these surprising results when voters turned on incumbents and so obviously voiced a frustration with government? These were faux-populist measures. Rather than arising from a local grassroots movement and popular demand for change, these initiatives owe much to out-of-state supporters. Most petitions were circulated by out-of-state groups. Campaigns for and against them were also largely financed by out-of-state money. This fact was widely criticized in the media. Out-of-state influence in initiative campaigns is certainly not a new tendency, but has been growing steadily over the past decade. Perhaps voters finally said "enough is enough."

Another negative influence affecting the vote in these anti-government initiatives may have been the large number of similar measures that were blocked from the ballot by the courts for irregularities or outright fraud in the petition process (there were at least eight TABOR and regulatory takings measures blocked in five states). Again, this was widely reported in the media, and contributed to negative voter attitudes toward these issues this year.

OTHER CONSERVATIVE-LEANING MEASURES

Most other conservative-leaning measures, with the exception of abortion, fared well in the polls. Although voters said no to all three abortion restrictions on the bal-

lot, they approved most bans on same-sex marriage. The single exception is Arizona, where voters for the first time in any state rejected such a ban. Coloradans rejected creating domestic partnerships.

All immigration measures on the ballot in Arizona and Colorado also passed, along with a ban on affirmative action in Michigan.

LIBERAL-LEANING MEASURES

Liberal-leaning measures generally fared well this year, with a few exceptions. Minimum wage hikes passed in all six states where they were on the ballot. Missouri's stem cell research measure narrowly passed.

A measure increasing usage of renewable energy in Washington passed. California voters rejected an oil tax to fund alternative energy research incentives.

OTHER NOTABLE MEASURES

- While the property rights measures on regulatory takings didn't fare so well, all of the straightforward eminent domain measures passed. (These prohibit using eminent domain for economic development.)
- In Arizona. Nevada and Ohio, voters faced competing smoking bans. They chose the stricter in all three. Now 16 states have state-wide smoking bans.
- There were mixed results on tobacco tax increases. They passed in Arizona and South Dakota and failed in California and Missouri.
- Expanded access to the Oregon prescription drug program passed.
- Across the nation, voters authorized bonding that totals more than $43 billion.
- Arizona voters rejected both the $1 million voter lottery and vote-by-mail.
- Rhode Island passed a measure automatically restoring voting rights to felons when they're released from prison.
- Criminal justice measures passed in three states. There will be no more probation for methamphetamine offenses in Arizona. Californians called for strict monitoring of sex offenders and placed restrictions on where they can live. Voters in Hawaii passed stricter punishment for sexual assault crimes against children.

• Education measures saw very mixed results. Colorado's "65% solution" proposals both failed. They would have required 65 percent of education budgets to go to classroom instruction. Funding increases for early childhood education were approved in Arizona and Nebraska. Nevada passed a requirement that education be funded before any other budget item. All education-related bond measures passed. And an estate tax repeal that would have cut education funding was rejected in Washington. But tax increases to fund education were rejected in California and Idaho. Mandatory funding levels for education failed in Michigan. A slot machine program generating revenue for scholarships failed in Ohio.

DID BALLOT MEASURES AFFECT CANDIDATE RACES?

There was much discussion leading into this year's election about how same-sex marriage, minimum wage, and other clearly partisan measures might increase voter turnout and help one party or the other's candidates. There is no clear picture on this.

Unlike the 2004 election in Ohio, when a same-sex marriage ban was the only statewide issue on the ballot and its influence was easy to see, this year's ballots were crowded, with plenty of measures on both ends of the political spectrum and in between.

It is difficult if not impossible to untangle the results of ballot measures and candidate races to determine how they might have influenced each other.

7

Direct Democracy's Disaster

John A. Straayer

Colorado learns the hard way that ballot initiatives don't always give the people what they want.

On Nov. 7, 2006, Colorado voters handed critics of direct democracy the gold-standard example of the foolishness that the initiative process can produce. Nearly 100 years ago, Grove Johnson voiced his disdain for direct citizen lawmaking, which his son Hiram was so successful promoting in California, when he quipped, "the voice of the people is not the voice of God, for the voice of the people sent Jesus to the cross." Coloradoans haven't yet sent anyone to the cross, but they have made a prophet of the senior Johnson by endorsing a measure that has produced a confusing and comical mess rather than new and improved political "ethics," as promised by the sponsors.

Colorado's Amendment 41 carried the short title, "Standards of Conduct in Government," and passed with 62.6 percent of the vote. A constitutional amendment, 41 was intended to restrict gift-giving by interest groups and lobbyists to elected public officials and others in positions of public trust. It was also designed to prevent legislators from immediately becoming lobbyists after their terms of office.

But its consequences to date include issuance of official opinions to the effect that scholarships for children of public employees and performance awards for employees are probably illegal; the resignation of more than a half-dozen legislators; questions as to whether the newly elected governor may legally recruit legislators for positions in his cabinet; and the curtailment of Capitol breakfasts, which had been enjoyed by legislators, staffers and student interns for decades.

Most voters, and indeed, even Amendment 41's sponsors, saw the measure as a reasonable way to curtail questionable connec-

From *State Legislatures,*
March 2007

tions among interest groups and public officials and remove even the appearance of such where none existed, and to keep departing legislators from becoming instant lobbyists. Voters might be forgiven for what has resulted, since the actual language of the new law was lengthy and complex and 41 was just one of 14 ballot measures. But for amendment sponsors Common Cause and millionaire political activist Jared Polis—who following the adoption of their measure, said that they didn't really mean what it said—forgiveness may be more difficult.

THE POWER OF THE INITIATIVE

Amendment 41 was placed on the Colorado ballot through the initiative process. As described in the ballot title, which ran just under 200 words, and in the full constitutional text, the measure bans gifts to all public elected public officials and all employees of all local and state governments and agencies and their immediate families insofar as the gifts have a cash or in-kind aggregate yearly value of more than $50. Governments and governmental units covered are cities, counties, colleges and universities, executive branch agencies, the legislature and the courts. Employees, from the governor to professors, state cops, receptionists, janitors, prison guards and legislative staffers are covered, and so are their spouses and kids.

In addition, legislators may not "personally represent another person or entity for compensation before any other such officeholder or members for a period of two years following departure from office." The measure makes it illegal for a lobbyist to give even a penny's worth of literally anything to a public official or public employee, including gifts, meals or drinks. The constitutional language reads, "No professional lobbyist ... shall give or arrange to give ... any gift or thing of value ... whether or not such gift or meal, beverage or other item to be consumed is offered, given or paid for in the course of such lobbyist's business or in connection with a personal or social event ...".

University of Colorado President and former U.S. Senator Hank Brown interpreted the gift ban as prohibiting Nobel prize-winning professors from accepting the financial award that would accompany the prize. On Brown's request State Attorney General John Suthers reviewed the matter and concurred; a Nobel winner could not accept the award. A fire-fighters association

official indicated that the organization might have to close its foundation, which had made scholarships available for fire-fighters' children and provided funeral assistance for fire-fighters' survivors. Lobbyist Frank DeFilippo, who also serves on the governing board of the Colorado School of Mines, wondered if he would be in violation of the law for buying his own groceries since that would amount to a lobbyist gift to a public official. With respect to the curtailment of legislative breakfasts, Representative Alice Borodkin quipped to a *Rocky Mountain News* reporter, "For God's sake, this whole thing is stupid. All this for a free doughnut?"

The two-year lobbying prohibition prompted more than a half-dozen lawmakers, who were term-limited out or lost their elections, to resign their offices early in advance of gubernatorial certification of the election. Some intended to go into lobbying but others, referring to the language "personally represent," worried that even communicating with lawmakers on matters of concern to an employer or association with which they might be connected would constitute a violation. Senator and pediatrician Kiki Traylor told the *Rocky Mountain News* that she was resigning because she wanted to "protect my ability to advocate for kids and health care issues."

As the full implications of Amendment 41 came into focus, its sponsors explained that they didn't really mean what the plain language of their measure said, and they hired an attorney to try to help the legislature clarify the sponsors' true intentions. Government officials asked the attorney general to interpret the new law. He concluded that the measure means what it says, not what the authors now say they meant it to say. The attorney general lamented that his conclusions were "extremely unfortunate, yet unavoidable" and that the measure's results were "absurd." Government lawyers and administrators went about issuing warnings and behavioral guidelines for public employees. The mix of the plain legal language and the measure's intent as expressed after the fact by its sponsors caused enough worry and confusion that when a Denver law firm arranged a seminar on the new law, 100 people signed up.

NO EASY FIX

But fixing the new constitutional law will be difficult, both legally and politically. Legally, there is a limit to what the legislature can do by statute to clarify a constitutional provision. The amendment states that legislation may not "limit or restrict the provisions" of the law. And politically, lawmakers risk appearing disingenuous and self-serving if they tinker too much. Some members, along with the amendment's own sponsors, seemed optimistic that legislation designed to implement and/or interpret the measure could steer it more clearly toward the authors' intent.

Others were not so sure. Deborah Fallin, a spokesperson for the Colorado Education Association echoed the view of many others, noting that "it doesn't really matter what they meant. It matters how the courts interpret the language." Senator Shawn Mitchell, an attorney, told *Rocky Mountain News* columnist Peter Blake that the amendment is "a poorly drafted pile of quicksand," but "the legislature can't convert it into an innocuous, reasonable measure." Mitchell added that if the legislature redefined the broad coverage of the measure so as to target lawmakers but not all government employees, "… that simply ignores the plain and simple language of the amendment."

Attorney General Suthers is on the side of Fallin, Mitchell and other skeptics. In his words to the *Rocky Mountain News,* "Legislative action can't supplant the clear language of the measure, nor will a reviewing court necessarily be bound by the legislature's interpretation." As the start of the 2007 legislative session approached, lawmakers were already at odds on both the wisdom and legality of tinkering with 41.

To oversee the new ethics law, Amendment 41 established a commission, which is itself a matter of some confusion and controversy. A lengthy portion in the amendment describes the commission, but the basics are these. There are five members, one each appointed by the Senate, the House of Representatives, the governor and the chief justice of the Colorado Supreme Court, with the fifth member selected by the other four on a vote with a minimum majority of three. All must be registered voters in the state, with no more than two from one political party. The commission is authorized to "hear complaints, issue findings, and assess penalties, and also to issue advisory opinions, on ethics issues arising under this article."

UNFORESEEN CONSEQUENCES

The constitutional wording provides commission "members" with subpoena power but it is unclear whether that power belongs to them individually or collectively. The law stipulates that "Any person may file a written complaint" and this, combined with the possibility that any one of the commissioners may individually issue a subpoena, has led some to worry that the whole process may have political witch-hunt potential.

This is not the first time voters in Colorado, like those in other states, have endorsed initiated measures that had great "curb appeal" but turned out to be problematic with unforeseen consequences. And it is not the first time direct democracy critics have had reason to question both voter competence and the wisdom of legislating through a process lacking in hearings, testimony, compromise and amendment. Through a series of initiated measures, Colorado voters have stripped the state legislature of much of its fiscal authority, deprived it of an institutional and policy memory by limiting legislative terms, and helped give birth to unaccountable independent campaign groups through highly restrictive campaign finance "reform." And now, with Amendment 41 in place, the voters have made it legally problematic for a college janitor's kid to receive a scholarship or for a lobbyist to invite the neighboring policeman and his family over for Easter dinner.

8

Push for Paper-Based Voting Divides Advocates

Kat Zambon

States pushed hard for high-tech electronic voting machines—only to find out that low-tech has its advantages.

The 2006 elections caused officials and activists alike to reconsider the future of electronic voting. Tight races like Florida's 13th Congressional District, where 18,000 Sarasota County votes were lost in the race (ironically) to fill former Secretary of State Katherine Harris's House seat, caused them to rethink their prior recommendations.

Sarasota's machines, paperless touch-screen systems, had no ability allow auditors to see individual votes independently from the voting machine's memory.

Once, the answer to paperless voting was to add a paper aspect to electronic voting machines—namely so-called voter-verified paper audit trails (VVPATs), which allow voters to confirm their choices on screen as well as on a piece of paper behind glass before casting their ballot.

Now, it would seem the winds have shifted again. Direct-recording electronic (DRE) machines, the touch screens common in Maryland, Georgia, Virginia, Florida and many other parts of the country, should go the way of the punch card, some advocates say. That is, to the scrap heap of election history, in favor of a return to the paper ballot.

Before the election, VotersUnite.org, a national grass-roots organization, supported the use of electronic voting, provided paper was backing up electronic totals.

But not anymore, according to John Gideon, executive director. "We are convinced that DREs are not the way to go and adding a VVPAT to a DRE is nothing more than a placebo," Gideon said.

From *Campaigns and Elections*
January 2007

Gideon spent Election Day posting reports about problems at the polls on VotersUnite.org and said that the problems not just in Sarasota County, but all over the country have motivated activists to pursue the implementation of optical-scan systems.

Some voters using DREs with VVPATs faced low-tech issues such as paper jams, Warren Stewart, VoteTrustUSA.org policy director explained, because vendors simply added printers to existing DREs instead of developing an integrated system.

"Printers were fielded for the first time in this election cycle ... and they're unsatisfactory," he said. Noting some DREs support printers, such as those produced by Micro Vote, "you have a lot of places where a federal requirement for a VVPAT ... [will require] a whole new system," Stewart said.

The new system that many advocates are pushing for is optical-scan, a system common in many parts of the country, which uses darkened circles or arrows to indicate vote choices. The completed ballots are then scanned at a precinct, identifying over-votes, stray marks or other potentially ballot-spoiling problems.

But they have drawbacks, said Jim Dickson, head of the American Association of People with Disabilities. For starters, they have no ability to allow people with some disabilities to vote independently and secretly, a requirement of federal law.

"As for optical-scan, there is nothing on the market that makes optical-scan accessible so moving to optical-scan is in violation of HAVA. Plus, I think there are real questions about the accuracy of optical-scan and the security of optical-scan ... I think that people who get rid of an accessible system for something that isn't accessible are violating the law and if they don't hear from the Department of Justice, they'll hear from the disabilities community," Dickson said.

On December 7, the EAC voted unanimously to adopt the first-ever federal testing and certification manual for DRE's, allowing the EAC to decertify machines that don't meet security standards. Though the guidelines will be voluntary, InfoWorld.com reported that more than 35 states have passed laws requiring that machines receive federal certification. TGDC will deliver new guidelines to EAC in July. However, NIST said that the guidelines will likely not be implemented until 2009 at the earliest.

"We as the public should really demand a voting system," Strickland Bhatia said "and we should be concerned when one of those doesn't happen ... we should refuse to accept trade-offs."

9

Connecting Kids and Lawmakers

Jan Goehring and Stephanie Walton

Young people don't vote. Some state programs are trying to change that.

The younger generation typically skips Election Day. Their interest in politics and government is dismal. But this past election, 2 million more young people voted than in the 2002 midterm election, a 24 percent increase.

What's going on? Programs inspiring students to get involved with the legislative process and appreciate American democracy may be working.

A Wyoming high school student served as a legislative aid, a Utah teen got involved in a precinct caucus and others help craft legislation. Young people's voices are being heard through legislative youth advisory councils that are popping up in states across the country.

America's Legislators Back to School Program, sponsored by NCSL, is having an impact. Each year some 1,500 legislators all across the country bring civics to life by talking with students about what it's like to be a legislator and how our system of democracy works. In many cases the lesson continues beyond the classroom, as inspired young people get involved in the legislative process.

"We need to reach young people. They are very skeptical of politics in general and the legislative process," says Wyoming Senator John Schiffer who regularly visits classrooms through the Back to School Program. "You never know what's going to result from a classroom visit," he says. Last year, Brianna Straub, a junior at Kaycee High School told Schiffer she was motivated to get more involved by his visit to her school and her government class. Straub served as the senator's legislative aid this past year and calls the experience "an eye opener." She says she knew the logistics of the process, but not how it really works.

From *State Legislatures*, February 2007

After a classroom visit from Utah Representative Sheryl Allen, Bountiful High School student A.J. Jones attended his precinct caucus and was elected a county delegate. He worked on a couple campaigns. Allen tells students about the caucus process and stresses that they "can have a voice."

Jones is passionate about citizen participation. "People don't value the power of their vote. The worst thing you can do is not vote. If people have no say, it's not a democracy anymore," he says.

CRAFTING LEGISLATION

Last September, Louisiana Senator Gerald Theunissen visited an 8th grade classroom at Hathaway High School where he participated in a mock debate with the students and listened to their ideas and suggestions on a number of issues. He was so impressed with their enthusiasm that he challenged the class to be his "partner" and help develop legislation of importance to young people. He stressed that their ideas do count and are important to lawmakers, but they must take the initiative to let their voices be heard.

Rising to the senator's challenge, the students will help craft a bill to establish the Louisiana Legislative Youth Advisory Council. The proposed council will examine and advise the legislature on issues such as education, school violence, substance abuse, youth employment, and ways to motivate young people to actively participate in their community and government.

The bill will be modeled loosely on legislation recently passed in New Hampshire. Senate staff will work with the class on the details of the bill, to be introduced this session. Students will testify before the Senate committee hearing the proposed bill.

"With this class, I wanted to find a way to encourage that enthusiasm and interest beyond my visit to the classroom. We're taking the 'back to school' effort to the next level," Theunissen says.

YOUTH COUNCILS GROW

Washington has a legislative youth advisory council because of the persistence of one young person, "I've always been interested in politics," says Alex Jonlin, "and I wrote letters but my legislators didn't listen to me because I was so young." When he was 11, he began researching how other governments provided opportunities for young people to express opinions, and learned that Maine and New Mexico have legislative youth advisory councils. Senator Ken Jacobsen sponsored Washington's legislation in 2005. He and Representative Dave Upthegrove have been strong supporters of the council. "If we want government that is accountable, people need to know their rights and responsibilities." Upthegrove says. "The youth council is a hands-on way for young people to learn how to participate in government."

Maine Senator Elizabeth Mitchell, current co-chair of her state's council formed in 2002, believes "a youth advisory council can be very meaningful if it's done right. We make sure council members represent all Maine youth by hosting regional forums to get the viewpoints of their peers."

Seventeen-year-old Meghan Brewer, the current youth co-chair, says the council can help change adult attitudes regarding the value of listening to young people, but "we have to be stubborn about it."

Maine's council includes 16 young people representing high schools and colleges; and four legislators—two each from the House and Senate. The speaker and the Senate president make the appointments. The Maine council is unique because it has the authority to introduce legislation. In 2006, the council introduced and got passed legislation that clarified the guidelines for appointing youth members, taking into account geographic diversity and requiring that at least two members represent nontraditional education programs.

"It's critical to have good staff support to keep the legislators focused on the youth council," Mitchell emphasizes. "Without dedicated staff at the legislature, we wouldn't be able to make this work."

The New Hampshire legislature formed a legislative youth advisory council last year. "We didn't have young people at the table, talking about issues that affect them, like student testing, graduated driver's licenses, and underage drinking laws" says Senator Bob Odell, who sponsored the legislation, "We needed a process to involve them and get feedback from their peers."

The Alliance for Civic Engagement will donate staff time to the New Hampshire council, and has secured Help America Vote Act (HAVA) funding to cover initial funding. Young people are being recruited to serve on the council this session.

New Mexico's Youth Alliance is slightly different. It acts as an advisory group to the governor and Children's

Cabinet, as well as working with legislators, according to Senator Cynthia Nava, who co-sponsored the legislation that created it. "The idea behind the Youth Alliance was to create a core group of young people to reach consensus on policy issues and give advice and input to the legislature," she says. "We also wanted to help young people realize their own lifelong leadership potential, and develop a commitment to service in their communities—that is even more important than providing input to state policymakers."

The alliance is staffed and funded through a public/private partnership with the New Mexico Forum for Youth in Community. Membership mirrors the legislature, with up to one young person allowed to participate from each legislative district. Youth members co-apply with an adult partner who provides mentoring, transportation to meetings, connections to other community resources and other assistance. Unlike Maine, Washington and New Hampshire, legislators do not serve on the committee.

GETTING RESULTS

The councils have made a difference. Senator Nava says that New Mexico's Youth Alliance has provided input on issues ranging from truancy, to early education and teen pregnancy. Meghan Brewer of Maine says the legislature passed several bills, including one to strengthen the rights of siblings in foster care to visit one another, and another standardizing permission forms for youth in state custody to participate in school field trips and other extracurricular activities.

"I have had the opportunity to create new connections with people in my community, and I've learned a lot." Brewer says. Other young members echo her sentiment. "I've learned to work with different kinds of people, and I've had the opportunity to work with adults on a more level playing field," says 17-year-old Kate Berry, co-chair of Washington's youth council, "It's an amazing opportunity for kids to get involved even if they can't vote."

Political Parties and Interest Groups

The key words for political parties and interest groups these days are "opportunity" and "accountability." As we learned in the last section, Democrats have seized the upper hand over Republicans in state legislatures and governors' mansions. The question for these newly empowered Democratic officials is what are they going to do with their newfound status?

While Democrats in state and local governments are pondering the opportunities presented by newly elected majorities, Republicans are feeling the sting of accountability. Elections in 2006 found voters not particularly happy with the way things were going, and that translated into bad news for the Republican leadership who had characterized a broad swath of state governments for a decade or more.

The two political parties, however, are not necessarily on opposite sides of the opportunity and accountability spectrum. In reality, they are fairly evenly matched, and Democrats are fully aware that Republican setbacks are likely to be temporary. Both parties are positioning themselves for the near future, and they both have a vested interested in making sure that no third party develops as a major rival to either of them.

Special interest groups, however, increasingly are facing less opportunity and more accountability. States are discussing and enacting ever more stringent constraints on interactions between lobbyists and legislators, and new laws and regulations are being enacted to limit the impact of special interest influence on state government. There is debate over how effective such restrictions are likely to be. What there is no debating is that higher accountability rules for special interests are becoming more popular with the states.

POLITICAL PARTIES AND INTEREST GROUPS: DIFFERENCES AND SIMILARITIES

To the uninitiated, it can seem like there is not much difference between a special interest group and a political party. And, in truth, the lines between the two types of organizations can be a little blurry: both political parties and special interest groups raise money, endorse candidates, and mobilize support or opposition for particular issues and causes.

Nonetheless, fundamental differences do exist. The most important of these is that political parties run candidates for office under their own label and help organize the government. Special interest groups might try to get candidates elected, and they certainly try to influence government, but they do not nominate candidates nor do people organize the government under their name. For example, the National Rifle Association (NRA) may contribute to a candidate's election campaign and may try to persuade that candidate to support a favored position on legislative proposals if elected to office. That candidate, however, will like as not be elected as a Democrat or a Republican and not be formally identified as an NRA representative. If elected, that candidate's role in the legislature—committee assignment, relative power—will be determined by his or her party, not by the NRA.

Even in nominally nonpartisan governments, and this includes most local governments and Nebraska's unique unicameral legislature, candidates often are not shy about declaring their partisan credentials and seeking party endorsements. In effect, informal party systems can exist even where they are formally prohibited. Political scientists view political parties as one of the natural byproducts of representative democracy: establish the latter, and the former will arrive sooner rather than later.

The same might be said for special interest groups. Although interest groups do not run candidates for office or play a formal role in organizing the government, give people a representative form of government along with freedom of expression and assembly and the right to petition government for redress of grievances and what you have is a gold-plated invitation to form a special interest group. It's an invitation enthusiastically accepted by citizens supporting every conceivable political issue or position.

While natural outgrowths of representative democracy, political parties and special interest groups have never been particularly popular with citizens. What often is ignored in such judgments are the positive services these organizations provide to democracy. Both organizations play a critical role in aggregating interests and connecting them to government. A single individual is unlikely to gain the attention of a legislator or a governor. A well-organized interest group that can mobilize voters, gain prominent news coverage, and wage effective public opinion campaigns is much harder for government to ignore. A team of candidates elected under the same label with a mandate to pursue particular policies or issues not only gains the attention of government, it *is* the government.

Yet while they provide important services to democracy, political parties and special interest groups are viewed with suspicion, especially when it comes to their relations with each other. The scramble to win elections, control the key offices and institutions of government, and influence the decisions of policymakers tends to create a negative image of political parties and special interest groups. And the fact is (as we shall see in the readings that follow), political parties do try to tip the electoral scales in their favor, and lobbyists sometimes do cross the line from persuasion to less ethical—and less legal—means of trying to line up legislative support for their favored policies.

Historically, political parties and interest groups have been regulated relatively lightly. Most states view political parties as something akin to public utilities, that is, as organizations that provide a necessary public service. As such, laws generally seek to ensure that in providing such services certain people or groups do not unduly profit, and they make sure these same people do not unfairly exclude other people and groups from the political process.[1] Special interest groups have been hard to regulate because of the constitutional issues involved. In short, it is difficult to place constraints on special interest groups without also putting constraints on the freedom of speech and assembly and the right to petition government for redress of grievances. Regulating interest groups mostly has been about registering and reporting, rather than about placing limits on behavior.

RECENT TRENDS

The readings in this section reflect recent trends in what political parties are doing at the state level. They also explore how states are struggling to regulate lobbying to effectively address concerns about bribery and corruption but not trample any constitutionally guaranteed freedoms.

The essays by Josh Goodman and Celinda Lake, Joshua Ulibarri, and Dan Kully reflect on the big partisan story of late: the Democratic surge in state government. Goodman's essay examines the breadth of Democratic gains at the state level and probes the opportunities and the risks these gains pose for both major political parties. The piece co-written by Lake, Ulibarri, and Kully distills the key electoral lessons of the Democratic surge. Democrats, it seems, have figured out ways to win predominantly Republican and conservative states.

The essay by Alan Ehrenhalt, however, suggests Democrats are going to have to do more than simply win votes to make significant gains in swing states. The party that controls a state legislature for the most part also draws the lines for political jurisdictions. The temptation to gerrymander districts at the state and national levels is hard to resist. Ohio—long a Republican stronghold—shows clearly that strategically drawn districts can make it very hard for the minority party to make legislative gains, even when they pick up more votes.

The essay by Theodora Blanchfield details some of the fund-raising activities that often give political parties and special interest groups a bad name. Want to play ping-pong with Arnold Schwarzenegger? Maybe you can if you pay enough. Maybe you could put it on your official Montana Democratic Party Master-Card. Fund-raising is a fact of life in politics, but it rarely reflects positively on candidates, parties, or interest groups.

Lastly, Rob Gurwitt takes a look at the recent trend toward tougher lobbying laws. A number of legislatures have been stung by lobbying scandals, and in response they are trying to crack down on special interest group activity. As the essay makes clear, this can be easier said than done. Looking on the bright side, reformers see a real opportunity to clean up government. Skeptics wonder if the new the rules and regulations will be able to make a significant dent in politics as usual.

Note

1. Malcom E. Jewell and Sarah M. Morehouse, *Political Parties and Elections in American States,* 4th ed. (Washington D.C.: CQ Press, 2001), 76.

10

Blue Challenge

Josh Goodman

Democrats hold power now in places where they have been on the outside a long time. The question is what they will do with it.

John Shea, of Nelson, New Hampshire, is nothing if not persistent. For many years, he has wanted a seat on the state Executive Council, the five-member body that has veto power over gubernatorial appointments. He ran in 1998 and lost. He tried again in 2002 and 2004—and lost both times. In 2006, he tried once more, but he was something of a fatalist about his chances. Not only did he refuse to accept campaign donations, or spend much time appealing to voters, he left on Election Day for a vacation in Europe. "I had a ticket that I had to use by the end of November," Shea explains. When he arrived at his hotel in Belgium, there was a surprising message waiting for him: He'd won.

A long shot such as Shea could win in New Hampshire last year for one reason: He's a Democrat. His party won victories in New Hampshire in 2006 that justify almost any metaphor of sudden upheaval. Blizzard, landslide, tsunami, earthquake—they all fit. Democrats gained 89 seats in the 400-member state House and erased a 2-to-1 deficit in the Senate, taking both chambers of the legislature for the first time since 1874. They ousted both incumbent Republican U.S. House members, reelected Governor John Lynch with 74 percent of the vote and, thanks to Shea's win, gained control of the Executive Council. In one dramatic day, New Hampshire Democrats acquired more influence over state politics than they had had since the 19th century.

No one saw this coming. Lynch was a strong favorite for reelection, and Democrats knew they had recruited good state Senate candidates, but a sweep of this magnitude seemed utterly unthinkable. In the final week before the election, the chairman of the state

From *Governing,*
January 2007

Republican Party declared that Democrats wouldn't gain more than five seats in the House.

The events that took place in much of America on November 6 took place in greatly magnified form in New Hampshire. But they raise essentially the same question: Was this a fluke occurrence or a hint of things to come?

It's a question that's being asked in quite a few states right now. In two years, President Bush will be on his way out, Jack Abramoff and Mark Foley may be receding from public consciousness and popular figures such as John Lynch might not even be on the ballot. Unless something bigger than these fleeting factors is at work, Republicans may be well positioned to regain the ground they lost.

But if there was a more fundamental reason for the results on November 6, the consequences could be dramatic. That's because the places where the Democrats made the biggest inroads are nearly all bellwethers in state and federal elections. New Hampshire, Iowa, Minnesota and Colorado are presidential swing states; Democrats triumphed in all of them in 2006 (the lone exception being the reelection of Tim Pawlenty, Minnesota's GOP governor). Michigan, Wisconsin, Ohio and Pennsylvania, large and crucial states, each voted for a Democrat for governor and imposed Republican losses at the legislative level. If Democrats can consolidate those gains, they are likely to become the dominant policy-making party in American state government over the next decade—and perhaps gain a natural advantage in presidential politics as well.

LOYAL TO LYNCH

Everyone agrees that the New Hampshire shock of 2006 was linked, like other Democratic victories, to the unpopularity of the Iraq war, President Bush's sagging poll numbers and Republican scandals on Capitol Hill. But it remains to be explained why Republicans were humiliated so much more thoroughly in the Granite State than anywhere else.

To start with, there were some highly specific local provocations. They go back to the election of 2002, which, ironically, was an awful year for Democrats in New Hampshire. Republicans won almost every office that year, but they made two big mistakes: They broke federal law by hiring a telemarketing firm to jam Democratic phone lines, and they elected Craig Benson governor.

The phone-jamming scandal, which led to a prison sentence for the executive director of the New Hampshire Republican Party, did more than tarnish the image of the GOP in the state. In paying for legal expenses, the party nearly went broke, cutting into its campaign budget and making it more difficult to recruit quality candidates, who knew they couldn't expect much financial help. Last month, state Republicans agreed to pay the Democrats $125,000 over five years in a settlement.

When Benson, a wealthy computer entrepreneur, took office after the 2002 election, he seemed to be assured of at least four years in office. Although New Hampshire is one of only two states that have two-year gubernatorial terms, no governor since 1926 had lost his first reelection bid. Nevertheless, Benson lost. Standoffish in personal manner and plagued by ethical accusations, he was beaten by Lynch in November 2004. In many ways, that was the key ingredient in the 2006 result.

Lynch, a political newcomer, came to office promising nonpartisanship and largely delivered. When a centrist coalition from both parties chose moderate Republican Doug Scamman as the House speaker, Lynch opted to work closely with him to fix a budget deficit, replenish the state's rainy-day fund and approve an ethics reform law.

The Democratic governor won plaudits for his handling of two major flooding events. He abandoned a trade mission in Germany to return home and supervise the cleanup work and handed out his personal cell phone number to citizens who had been affected. Lynch's overall record built goodwill toward the Democratic Party as a whole, especially in contests for the Executive Council, whose traditional function as a counterweight to gubernatorial power no longer seemed crucial to voters with the popular Lynch running the state. The governor's coattails were even more important because voting a straight party ticket is as easy as checking a box in New Hampshire.

But Republicans seemed to have a few advantages of their own in 2006. Two months before Election Day, the state Supreme Court appeared to hand the GOP a gift by invalidating the state's school funding system. This wasn't much of a shock, since over the past decade it's been routine for the court to invalidate every school funding plan sent its way. But Republicans expected the decision to work in their favor. To understand that, you

The Nation in a Nutshell

Democrats made historic gains in state politics last year—or didn't—depending on which statistics you consider.

The total gain in legislative seats for the Democrats, around 325, wasn't among the biggest on record—the parties routinely traded more seats throughout the 1940s, 50s, 60s and 70s. Even the 325 figure in some ways overstates the shift that occurred, since Democratic advances were primarily in small and medium-sized states, including 95 in New Hampshire alone. A Republican disadvantage also could have been expected this year, since the party that holds the presidency has lost seats in every midterm election (with the exception of 2002) since at least 1938.

On the other hand, the Democratic gains are more impressive when compared with recent history. The party netted a bigger gain than it had since the post-Watergate election of 1974 and gained more ground than either party had since the 1994 Republican landslide. This result is especially impressive because Democrats captured some of the easiest targets in 2004, when they bucked the national Republican advantage and gained 60 seats.

The best states for Democrats were spread across every region of the country—from the Northeast (New Hampshire and Vermont) to the Midwest (Michigan, Minnesota and Wisconsin) to the West (Alaska, Arizona and Washington)—except for the South. Nevertheless,

Deeper Blue
Legislatures with the largest Democratic gains, 2006*

State	Gain
New Hampshire	22.41%
Minnesota	12.44
Wisconsin	9.09
Washington	8.84
North Dakota	8.51
Arizona	7.78
Maine	7.53
Michigan	6.76
Alaska	6.67
Iowa	6.67
Vermont	6.67
Ohio	6.06
Colorado	6.00
Idaho	5.71
South Dakota	5.71

*Gains were calculated in proportion to the total number of seats in the legislature.
Source: National Conference of State Legislatures

Democrats there were satisfied with their legislative performance. The party posted a net gain in the region for the first time since 1982.

As for gubernatorial politics, there's no denying that Democrats made substantial gains, picking up the executive office in six states with a combined population of more than 50 million—New York, Ohio, Colorado, Massachusetts, Maryland and Arkansas—while losing none. These results mean that a slight majority of Americans now reside under one of the 28 Democratic governors. That was also the case as recently as 2003, before the California recall election brought Republican Arnold Schwarzenegger to power.

The statistic that's perhaps most telling, though, is the number of places where each party has complete control of government, meaning the governorship and both houses of the legislature. In this regard, Democrats reversed a disadvantage and now hold 15 states with a population of more than 73 million, compared with Republicans, who have 10 states and preside over around 66 million residents. That means that Democrats will have more policy-making power than Republicans in state government over the next two years, but the majority of Americans live in places with divided government.

—*Josh Goodman*

have to take into account New Hampshire's deeply entrenched political culture.

TAXES AND SCHOOLS

That culture is immortalized for anyone who visits the Governor's Office by a sign in the official portrait of Meldrim Thomson Jr., "Low taxes are the result of low spending." Thomson, a Republican who served from 1973 to 1979, believed in this warning above anything else. He made himself popular as the opponent of almost any new tax, on anything, at any time, for any reason. Keeping taxes low has long been an overriding goal for the state's leaders. That's been accomplished by refusal to enact any broad-based income tax or sales tax.

The acceptance of this anti-tax ethos kept New Hampshire Republican, even as the rest of the Northeast trended toward the Democrats. To prevent anyone from forgetting the lesson, a large map in the window of the Republican Party offices, just across the street from the capitol, shows Vermont, Massachusetts and Maine, all with sales and income taxes, and New Hampshire without either. "Lowest tax burden in the nation," it crows. "Republican leadership working for you!" Thomson would be proud.

Over the past two decades, however, this culture has been challenged by the ongoing school funding dispute. Without a sales or income tax, schools lean especially heavily on local property taxes, adding to inequalities between rich districts and poor ones. The poor districts challenged this situation on constitutional grounds, and the state Supreme Court has consistently agreed with them. In the past several years, a statewide property tax has invested modest amounts of additional money in poorer communities and mid-wealth districts have filed their own suit, claiming the state still isn't meeting its obligations.

In September, the court ruled in favor of the middle-income plaintiffs. Even more significant, the ruling warned that if the legislature didn't define an "adequate education" and then fund it by July 2007, the court would impose its own solution.

This decision served as a rallying cry for Republicans. They finally seemed to have an issue of sufficient strength to counteract Lynch's growing popularity. Conservative Republicans began promoting a solution many of them had advocated for a long time: amend the state Constitution to remove the court's jurisdiction over school funding. Plans to place a court-limiting amendment on the state ballot in 2006 fizzled out, but the Republican gubernatorial nominee, state Representative Jim Coburn, and other GOP candidates made the issue central to their fall campaigns.

The specter of broad-based taxes had hurt Democrats in the state before. In 1999, the only time in recent history the Democrats held the state Senate, they voted for an income tax and then saw their majority erased at the polls in 2000. The Democratic nominee for governor in 2002, an income-tax supporter, lost in a landslide. This time, though, the anti-tax strategy didn't work.

Most observers don't think this is because New Hampshire's libertarian streak is waning. "They don't want an income tax, they don't want a sales tax," says Scamman.

"They don't want the government to tell them how to blow their nose." But Lynch promised repeatedly to veto any tax increases that reached his desk. In addition, many voters seemed to feel uncomfortable with the idea of amending the state constitution to strip away the jurisdiction of its highest court. Equally important, the image of Republicans in power at the national level had increasingly come to be one of fiscal profligacy, not restraint.

To put the matter in only slightly simplified terms, Democrats stole the mantle of fiscal conservatism from Republicans in New Hampshire. They successfully presented themselves as the party best able to protect the public pocketbook.

DEEPER ROOTS

But there's a strong case to be made that the Democratic takeover has roots much deeper than the popularity of Lynch or the blunders of Republican strategy. In many ways, the events of November 6 represent the final stage of a long transformation that in five decades has changed New England from one of the most Republican regions of the country to the most Democratic. Democrats now control every legislative chamber in the region and all but one seat in the U.S. House of Representatives. "The Yankee moderate Republicans are going the way of the dinosaur," says Dante Scala, a political scientist at Saint Anselm College in Manchester.

In a sense, what's happened in New England is a mirror image of what's taken place in many Southern states since the 1960s. The changes begin at the top, then filter down to lower-level offices. Bill Clinton won New Hampshire's presidential vote in 1992, only the fourth Democrat in the 20th century to do so; Clinton carried it again in 1996 and John Kerry did so in 2004. Jeanne Shaheen claimed the governorship for Democrats in 1996 after nearly two decades of Republican control, and held it twice. Finally, this year, the party made major gains at all levels of office.

Increasingly, Republicans are associated in New Hampshire with a Southern-based and socially conservative national party—a party that believes government has a role in promoting traditional morality, in opposition to New Hampshire's libertarian inclinations. Democrats now seem to be the party of smaller, more permissive government, which is what most New Hampshirites still want.

For all these reasons, the gains in New Hampshire in 2006 look different from the ones that Democrats made elsewhere. New Hampshire was making a dramatic break with its partisan past; states elsewhere were moving back to past Democratic loyalties that had slipped away in recent years. Iowa and Minnesota, among the most Democratic states in the country two decades ago, had been trending steadily Republican, to the point that, in 2004, Bush was the first GOP presidential candidate to carry Iowa since 1984. That trend reversed itself in 2006. Democrats swept to power in both houses of the Iowa legislature and gained 19 seats in the Minnesota House, taking control of that chamber as well.

Because the 2006 upheaval in Iowa and Minnesota came as a reversal, rather than an evolution, political analysts are more likely to view it as a temporary event. They say Democrats won because their voters were more motivated, because the party recruited good candidates and because the national mood had an impact. What they don't see, at least not yet, is anything to make them believe a lasting political realignment has occurred.

LEFT OR CENTER?

Whatever the local situations that might have contributed to the 2006 result, however, the issue of whether Democrats can consolidate it hinges mostly on what they do now. In state after state, Democrats have a choice: to pursue the goals that have energized their party's activists during their time in the wilderness or to chart a cautious course of moderation and compromise. Nowhere is that choice starker than in New Hampshire, with the looming deadline on school finance imposed by the state Supreme Court.

Despite the pledges of Governor Lynch, the Democrats who now run the New Hampshire legislature might be expected to respond to this mandate with a sales or income tax. Both new Democratic lead-

ers, Speaker of the House Terie Norelli and Senate President Sylvia Larsen, have supported income taxes in the past. In the opinion of Andru Volinsky, lead attorney for the low-income school districts, "If the legislative leaders in the House and Senate follow their own lead, we'll be fine."

But the legislative leaders seem likely, at least at first, to follow the governor's tax-cautious lead. Part of the reason is that Democrats in the legislature owe so much to Lynch for their victory that they are not inclined to undermine his leadership. But, more than that, there's a sense that the party has spent so long waiting for its chance that it cannot afford any move that might return it to minority status. For example, Martha Fuller Clark, a veteran Democratic legislator who used to support an income tax, is backing away from that stand now. "If anything would ensure that Republicans would recapture the majority," she says, "it would be to expect the governor to break his promise."

Difficult and politically symbolic choices await Democrats in almost every state where they gained ground in 2006. In Maryland, where they now have the governorship in addition to their lopsided legislative majorities, an increase in education spending several years ago that didn't come with any funding source is now creating a budget crisis. That means new revenue will have to be raised or spending will have to be cut. Deval Patrick, Massachusetts' first Democratic governor in 16 years, may face pressure to accept a reduction in the state income tax to 5 percent, which voters approved in 2000 but which has never been implemented. In Michigan, lawmakers have already agreed to eliminate the state's Single Business Tax, which brings in $1.9 billion annually, meaning Governor Jennifer Granholm and her fellow Democrats, who have a freshly minted majority in the state House of Representatives, will immediately have to overhaul the state's tax system. The way they choose to do that work will send clear signals about where on the ideological spectrum they wish to settle.

> "There's a sense among the Lynch leadership that they are pretenders to power—if they don't act like good Republicans, they won't stay in power."
>
> —Andru Volinsky, lead attorney for the low-income school districts

In Iowa, the debate goes beyond taxes. Democrats are wondering whether, now that they have complete control of state government for the first time since the 1960s, they should pursue the policies of dramatic change that many of them have been advocating for years. The last time they had a similar opportunity, in the aftermath of the 1964 election, Democrats altered the tax system and abolished the death penalty. Their one-party rule lasted only two years.

This time, the Democratic wish list includes initiatives such as a cigarette tax increase and a repeal of anti-union right-to-work laws. But that agenda may not get very far. That's partially because the victories in Iowa in 2006 were due in large part to the recruitment of moderate Democrats skeptical of drastic change, and partly because even Democratic ideologues don't want history to repeat itself. "They got this majority," says David Yepsen, a *Des Moines Register* columnist, "not by running as crazy Deaniac liberals but by being centrists. They know that."

DEMOCRATIC DILEMMA

It's a mistake, however, to think that the preference for caution isn't fraught with dangers of its own. If the Democratic Party's most loyal supporters, many of whom don't view "Deaniac liberal" as an epithet, see no progress toward their long-cherished policy goals, they are likely to become disillusioned and decide that all the hard work of 2006 was a waste of their time.

This isn't merely a theoretical concern. Volinsky, who has been fighting for a new education funding system in New Hampshire for nearly two decades, is already talking about his disappointment with the party. "There's a sense among the Lynch leadership that they are pretenders to power," he says, "and that if they don't act like good Republicans, they won't stay in power."

Volinsky may still get his way, however, if only after what he terms a "constitutional calamity." Governor Lynch appears likely to offer a school funding plan similar to what he proposed two years ago, when his suggestions were approved only in part by the legislature. This could entail more targeted aid, improved funding formulas and school accountability measures—but no new broad-based taxes to fund educational improvement.

The question is what happens if, as seems probable, these proposals don't win court approval. The only obvious options then would be new state taxes, which the court might impose on its own, or the court-limiting constitutional amendment conservatives prefer. Lynch has said he would consider a narrowly crafted constitutional amendment, but the new legislature seems even less inclined to support it than the previous one. Furthermore, such an amendment would require a vote of the people, which likely couldn't take place until 2008.

If the new Democratic leaders find themselves under court order, will they accept a sales or income tax, knowing it might cost them their majority? If not, would they be willing to create a confrontation between the legislative and executive branches of government—and between factions of their own party? No one knows, and that uncertainty gives Republicans reason to hope. "I think it's going to be their Waterloo," says state Representative Fran Wendelboe, a candidate to chair the state GOP.

Democrats in New Hampshire, like their counterparts in Minnesota, Iowa, Massachusetts and other states where the blue tide came in last November, are fully aware that two dangerous years lie ahead of them. But they also are aware that Republicans, who are licking their wounds and trying to heal their own split between moderates and conservatives, would gladly switch places. And they know one more thing: that if they find a way to deal successfully with their one overriding dilemma, they could stay in power for quite a while. In the words of John Shea, back from Europe and ready to be an executive councilor, "It's going to be fun."

11

How Democrats Can Win in Red States: Ten Lessons from Winning in Montana and Other Senate Races

Celinda Lake, Joshua Ulibarri, and Dan Kully

"Blue" candidates in "red" states. How Democrats are learning to win in states that lean Republican.

In 2006, we had the great privilege of working with the successful Jon Tester for Senate campaign. That campaign built on a number of races in Montana that can help redefine winning strategies for the Democratic Party. In 2000, despite Bush carrying the state with 58 percent of the vote and losing the top races, Montana Democrats still won a number of lower level statewide offices, including attorney general, auditor and superintendent of public instruction. In 2004, when Bush won Montana by 20 points, Brian Schweitzer won the governorship, and Democrats took control of the state Senate. In 2006, Jon Tester won the Senate seat, beating an incumbent, and, of course, Max Baucus has continued to win re-election. Other Democrats—Jim Webb and Claire McCaskill—also won Senate seats in so-called red states. What can we learn from these races on how to turn red states blue? Here are ten lessons:

LESSON 1: VOTERS DO NOT VOTE FOR ISSUES— THEY VOTE FOR PEOPLE

Voters choose the candidate they are most comfortable with—most willing to have a cup of coffee with or sit down and talk to. Likeability was the strongest predictor of the vote in the Burns-Tester race, far ahead of job performance. Schweitzer wore blue jeans, rode a horse, and carried a rifle, not to fool or tease voters, but because it was all part of who he was. Similarly, Tester wore a flattop buzz cut, spoke of greasing a combine and lifting hay bales, enjoyed his fries, and admitted he did not look like a typical Senator because it spoke to his upbringing, his values and his deep roots in the state.

From *Campaigns and Elections,* February 2007

A key part of many of the candidates' successes in red states is firmly establishing their roots in the state. Tester ran as a third generation Montanan. Schweitzer also ran from the family farm. McCaskill established her firm roots in rural Missouri. They firmly rooted themselves in "place", and in so doing communicated values, likeability, and character.

LESSON 2: CANDIDATES MUST ESTABLISH CULTURAL BONDS WITH THEIR VOTERS

Successful candidates in red states establish cultural bonds with their voters. Tester talked about his opposition to gun control. Schweitzer had done the same and also talked about hunting, fishing and protecting public lands. Jim Webb wore combat boots and chewed tobacco. The key point is that through these actions and traits the candidates were able to illustrate their values and strength of character more convincingly than any policy positions they could have favored.

Successful Democrats also found ways to distinguish themselves from national Democrats. In Montana, the obvious issue to accomplish that was gun control.

LESSON 3: THE VALUES OF THE WEST AND MIDWEST ARE NOT THE VALUES OF THE SOUTH

Much of Democrats' talk and strategy around values has been developed with southern, not western, states in mind. The West is the frontier of the Democratic Party and a lot easier to deal with than the South. The southern states are 50–60 percent evangelical Christian. Montana is 36 percent evangelical Christian. These are far more libertarian and secular states. Arizona was the first state to defeat a ballot initiative banning gay marriage. Brian Schweitzer won soundly, even with a gay **marriage** initiative on the ballot.

LESSON 4: THE OPTIMIST WINS

A number of presidential studies show that the more optimistic candidate has always won the presidency. Similarly, the candidates who won in Montana exuded a "can do" attitude and optimism. Jon Tester's slogan as the state Senate leader had been, "We'll get 'er done."

Bill Clinton had showed Democrats how to be critical yet optimistic.

LESSON 5: IDENTIFY WITH CHANGE AND ANTI-CORRUPTION

Both Tester and Schweitzer communicated "change." Tester said he wanted to bring about change and make Washington look more like Montana. Schweitzer said "it was a new day in Montana."

Corruption was also a big issue in Montana in both races. In Schweitzer's campaign for an open-seated governorship, voters were angry about incompetence and scandal that compelled them to ask for whom their governor was really working. In the Senate race, voters continued to believe that Burns delivered for Montana even after the Abramoff scandal broke. If Burns delivered, we asked voters to question for whom he was really delivering. Tester also raised questions about who ultimately paid for the earmarks that Burns kept including in legislation.

LESSON 6: POPULIST ECONOMICS WINS

Voters in Montana, Missouri and Virginia responded to populist economics. Tester and Schweitzer both ran on taking on big corporations and big government on behalf of ordinary people and middle-class families. Tester said that he got into politics to take on the deregulation of Montana Power. Schweitzer talked about taking on pharmaceutical companies over prescription drug prices and how wrong it is for seniors to be forced to choose between food and drugs. Webb made a strong populist economic argument that the biggest divide facing our country was not over Iraq but over economic trends.

Candidates who won also paid attention to taxes as an economic issue for families. Schweitzer talked about a tax rebate for homeowners and not out-of-state corporations. Tester emphasized his record of giving tax breaks to 13,000 small businesses in Montana. Both talked about keeping taxes low for working families and making sure the wealthy pay their fair share.

LESSON 7: SEVERAL-YEAR SUCCESSES

In most cases, the winning candidates ran for over a year—getting out to voters, becoming better known, and getting their messages out. Schweitzer ran for Senate and then ran an intensive grass-roots campaign for two years for governor. Tester had an aggressive primary that he won with grass-roots support. Democrats got out and defined themselves at the grass-roots level.

LESSON 8: GOVERNORS MAKE A BIG DIFFERENCE

Governors make a huge difference in turning a red state blue. They are the local face of the Democratic Party. When Tester was accused of being a national Democrat, he said, "No, I'm a Brian Schweitzer Democrat." Similarly, Webb was able to say he was a Warner/Kaine Democrat. Governors also helped build grass-roots operations in their states. This is a major asset to picking up more seats in the Rocky Mountain states where we now have five Democratic governors.

LESSON 9: CAMPAIGNING TO INDEPENDENTS

To be successful, Democrats ran grass-roots efforts aimed at independent voters, not just television ads.

Montana ran the most extensive identification and re-identification campaign the state had ever seen, identifying most independent voters and then aggressively talking to them on the phone, at their doors, and through the mail.

LESSON 10: GOTV

In red states, winning campaigns cannot rely on just base voters. On the other hand, there is not a vote to waste. In Montana, there was a successful and unprecedented effort to get Democrats to vote early by mail, and tracking showed Tester winning those voters overwhelmingly. Also, young voters were instrumental in both Tester's upset primary victory and the win in November. There were also intensive efforts to turnout Native Americans in Montana. In Missouri, turnout among African American voters was at a record high, especially for an off-year election. In 2004, 8 percent of the electorate was African American, but in 2006 it was 13 percent. Minimum wage initiatives in both Missouri and Montana helped mobilize voters.

12

Party Lines

Alan Ehrenhalt

Gerrymanders make the odds against a successful challenge very hard to overcome—and to an extent dilute the political expression of voter discontent.

From *Governing,* January 2007

Democrats were expecting a big year in Ohio in 2006, and they got one. With the Republican Party crippled by both financial scandal and widespread disdain for the retiring GOP governor, voters elected Democratic candidates to almost every major office: not only governor but also U.S. senator, secretary of state, treasurer and attorney general—ending more than a decade of Republican control in each case. None of these elections was even close. "There will be a sea change in Ohio at every level," one of the state's most prominent Democrats exulted on election night. "The significance of this is almost indescribable."

It was, indeed, the Great Blue Sweep of 2006, in Ohio as in much of the country. But as the votes poured in, the Democratic Party found itself puzzling over the one big prize that got away: the legislature. Not only did Democrats fail to capture the Ohio House or Senate—which some thought might happen—they didn't come near it. When the legislature convenes again this month, the House will still be Republican by a margin of 53-46. And the Senate, which was Republican by a lopsided 22-11 before November, scarcely moved at all. It's now 21-12. The Democrats gained one Senate seat. The voter discontent that installed their candidates in nearly all the major statewide offices in Columbus failed to produce a remotely similar result on the legislative side.

Why would voters cast Democratic votes at the top of the ballot and then change their minds in the next column down? Actually, there's a simple answer. They didn't.

If you take out a calculator and add up the votes cast for the Ohio Senate in 2006, you will find that there was something indeed resembling a blue tide. Returns from the Secretary of State's Office (they are unofficial and will change, but not by much), show that Democratic Senate candidates drew more than a million votes—1,007,284. Republicans drew 731,168. That's close to a 60-40 split.

So how did the GOP end up with a 21-12 majority in the chamber? Well, only 17 of the 33 Senate seats were up this year. And Democrats already held eight of those. So the best they could do mathematically was pick up nine. And you're never going to win all of the other party's seats, no matter how strong a tide there is. So that explains part of it.

But still, one measly seat? The Democrats draw 60 percent of the statewide Senate vote—a plurality of 300,000—and all they get out of it is a one-seat gain? That makes no sense.

Or, rather, it doesn't make sense until you look at the margins of the winning candidates. All eight of the Republicans who won survived competitive campaigns by relatively narrow spreads. Six of the eight were in the 50 to 59 percent range. On the other hand, the nine Democratic winners all coasted home. Two weren't even opposed. The *lowest* Democratic winning percentage (60.8 percent) was very close to the *highest* Republican percentage (61.9 percent).

What's the explanation for that? I won't keep you in suspense any longer. In fact, I imagine you've figured it out by now. The Ohio Senate map is an elegant 21st-century gerrymander, drawn by Republican mapmakers to squeeze out as many Republican victories as possible by packing Democrats into a limited number of one-party enclaves with huge Democratic majorities. They did a pretty good job with the Ohio House, too, by the way: Democrats drew about 125,000 more votes than Republicans in the state's 99 House districts, and still fell four seats short of control.

This sort of thing is nothing new, of course. It has been a staple of legislative mapmaking since Elbridge Gerry invented it in Massachusetts in 1812 and lent his name to the practice. Both parties do it. Republicans were able to do it in Ohio in 2001 because they held all

> *Redistricting will always be unfair to somebody. The best we can hope for is that it isn't systematically unfair to the same people and groups, election after election.*

the major statewide offices, which gave them control of the state Apportionment Board that drew the map.

"It's definitely one of the most effective partisan plans," says Tim Storey, of the nonpartisan National Conference of State Legislatures. "It's one of the top two or three. The Republicans controlled that board, and they took advantage of it." As Storey is quick to add, Democrats would have been just as political had they been in charge—and likely will be if they hold on to their newly won state offices and control the board in 2011.

I went back and looked at the numbers in Ohio because I was curious what effect gerrymandering really had on the 2006 results. I have to confess that I've always been a skeptic when it comes to the notion that parties can draw districts skillfully enough to rig the political process for any significant length of time.

One thing I know for sure is that no set of districts can be drawn cleverly enough to provide a guarantee against a powerful shift in the mood of the electorate. Republicans drew most of the district lines in current use for the U.S. House, and many experts proclaimed that the political artistry of those lines precluded any possibility of Democratic congressional control in the current decade. But public revulsion over the Iraq war proved too much for the maps to handle, and the House went Democratic.

Those discontents had their effect at the state legislative level as well. Republicans in Michigan and Pennsylvania had the same cartographic opportunities as their counterparts in Ohio in 2001, and they drew House and Senate district maps that seemed just as impervious to Democratic challenge. But it didn't work out that way. Gerrymander or no gerrymander, Democrats picked up nine House seats in Michigan and eight in Pennsylvania in 2006, and (pending a recount in Pennsylvania) hold majorities in both chambers.

But those results simply frame the most important question: Is the power of gerrymandering overrated, or did the skill of Republican mapmakers at the state level save the GOP from a 2006 electoral debacle far more humiliating than it actually turned out to be? At this point, I'm inclined to think the answer is a little of both.

Gerrymanders aren't impregnable. In the right year, with the right issues, the right candidates and enough money, either party can break through the best of them. But even in a year like 2006, they make the odds against a successful challenge very hard to overcome—and to an extent, at least, dilute the political expression of voter discontent.

That's a legitimate problem for American democracy. The question is what to do about it. For decades, the forces of good government have been promoting a simple answer: Take mapmaking out of the hands of elected officials and turn it over to a nonpartisan commission.

Several states, most famously Iowa, have been doing this for many years, and the results have been generally positive: no skewing of votes-to-seats like the one that happened in Ohio this year.

But when citizens are asked if they want this sort of reform, they usually say no. That's what they said in a referendum in Ohio in 2005. In California, the voters have turned down five different proposals for nonpartisan redistricting over the past quarter-century. Still, the reformers never seem to give up. Republican Governor Arnold Schwarzenegger hopes to persuade the Democratic legislature to pass a nonpartisan redistricting plan later this year. The odds would seem to be against that happening.

But what if public sentiment changes? What if voters in states around the country become so tired of blatant partisan mapmaking that they finally decide to give the nonpartisan idea a try? Would that solve the problem?

To a degree, yes. In a small state such as Iowa, with a largely homogeneous population, it's easy to imagine a group of disinterested experts—or a computer—coming up with a map that doesn't tilt toward either party or disenfranchise any bloc of voters.

It's not so easy to imagine in a big, diverse state with highly concentrated minority populations—a state, for example, such as Ohio. If you look at the districts where Democrats won the most lopsided victories for the Ohio Senate in 2006, you'll find that they are almost all densely populated urban constituencies with big blocs of minority voters. Republicans were delighted to pack these voters together in 2001, but even the most nonpartisan group of mapmakers would have had some difficulty figuring out how to unpack them.

The only sure way to create more competition in a city such as Cleveland would be to create districts shaped like slices of pizza, narrow wedges in the inner city that broaden out and take in enough suburban territory to make them politically competitive. That's been suggested, and Democrats would no doubt like to do it in 2011 if they could, but such a scheme would almost certainly fall victim to legal objections that it would reduce the number of minority candidates strong enough to win election.

The harder one looks for an ideal solution to the redistricting problem, the more one concludes that there is no ideal solution: Redistricting will always be unfair to somebody. What we can hope for is that it isn't systematically unfair to the same people and groups, election after election. Perhaps we're inching closer to that goal.

13

Make a Deal, Get a Donation

Theodora A. Blanchfield

Life takes Visa. For just about anything else politically related, candidates in Montana will take the official party MasterCard.

It's a commonly held notion that politicians will do almost anything for money. And some politicians earn that money in interesting ways.

Want to play pingpong with California Gov. Arnold Schwarzenegger? If you promise to donate to his campaign, he just might agree to a match. Byng Forsberg, an 80-year-old superstar on the 75-plus table tennis circuit, received a fund-raising letter from the governor's campaign. Forsberg wrote back that he would donate if the governor would agree to a pingpong match. A reporter from the *Stockton Record* in California asked the governor's staff about the letter, and Schwarzenegger agreed to the match.

In 1995, Democrat Ruth Messinger hoped to start a new trend: giving up treats for campaign season. The then-Manhattan borough president, who planned to run for mayor in 1997, urged supporters to give up an ice cream cone a week, a Big Mac meal, a CD and a T-shirt to "invest" in her campaign. Giving up an ice cream cone a week netted a campaign donation of $10 a month to Friends of Ruth Messinger '97; the Big Mac meal, $20; a CD, $40; and a T-shirt, $80. But she lost the race. No word on total dollars raised or pounds lost.

If you're not willing to make sacrifices for your candidate, consider adding them to your Christmas list. Last Christmas, Kayla Moore, wife of Roy Moore, the Republican candidate for governor of Alabama, sent out fund-raising letters on her husband's behalf saying that Christmas was an appropriate time to begin their campaign "to return morality to our country and God to our public square."

Sometimes the candidate will sacrifice for you. Those who were sad to hear that the congressional jalapeño-eating contest is no

From *Campaigns and Elections,* September 2006

more will be happy to know that U.S. Rep. Steve Pearce, R-N.M., lets them fulfill their penchants for watching lawmakers down cringe-inducing spices. Pearce held his second annual Green Chile Fest fundraiser this June.

The Montana Democratic Party isn't asking anyone to sacrifice anything. Just sign up for their Montana Democratic Party MasterCard and one out of every hundred dollars spent will go towards the party. The party also gets a donation from every new card member.

In a job where the other guy is always out to embarrass you with some detail from your past, some candidates are willing to embarrass themselves first in the same good, old-fashioned way the rest of us might after a few drinks: karaoke. Melody Damayo, a Republican who recently lost the primary for governor of Nevada, hosted a campaign fund-raiser where she treated attendees to her karaoke rendition of "Material Girl" as well as a limbo contest.

In St. Louis, the Women's Political Caucus upped the stakes by holding a karaoke auction with Missouri politicians, auctioning off the song choice to the highest bidder. Attendees paid an entrance fee and then bid to hear politicians such as U.S. Senate candidate Claire McCaskill, state representatives Russ Carnahan, Margaret Donnelly, Barbara Fraser, Rick Johnson, Robin Wright Jones and Sam Page croon some embarrassing tunes.

Of course, paying for someone else to embarrass him or herself isn't quite as fun as paying to embarrass yourself. Republicans in the Utah House of Representatives held a speed-dating fund-raiser, allowing lobbyists five-minute dates with the 56 representatives, as long as the lobbyists donated to the representative's political action committee.

Puts the fun back in fund raising.

14

Cookie-Jar Clampdown

Rob Gurwitt

Tougher lobby laws are being discussed all over the country. A few states have enacted them. Whether they will work remains to be seen.

Until last year, the North Carolina legislature did not spend a lot of time worrying about its reputation. It had never gone through a scandal on the order of South Carolina's 1989 "Operation Lost Trust" vote-buying affair, which led to indictments against one-tenth of the legislature, or of the "Tennessee Waltz" scandal of 2005, which led to the arrest of seven state legislators on federal bribery and extortion charges. "We've been lucky to have clean government for most of North Carolina's history," says Tom Ross, president of the Z. Smith Reynolds Foundation in Winston-Salem.

Indeed, when a bipartisan citizens' commission named by the secretary of state proposed in 2004 that the legislature close a gaping set of loopholes in its lobby laws, its ideas went nowhere. "I don't think there was enough interest, and certainly there was no pressure to do anything," says Bob Phillips, who heads Common Cause North Carolina.

That all changed in late 2005, when a series of newspaper stories began detailing a raft of unsavory doings by aides and associates of House Speaker Jim Black, and the federal and state investigations into them. Black had held the post for four terms, riding herd over a slim Democratic majority, earning respect as a consensus-builder and loyalty for his prodigious fundraising efforts on behalf of colleagues.

The catalog of misdeeds, however, was a long one. The woman who ran the House page program had arranged to have teenage pages stay with her son, a felon with a history of drug and alcohol problems; when that became public, Black made her House historian, but after $80,000 in payment, she produced only a 23-page report filled with mistakes and grammatical errors. Last year, a

From *Governing*,
April 2007

Republican-turned-Democratic legislator named Michael Decker pled guilty to taking $50,000 from an unnamed Democrat to switch parties in 2003, thus putting him in position to cast the deciding vote that kept Black in power as co-speaker after the Republicans had appeared to take the majority. Black's former political director pled guilty to failing to register as a lobbyist on behalf of a company seeking the contract to run the new state lottery—which Black had played a key role in creating. Similarly, one of Black's first appointees to the lottery commission was forced off after it was revealed he, too, had failed to report financial ties to the same lottery vendor.

Black himself remained only circumstantially touched by the scandals—until two months ago, when he stunned Raleigh by pleading guilty to accepting $29,000 from three chiropractors in exchange for pushing legislation they wanted. He followed that up a few days later by accepting a plea agreement to state charges that the party-switching bribe to Decker had come from him.

By then, though, events at the capitol had passed him by. Well before his court pleas, Black had stepped down as speaker and had unwittingly served as the catalyst for a sweeping ethics reform package. The 2006 legislation, shepherded through the House by Joe Hackney, who was then majority leader and this year became speaker, tightened the state's lobby disclosure laws, enacted a gift ban, made it harder for lobbyists to bundle campaign contributions and strengthened the state's ethics commission. "The scandals," says Tom Ross, "gave light to other kinds of issues and concerns people had. No one saw it as just a problem that the speaker had that had to be fixed. It was seen as a more systemic problem—a recognition that we just weren't as open and transparent as we should be, that there was a lot happening that wasn't disclosed."

PETRI DISHES FOR NEW IDEAS

North Carolina isn't alone in that realization. Capitol hallways from New York to Alaska are awash in virtuous intentions this year, which is hardly surprising in the wake of voters' focus on legislative integrity in last November's elections. While their ire might have been aimed first at a tarnished Congress, state legislative leaders paid attention. "This has been cutting a broad swath," says Peggy Kerns, director of the Center for Ethics in Government at the National Conference of State Legislatures. "Even if states have had no scandals, they're interested in making sure their general assembly and legislators are ethical, and that there's an ethical environment there."

Yet the dynamics of reform are also being fed by circumstances peculiar to the states: in some, their own homegrown scandals, and in many, a growing sense that longstanding capitol folkways need refurbishing. As state Senator Kate Brown, an Oregon Democrat, puts it, "The states have become the petri dishes for new and evolving ideas," and the increasing importance of legislatures as engines of domestic policy has brought with it a pair of pressures that demand attention: increasingly expensive legislative campaigns that push legislators to act more like members of Congress in their search for funding; and growing numbers of highly paid lobbyists seeking whatever edge they can find. States where a few years ago a legislative campaign topping $50,000 would have raised eyebrows are now seeing campaigns requiring well into six figures, and in closely fought states, the most expensive races can top $500,000 or even $1 million. Some 40,000 lobbyists now focus on the 50 statehouses and help fund those campaigns, according to the Center on Public Integrity in Washington, D.C. In 2005, lobbying expenditures totaled $1.16 billion in the 42 states that reported them, a 22 percent increase over the year before.

In that atmosphere, it is hardly surprising that a growing number of legislative reformers look askance at the gifts, trips, meals and other forms of social lubrication that spill from the pockets of well-heeled interests. Nor do they like the close-mouthed, none-of-your-business legislative culture in some states that leaves ordinary citizens wondering just what all that cash is buying. To the most determined reformers, indeed, the recent spate of rules changes and ethics legislation should be considered just the beginning. "You start with compliance, because if you make it illegal to take free sports tickets and travel, then people won't be doing it," says state Representative Deborah Ross, a North Carolina Democrat who has played a prominent role in implementing that state's reforms. "But you have to ask, what kind of culture did you have that made people think that would be acceptable in the first place? So the question is, after we do this compliance, will the culture fundamentally shift to where the public good is considered the primary concern of legislators?"

It's a fair question. And if three states where reform has dominated the agenda this year—North Carolina, Pennsylvania and Oregon—are any guide, it will not be answered anytime soon.

HABITS AND TRADITIONS

Since the passage of North Carolina's new ethics law, attention in Raleigh has understandably focused on what it means for legislators and lobbyists. Every legislator has had to attend a two-hour training session—and, says Deborah Ross, all the sessions have lasted longer because members have had so many questions. "We didn't have that opportunity in the past," she adds, "because that wasn't the kind of culture we had, where ethics was front of mind."

The question, of course, is whether the new legislation will change for good what Hackney calls "a habit, a tradition in the way that entertaining and lobbying are done." The issue, reformers agree, was never so much the meals or the travel that lobbyists were able to buy as the exclusive access to legislators' time and attention that a meal or golf outing secured—time and attention that ordinary citizens and non-profit lobbyists found harder to get. Deborah Ross is optimistic, if only because many members of the legislature are relatively new and haven't yet risen to positions of influence where they'd expect or solicit the little kindnesses of lobbyists. "If you change the culture for half the House this session," she says, "then that's a new culture they'll perpetuate."

Common Cause's Bob Phillips, however, isn't so sure. "We'll have transparency that we never did have," he says, but points out that last year's legislation still allows lobbyists to raise funds for legislative campaigns. "The real action and power now comes in the campaign contributions. Lobbyists raising money for elected officials is where they gain their power. They develop relationships that the average citizen can't have with legislators."

WHO'S PAYING FOR DINNER?

Lobbyists' influence also is at issue in Oregon. There, newspaper reports last year revealed that the Oregon Beer and Wine Distributors' Association had treated seven leg-

> *"I wanted to say from day one, 'Let's change the culture.'"*
>
> —Jeff Merkley, Oregon House Speaker

islators to trips to Maui in 2002 and 2004—gifts that neither the lobbyists nor the legislators reported. The subsequent coverage was careful to note that beer-and-wine lobbyist Paul Romain had successfully fended off any increase in the state's beer tax, which hasn't changed for 30 years.

The scandal actually broke in the midst of a low-profile effort to update Oregon's ethics code, which has been in place slightly longer than the beer tax. The Oregon Law Commission, a bipartisan group of lawyers, legislators and academics, had been asked by Democratic Governor Ted Kulongoski in 2003 to look at improving the code and was readying its recommendations for the 2007 session. These were mostly incremental changes: restricting the use of campaign contributions, increasing fines for violations and requiring more frequent disclosure of lobbyists' gifts.

Not surprisingly, the stories about the Maui trips blew a hole in that discussion. "Those stories raised questions like, jeez, all we want you to do is report, and you're not even doing that," says Janice Thompson, director of the Money In Politics Action Research Project in Portland. "But the real issue in the public's eye wasn't that they weren't reported, it was why are they doing these trips in the first place."

That was essentially Jeff Merkley's response. Merkley, the Democratic leader while Republicans ran the House, became speaker after Democrats won a majority in last November's elections. He decided that rather than wait to craft ethics legislation, he would work to change the House rules at the start of the session. "When you get into the nitty-gritty of legislation, it's very easy to get distracted by 'what if' arguments," he says. "I wanted to say from day one, 'Here we are, let's change the culture.'"

So the House banned trips paid for by lobbyists; banned entertainment paid for by lobbyists; and instituted a $10 maximum on gifts, including meals. "Overnight," says Merkley, "behavior changed. Lobbyists told me that before, they'd been beseeched by members, 'Why don't you take me to lunch? Who's going to take me to dinner?' That changed. As one lobbyist put it, he's going to save $20,000 over the next six months."

The Senate, meanwhile, has opted to go the legislative route, building off the Law Commission's recommendations. Although it has tightened up limits on lobbyist-sponsored gifts, meals and travel, its preferred approach has been to strengthen disclosure laws. This, in turn, has meant strengthening the state ethics board, known as the Government Standards and Practices Commission, which ostensibly oversees the behavior of some 160,000 elected, appointed, hired and volunteer public officials at every level of government in the state. This is a tall order under any circumstances, but the legislature made it much harder in recent years by cutting the GSPC's funding and capabilities, mostly as retaliation for commission inquiries into ethics complaints.

The response, led by Senate Rules Committee Chair Kate Brown, has been to try to find an independent source of funding for the commission. "It's deplorable to me," she says, "that we as a legislature would hold the purse-strings to the very agency that holds us accountable."

Still, it is unclear to what extent the new rules and legislation will convincingly stem the cozy insiderness of "the lobby," as it is known in Salem. As Merkley points out, in one 2006 House race, the two candidates spent $1.4 million on their campaigns. "It's hard to raise sums that large by just knocking on doors," he says. And in Oregon, fundraising tactics that are illegal elsewhere—such as using corporate funds to pay for legislative campaigns—are permitted.

OLD GUARD VS. REFORMERS

Pennsylvania, too, is awash in campaign cash: It places no limits on contributions, although it does prohibit corporations from making direct donations to candidates. It was also—until a few months ago—the only state with no law to regulate lobbying activities, and even now reformers dismiss the new law as pitifully weak.

So you'd think that overhauling campaign-finance and lobbying rules might stand atop reformers' wish lists in the Keystone State. And they do. But so does reforming pretty

> ## "There's a feeling that we have to move on this."
>
> —Rep. David Steil, co-chair of Pennsylvania's legislative reform commission

much everything about the state legislature, which until this year operated in a way that your average Gilded Age political boss would recognize in an instant. "The legislature here is an anachronism," says Barry Kauffman, the state's Common Cause director, "and it's locked into a history more than 100 years in the past."

Until 2005, not many people cared, outside a handful of reformers in Harrisburg. That summer, however, the legislature handed itself, state judges and a small number of state officials a pay raise that wound up causing the biggest political ruckus the state has seen in many years. Its reverberations still have not died down.

The issue wasn't so much the raise itself as how it was handled. Using another bill as a vehicle, a legislative committee convened late at night, stripped the bill's original language and substituted the raise, then reported it to the floor, where legislators at 2 a.m. voted without debate to pass it; even had they had time to read it, the bill wouldn't have told them much, since it essentially pegged officials' salaries to the money earned by their federal counterparts. Democratic Governor Ed Rendell quickly signed the measure.

The tactics weren't new. Control of the Pennsylvania legislature has long rested in the hands of a few leaders, and since the state sidestepped the Progressive Era reforms of the early 20th century, the only checks on their power are the governor and state supreme court justices—who, in Harrisburg's close-knit political community, tend to see disagreement merely as an opportunity for deal making. The public and rank-and-file legislators have usually been treated as mere annoyances. So, for instance, in 2004, a measure allowing slot machines into Pennsylvania that had been pushed by Rendell as a means of providing property-tax relief was substituted for another bill over the July 4 weekend, and passed with no public input. "A lot of folks wanted a public discussion about what is potentially the biggest change in social policy here since the advent of the automobile," says Tim Potts, a former legislative staffer who runs a reform group called Democracy Rising. "But everyone outside that building was prevented from having that discussion. A lot of people were really angry."

Not, however, as angry as they became a year later when the pay raise went through. The press, which knew a good story when it saw one, filled up not only with pieces about the legislature's close-mouthed ways but about legislative perks, from a monthly allowance for leasing a car to a $140 per diem for travel expenses no matter how close a legislator lives to Harrisburg. A few months later, voters for the first time in the state's history turned out a sitting Supreme Court justice, and shortly after that, the legislature rescinded the pay raise. But the hubbub did not die down, and in last year's elections, between defeats and retirements, fully one-fifth of the legislature's incumbents left office.

CAUTIOUSLY OPTIMISTIC

The result now is that political virtue is the coin of the realm in Harrisburg. "Everyone in the city is a reformer," says Terry Madonna, director of the Center for Politics and Public Affairs at Franklin & Marshall College in Lancaster. "This revolt from the voters genuinely has thrown the fear of God into legislators." One result is that, although Democrats took a one-seat majority in the House in November, their longtime leader, Bill DeWeese, was unable to win the speakership; instead, a Republican who was put forward as a reformer was made speaker—the result, ironically enough, of a backroom deal struck at the governor's mansion.

Reform is also now on the legislative agenda, in the form of a commission created by new Speaker Dennis O'Brien. Its Republican co- chair, David Steil, was part of an abortive reform effort about a decade ago to open up the rules and give legislators more time to consider bills before voting on them. "I think things are headed in a positive direction," Steil says. "There's a feeling that we have to move on this, that there'll never be a better time than now."

The commission is focusing first on rules changes internal to the House. "They are all focused on ensuring that issues or bills stand or fall on their merits," he says. "So that members can offer their ideas, assure themselves of having their day in court, and ultimately a vote." Once that work is done, Steil says, it will be time to discuss a long list of potential reforms, from establishing an ethics committee to trimming the power of the House Rules Committee—the leadership's choke point—to campaign finance reform, term limits, even cutting the size of the legislature.

Reformers believe that, as Potts says, "This is the best environment for improving the way our government works that I've seen in the 35 years I've been on this scene." But they are also cautious. Steil believes that the number of legislators committed to reform is still a minority, and despite the election of a wave of legislators who ran on reform, the old guard still holds considerable sway. "We absolutely cannot let our guard down," says Potts, "and we absolutely cannot assume good things are going to happen. I will believe it when I see it, and not one second before."

IV

Legislatures

Legislatures are one of the great ironies of representative democracy. They are arguably *the* central institutions of all republican systems of government. After all, legislatures are where democratically elected representatives get together to do the people's business.

The people, however, often aren't too happy with the results. Indeed, rather than doing the people's business, legislatures in many quarters are viewed skeptically as giving the people the business. Such cynicism about politics in general and legislatures (or at least legislators) in particular partly explains the popularity of legislative term limits in many states.

But do legislatures really deserve this reputation? Many observers of state politics would argue no. Legislatures have a tough job, and no matter how well they do it, their decisions will leave many unsatisfied and some apoplectic. It's just the nature of the job. The readings in this section highlight some of the better- and lesser-known sides of that job.

WHAT LEGISLATURES (AND LEGISLATORS) DO

Legislatures do three basic things: they pass laws, they represent the people, and they oversee public agencies in other branches of government. Sounds simple in theory, but in practice it is a phenomenally complex challenge. A state legislature deals with a thousand or more proposed laws in any given year.[1] Those bills can cover everything from the death penalty to property taxes, from water regulation to welfare. Legislators, in short, tend to have an awful lot on their plates, and are expected to be experts on, well, everything.

Representing people is no picnic either. Constituents outnumber state legislators by the tens of thousands, even hundreds of thousands, to one. Ever try pleasing a hundred thousand people? Most state legislators would likely tell you not to bother—it can't be done. It doesn't matter what side you take on an issue or proposed law, chances are somebody in your district disagrees with you and is only too happy to point out your faults on this matter to their friends and neighbors. Keeping an eye on public agencies and employees is another mission impossible. At last count state governments employed five million workers and local government employed nearly fourteen million.[2] Most college deans get a headache trying to keep track of less than a hundred faculty members.

You might say that passing laws, representing constituents, and keeping an eye on public agencies is a full-time job. And if you said that you'd be wrong, at least in some states. These states, including the great state of Texas, still have part-time legislatures. Which doesn't mean that these legislators are not expected to do any less than their full-time counterparts in other states. They're just expected to do it in less time and for less pay.

In thanks for all this hard work, legislators generally are viewed with considerable skepticism and cynicism by the public. Evidence of this comes from the success of the term limits movement. In ballot initiative states, voters have enthusiastically supported limits on the amount of time legislators can spend in office, regardless of how popular they are with their constituents.

As the reading by Rob Gurwitt in the previous section makes clear, some of this suspicion of legislators is not without reason. Corruption scandals are not exactly calculated to boost the public's esteem of legislatures. Generally, though, most legislators do a pretty tough job pretty well most of the time, and there is an emerging consensus among observers of state government that term limits have hampered the ability of legislators.[3] Voters don't seem to care, at least not yet. They appear to view experienced, professional legislators as the greater problem.

RECENT TRENDS

The essays in this section reflect some of the key issues and challenges currently facing state legislatures. Joe Kolman's essay takes a look at an underappreciated component of state legislatures: staffers. Legislative staff are key cogs in the machinery of democracy. They provide research for their elected bosses, do service work for constituents, draft bills, and often serve as institutional memory. Staffers mostly are taken for granted; it's fairly safe to say that the

average voter rarely gives a thought to the qualifications and responsibilities of a committee or legislative aide. That may change, however. There is an unprecedented wave of retirements about to happen among legislative staffers as baby boomers step down from these highly specialized positions. Kolman asks: Who is going to replace them?

Nicole Casal Moore's essay follows up on some of the readings in the previous section. Just as corruption and bribery scandals have prompted calls for tighter regulations on lobbyists, they also have precipitated a movement for tighter ethics requirements on elected officials and other public employees. This reflects a key oversight responsibility of legislatures, as it is part of their job to keep an eye on the rest of government. Thus legislatures are looking at broader ethics requirements and seeking to give ethics commissions the regulatory teeth to enforce them.

Jack Penchoff's essay takes a look at the pay of state legislators, and he finds that it tends to lag behind inflation. Legislators, in other words, are doing more work for less compensation. In fact for many legislatures, pay is falling when inflation is taken into account. Good luck calling for higher pay, though. Most elected officials who propose raising their own salaries find it a tough sell with voters.

In the final essay Dave McNeely takes a look at what can happen when a legislature is unable to resolve a tough issue. Property taxes are a difficult and complex issue that perennially tops the legislative agenda. Nowhere is this more true than in Texas, where court rulings forcing more equitable distribution of property taxes among school districts created band-aids and gridlock in the legislature for years. Gov. Rick Perry, frustrated by the lack of a sustainable solution to this issue, created a commission charged specifically with the creation of a comprehensive property tax package. The problem essentially was outsourced from the public legislature to a private legislature. In this case, it created a solution that worked. It took some work to sell legislators on the plan, but it ended up passing with large legislative majorities.

Notes

1. Kevin B. Smith, Alan Greenblatt, and John Buntin, *Governing States and Localities* (Washington, D.C.: CQ Press, 2005), 178.
2. Census Bureau. "Governmental Employment and Payrolls: 1982–2004." www.census.gov/compendia/statab/tables/07s0450.xls.
3. Alan Greenblat, "The Truth About Term Limits," *Governing,* January, 2006.

15

Brain Drain: Many Legislative Staffers Are Due to Retire Soon— Taking with Them a Ton of Experience

Joe Kolman

State legislative staffers are retiring. Who will replace them?

When it comes to legislative proposals, Eddye McClure and her counterparts in Montana Legal Services have seen it all.

"Don't try to reinvent the wheel," McClure tells rookie bill drafters. "There are no new ideas that haven't already been drafted in some form—ask one of us."

But what happens when wise veterans of a decade or more of legislative sessions lay down their codebooks, turn in their nametags, and saunter off to places where nobody cheers when somebody says "sine die?"

As baby boomers eye their golden years, employers across the nation face the prospect of losing folks who know how things work and why. The problem may be even more acute, however, in the relatively small world of legislative employment. Most of the positions are highly specialized, may appeal to only a few, and can take years to learn. The hours can be long, stressful and irregular. And many of the jobs rely heavily on relationships built over the years with lawmakers.

Why does it matter? While lawmakers make the big decisions, staffers do everything to make sure the giant machines known as state legislatures run as smoothly as possible. They provide research and context, write bill drafts in the proper style, explain budget information and dispense legal advice. They are versed in parliamentary procedure and rules. And those are only the most visible staffers; thousands of others make sure computer systems hum along and documents actually make it into print.

"It's a unique world, so experience helps," says Legislative Counsel of California Diane Boyer-Vine.

From *State Legislatures*, February 2007

But like other leaders of legislative staff across the country, Boyer-Vine sees many of her employees nearing the end of their careers. Nationwide, almost half of legislative staffers are more than 50 years old, according to a recent survey by the National Conference of State Legislatures. About one out of every three staffers surveyed has spent two decades or more working for a legislature.

"You have a lot of experience walking out the door," Boyer-Vine says.

Possible solutions range from convincing potential retirees to hang on a bit longer to establishing formal mentoring programs and succession plans. The pending glut of retirements also presents a chance to evaluate and possibly change the traditional structure of legislative organizations.

"We can bemoan it, but that's not going to stop them from retiring," says Susan Fox, a 15-year veteran of Montana Legislative Services recently hired as executive director. "This is opportunity knocking."

A LONG TIME COMING

How the boomer generation came to be more prevalent in the public sector than in the private world is complicated.

About 46 percent of government workers at all levels are more than 45 years old, according to a 2002 study by the Nelson A. Rockefeller Institute of Government. Among state workers, the figure is 45 percent. But less than one-third of private sector workers have seen their 45th birthday.

There are a number of factors contributing to the difference between the private and public sector, according to a 2003 report by The Center for Organizational Research in Massachusetts. Reasons cited in the report include:

- In the 1960s and '70s, government went on a hiring spree. Many of the employees hired during those years are approaching retirement.
- In the 1980s and '90s, governments did a lot of belt tightening. Positions likely to be filled by younger workers were left vacant and layoffs targeted newer employees. Reductions in training and development budgets didn't allow younger employees to gain skills needed to ascend into leadership positions.

- Public service as a career hasn't been cool for a while, especially compared to the private sector where pay scales can be more flexible, promotions more attainable and applications less cumbersome.
- Retirement polices in governments may be rigid, not allowing for phased retirements.

Some say there also are generational differences at work. For baby boomers, a steady job with good benefits and a secure retirement were reasons enough to become a lifer.

"Boomers were easy," says Fox, herself a member of that generation. "They planted themselves."

The study by the Center for Organizational Research concluded that the situation isn't completely dire. Boomers may continue working past retirement age, the job security and benefits of government jobs may once again be appealing to those burned by the private sector, and after the terrorist attacks of 2001, there may be a resurgence in the nobility of a career in public service.

Still, the fact remains that legislative leaders across the country seem to be realizing that their staffs are graying. In California, Boyer-Vine sees most of her supervisors nearing retirement age. In Connecticut, it is estimated that by 2011, almost 60 percent of the current staff could be retired. Until recently, the "rookie" attorney in Montana's Legislative Services was a veteran of 17 years.

Connecticut has a formal succession-planning program, and California is just starting one. In Montana, Fox has been on the job only a few months, but dealing with an aging staff is at the top of her list of things to address. Already, she has put out a call for mentors to help train new researchers.

SLOW TO RESPOND

Although other legislative agencies may be aware of the retirement problem, few are addressing it. "There's really no concerted effort out there in most legislatures to deal formally with this issue of baby boomers getting ready to bail out," says Brian Weberg of NCSL, who headed a task force on succession planning in 2005.

Successfully implementing plans often requires an inside champion, such as a human resources director and few legislatures have such a person, Weberg says.

An exception is Jim Tamburro. As the training and staff development coordinator for the Connecticut General Assembly, part of his job is to make sure people are ready to do their jobs.

A component of the agency's succession management plan is to identify and train future leaders. Anyone who thinks they may want to take a leadership role is free to enter the program.

Tamburro admits he was afraid the program would attract some for whom leadership may not be the best career option, while better candidates would stay away. But that hasn't happened. The program is intensive and only those who really want to be leaders stick with it.

Participants undergo an evaluation not only by supervisors, but also by peers and others. They take a personality test to identify communication and leadership style. And they must complete an individual plan that shows where they want to go in their job. Participants also receive office-specific training and are given some higher-visibility tasks or projects.

Even with the training, Tamburro says legislative agencies are still relatively flat organizations. There are just not many leadership positions available. However, creating more leadership opportunities may be part of an agency's goal. And obtaining leadership skills is valuable for any employee.

OTHER OPTIONS

There are other ways—short term and long term—to deal with the retirement bubble.

Postponing retirement is one option. In Idaho, the veteran director of legislative services, Carl Bianchi, announced his intent to retire before the 2006 session. That prompted House Speaker Bruce Newcomb and Senate President Pro-Tem Bob Geddes to plead for a bit more time. Geddes jokes that they sought permission from Bianchi's wife for one more session.

"Carl had a lot of experience we hated to lose," Geddes says. "We felt like we needed a bit more time to find and groom a person to replace him."

How to Deal with Retirements

While legislative agencies may be realizing that the baby boomer age bubble has the potential to deplete their staffs and result in a loss of institutional knowledge, leaders may not really know what to do about it.

The National Conference of State Legislatures' Legislative Staff Coordinating Committee established the Legislative Institution Task Force to examine the problem and come up with solutions. Its report, "Succession Planning in the Legislative Workplace—A Guide for State Legislatures" gives this advice:

■ Understand the current situation within your organization. Examine the staff and identify the key roles that only a few people perform. Estimate who may be retiring in the next two to five years and what roles they play. Try to gauge the level of commitment younger workers may have.

■ Work with staff to anticipate transition. Key parts of this include enlisting cooperation in succession planning, identifying the in-depth knowledge and tasks that need to be passed on, developing a resource notebook or manual for critical positions and devising a mentor program for younger staffers to learn aspects of other jobs.

■ Prepare the organization to change as needed during transition. This includes assigning responsibilities for succession planning oversight and leadership development and also developing a plan that identifies hiring and training needs. Before making decisions about new staff appointments, consider organizational changes. It's also important to keep employees informed about general plans and directions.

■ Work with emerging leaders to prepare them to assume critical roles. First, figure out a way to identify potential leaders. This may be done by current leaders or asking for volunteers. It's important that current leaders support the idea of succession planning as well as training and mentoring programs.

■ Guide emerging leaders toward new responsibilities. Some legislatures may not have formal succession planning programs. But employees who may inherit duties when co-workers retire can take steps to prepare themselves. That includes soliciting feedback from supervisors as well as peers on leadership potential, finding a mentor, participating in available training, asking questions of current managers and developing an individual career development plan.

Bianchi retired later in 2006 after the Legislature passed a resolution in his honor. He was replaced by Jeff Youtz, himself a 29-year veteran of the state's Legislative Services Office. Youtz, who has no definite plans for his retirement date, says Idaho's staff has a good age mix, but there are several key baby boomers in leadership positions.

Youtz says succession planning is always on his mind. "I try to hire people who I envision one day might be doing my job," he says.

Ohio also has used stopgap measures. Karen Burkey, the personnel officer for the Legislative Services Commission, says about a half dozen attorneys and researchers have retired and then returned.

"We'd like to keep those people who know how things work," Burkey says. "So far, we've been able to handle it with people coming back."

BEYOND BAND AIDS

Encouraging valuable employees to stick around and revising policies to allow for phased retirements and part-time employment are really only band aids.

Devising a plan to deal with retirements does not have to be a behemoth effort, according to a report from the NCSL Task Force on Succession Planning. It is really just an attempt to keep the organization focused on its mission as it undergoes major personnel changes. It should be viewed as a chance to review job descriptions, delegate responsibilities and change the organization to make it run more efficiently.

"This just sounds so tedious, but it gives you this place to become flexible and change as you need to," Fox says. "I see succession planning as opportunity. It's all about change, and change is what people don't like. When somebody leaves, you institute the change for that new person who doesn't know any better."

Evaluating the organization's need and the roles veterans play is key to tackling succession planning, according to the NCSL report and a study by the Center for Organizational Research. Providing opportunities for leadership training, mentoring and higher-profile assignments also is important, the studies say.

Recruiting new employees also must change. "Some generations are apt to move and not make this a lifelong career," says Boyer-Vine. But she and others say agencies should emphasize the benefits of legislative work and also provide some of the perks younger workers crave.

Although there may be long hours involved during the sessions, legislative employees often enjoy accumulated compensation time. The work is intense, but hardly dull. Schedules can be flexible, which is conducive to telecommuting, engaging in other interests, or taking college classes.

And whether it's dealing with current employees looking to move into management or training new recruits, Tamburro says veterans should be included in ensuring the institution continues to thrive long after they are gone.

"We have a lot of people who have been here a long time. These people basically built this place," Tamburro says. "Veterans need to be asked, 'How do you want to leave it? What's your legacy going to be?'"

16

Flexing the Ethics Muscle

Nicole Casal Moore

Can tough new ethics laws restore confidence in state government? State legislatures sure hope so.

They have names like Shrimpscam, Azcam, Bop Trot, Operation Lost Trust, Tennessee Waltz. They are investigations into political corruption and ethics violations that snare legislators and damage legislatures. In 2005, scandals in at least six states involved lawmakers. The fallout can be devastating to public perception and confidence and sullies the reputation of the institution—and those who serve in it. That's when ethics reform takes center stage.

In the year since four Tennessee lawmakers and others were arrested in a bribery sting and charged with extortion, their former colleagues in the General Assembly have been busy enacting new ethics laws.

Leaders appointed a bipartisan, joint ethics committee and called legislators into a special session where they created a new ethics commission with broad jurisdiction over lawmakers. They banned lobbyists from giving lawmakers campaign contributions or gifts. And they required lobbyists to report more details about their finances. These are among the more visible of the many ethics and lobbying provisions Tennessee legislators passed late last year and in early 2006.

But none of them would have prevented the scandal of 2005. Those crimes were already against the law, points out Tennessee Senator Jim Kyle, a member of the joint ethics committee that wrote the bills. So why did the legislature pass them? "We felt that if we didn't exceed the public's expectations, we could lose the moral authority to govern," Kyle says.

Though initiated in response to scandals, Tennessee's new laws aim for a higher purpose—to help restore public confidence in government.

From *State Legislatures*, July/August 2006

And Tennessee is not alone. Connecticut, Florida, North Carolina and other states reacted to scandals in the last few years that legislators felt violated the public trust.

SCANDAL BREEDS REFORM

State legislators across the nation have introduced close to 200 ethics and lobbying bills so far this year. At press time, five states—Colorado, Iowa, Maine, Tennessee and Virginia—had enacted new laws, with Tennessee's overhaul the most significant. It's too early to tell whether this will be a banner year for ethics reform. Some factors suggest that it might be. It's an election year. And the federal scandal involving former lobbyist Jack Abramoff and several members of Congress has cast a shadow over government.

A January 2006 Harris poll found that only 4 percent of U.S. adults believe the Abramoff scandal is an isolated case, compared to 86 percent who think he is just one of many who happened to get caught.

There's likely a connection between the Abramoff scandal and the long list of ethics bills being considered in state legislatures—75 of which deal with lobbying. It was behind Minnesota Senator Linda Higgins' ethics bill, which, among other things, would require more financial disclosure by lobbyists and would establish a two-year period before former legislators may lobby. The bill's purpose is to ensure the public knows how lobbyists are influencing the legislative process.

"I looked at the Abramoff scandal and thought that, even though it's in Washington, people might start to look at us and think maybe our branch of government is like that," Higgins says. "Maybe we also were getting golfing trips to Scotland paid by lobbyists. Yet in Minnesota, we can't even take a cup of coffee from lobbyists."

THE UMBRELLA EFFECT

Robert Stern, president of the bipartisan Center for Governmental Studies in Los Angeles, understands this umbrella effect. "The public puts everyone in the same

> *"We felt that if we didn't exceed the public's expectations, we could lose the moral authority to govern."*
>
> —Tennessee Sen. Jim Kyle

field and doesn't distinguish among the various levels of government," he says. "If the president and the Congress are seen in a bad light, so is every other public official."

Stern says legislatures rarely pass campaign finance or ethics laws unless there's been a scandal at some level of government. But, he says, we can't have a law for every situation. "There should be a standard that says you shouldn't embarrass the body."

Connecticut lawmakers were embarrassed not only by the misconduct of their governor, John Rowland, but by the inability of the State Ethics Commission to respond to it. Many of the commissioners recused themselves from the bribery investigations citing conflicts of interest with the former governor, who was ultimately sentenced to a year in prison.

The legislature passed laws in 2005 subjecting contractors to state ethics laws, including gift limitations and reporting requirements. It also abolished the nine-member ethics commission and fired its director. Now the state has an Office of State Ethics, with a Citizen's Ethics Advisory Board.

Not all ethics reforms are the direct result of headline-grabbing scandals. There hasn't been an FBI sting in North Carolina, but there has been a flurry of allegations over the past several years that lawmakers wanted to address. They formed an ethics study commission which, according to House Majority Leader Joe Hackney, who co-chaired it, succeeded in elevating the discussion of ethics, as it looked at the areas of lobbying and campaign finance. "We recommended 10 bills—a good package," he says.

Representative Hackney says that most members of the legislature are vigilant. "They do not violate our ethics laws," he says. "But we need these laws to tell the public that we mean business."

A LEVEL PLAYING FIELD

Florida tackled public perception when it enacted in late 2006 what Senate President Tom Lee calls "some of the boldest lobbying reforms in the nation."

Lee says he has always been uncomfortable with the "wining and dining" that takes place at receptions and events sponsored by lobbyists. "I saw how much money was being spent to influence how our laws were being made," he says. And even though the events were perfectly legal, they "just never seemed right."

He says he set out to change the cozy relationship between lawmakers and lobbyists because he believes it precluded the people from having a voice. Lee says the desired effect of the Florida laws was to give grassroots and constituent groups a more level playing field "without having to bear big checks or perks to gain admission to the process."

Lee says it's not always easy for legislators to support ethics legislation. The "gift-giving culture" can be very offended, he says. The new Florida law, which bans lobbyists from giving gifts or hospitality to legislators, is being challenged in federal court by the Florida Association of Professional Lobbyists who protests its requirement to report compensation.

DO THEY MAKE A DIFFERENCE?

What good are ethics laws? Do they increase the public's trust in government? Ironically, Americans' confidence in government has receded while legislatures have passed more and more ethics laws. According to the American National Election Studies' biennial poll, which tracks citizen confidence in government, public trust declined from more than 60 percent in the early 1960s to less than 30 percent by the year 2000. These aren't numbers to be proud of, but where would they be if legislatures had not focused on ethics?

Tennessee Representative Kyle says there has been a noticeable change in Tennessee since the legislature enacted ethics reform. He admits that there is still a fair amount of cynicism, but "as a whole, and I can only tell from my constituent communications, it's getting better. The tone has changed," he says.

Kyle says the FBI sting was a wake-up call. "It caused us to take a look at ourselves and see where we were in comparison to other states with citizen legislatures. When you go through this experience, it makes you reflect."

EMPHASIS ON DISCLOSURE

Many citizens may not trust their government today, but at least they can verify certain pieces of information, thanks to laws that require open meetings and legislators to disclose their economic interests.

Transparency is the word of the day, says Courtney Pearre, president of the Tennessee Lobbyist Association. New disclosure laws in Tennessee provide more windows through which its residents can observe the political process.

"I think this type of legislation is good for improving the perception, or really the reality of how the process works," Pearre says. "There is more reporting. There are more limitations on what lobbyists can do and what legislators can do, so I think everyone feels better about it."

In many states, disclosure by legislators and lobbyists is the answer to conflicts of interest. Forty-seven states require legislators to file regular financial disclosure forms showing the sources, and in some cases, the amounts, of outside income, as well as other details about property holdings and investments. This session, 26 states considered or are considering ethics legislation dealing with some aspect of disclosure.

In addition to reporting financial conflicts, rules in 66 of the nation's 99 legislative chambers require lawmakers to reveal any conflicts of interest they have with matters at hand either before abstaining from voting, before voting, or shortly after voting.

But disclosure doesn't erase the conflict, says Utah Representative David Clark. "Lawmakers should decide on their core values and use them to create a template to place over ethical decisions." Legislators often have conflicts of interest, Clark says. "It's how you handle them that counts."

"Ethics are like a muscle. They have to be used or they get a little soft," he says.

And when legislators flex their ethical muscle, they're strengthening public confidence, which Senator Lee says is vital to our system of government.

"The most important thing we can do as public officials is to enhance the public trust," Lee says. "It's at the core of our democracy. Democracy can't function if people don't trust their elected officials."

17

Legislative Pay Daze

Jack Penchoff

It just doesn't pay to be a legislator in some states. A new study shows exactly how far legislative pay lags behind inflation.

From *State News,* February 2007

N ew Hampshire and California sit on opposite coasts. They also sit on opposite sides of the legislative pay scale. New Hampshire's lawmakers are the lowest paid in the nation at $100 per year. Legislators in California, however, are the highest paid in the 50 state capitols with annual salaries of $110,880.

Yet, lawmakers in both states share something in common with their brethren in the other 48 states—their pay has not kept pace with inflation nor the average salary increases among the general population.

Those are some of the findings in a new publication from The Council of State Governments, *State Legislator Compensation: A Trend Analysis.*

Dr. Keon Chi, editor-in-chief of CSG's annual *Book of the States,* wrote the 38 page report. Using data compiled from *Book of the States* over the past 30 years, Chi and his staff took a comprehensive look at state legislative compensation and the various factors that influence salaries for state lawmakers.

"To my knowledge, this is the first longitudinal analysis that focuses on legislative salaries broken down by types, frequency of sessions and regions," Chi said.

SALARIES DECLINE

Chi's trends analysis shows that since 1975, when adjusted for current dollars, legislators' pay in the majority of states—28—has actually declined. In 22 states, salaries over that same 30-year period increased.

But even in states where salaries increased, pay did not keep up with inflation.

Between 1975 and 2005, per capita income in the 50 states increased 50.62 percent.

Meanwhile during that same period, annual salaries for legislators declined nearly 7 percent when adjusted for inflation.

In New York, for example, where the legislature is full-time, the annual legislative salary declined 8.63 percent between 1975 and 2005. Meanwhile, per capita income for residents of the Empire State rose 56.92 percent.

Even in some states where legislators' salaries increased in current dollars, gains were much smaller than per capita income in the state.

An example is Massachusetts. Legislative pay for legislators increased 18.29 percent since 1975 when adjusted for inflation.

Meanwhile, per capita income in the Bay State increased 85.19 percent when adjusted for inflation over the 30 years included in the report.

Although California's legislators are the highest paid, their inflation adjusted salary increased between 1975 and 2005 by 41.79 percent, about the same increase in per capita income for all residents, 40.41 percent.

Pay influences the interest level of potential candidates for legislative offices, said Chi.

"Even in California and other states with higher pay, compensation levels have an impact on recruitment, retention and the work of the legislature," said Chi. "If legislators are not paid adequately, then candidates are drawn from a smaller pool. High pay broadens that pool. You can't expect to attract good candidates with pay that is lower when compared to other jobs and professions."

> *"Even in California and other states with higher pay, compensation levels have an impact on recruitment, retention and the work of the legislature. If legislators are not paid adequately, then candidates are drawn from a smaller pool. High pay broadens that pool. You can't expect to attract good candidates with pay that is lower when compared to other jobs and professions."*
>
> —Dr. Keon Chi

TYPES OF LEGISLATURES

Among the factors that impact legislative compensation, according to the report, is the type of legislative body—professional, citizen or a hybrid of the two.

Professional legislatures are generally comprised of full-time legislators who have no legal limits on the length of their regular sessions. The nine states with professional legislatures also are the nine highest paid—California, Illinois, Massachusetts, Michigan, New Jersey, New York, Ohio, Pennsylvania and Wisconsin.

In 2005, the average salary in professional legislatures was $67,077.22. That's a 5.13 percent increase for those states since 1975. In four of those states—Illinois, New York, Ohio and Wisconsin—salaries during that period declined when adjusted for inflation.

Citizen legislatures are the lowest paid. Citizen legislators generally hold full- or part-time jobs outside the legislature and spend less time on legislative work. In 2005, legislators in those 18 states earned an average salary of $9,158, which was 12.4 percent lower than the average for those 18 states 30 years earlier.

Hybrid legislatures possess some of the characteristics of professional and citizen legislatures. In 2005, legislators in those 23 states earned an average of $22,907, a 16.22 percent decline in pay when adjusted for inflation.

REGIONS

The report includes regional information. Tables in the report show that in 2005 legislators in the Eastern Region were the highest paid. At $35,833, their salaries were nearly double the average legislators in the South are paid.

2005 Salary Comparison: Legislative, Executive and Judicial Branches

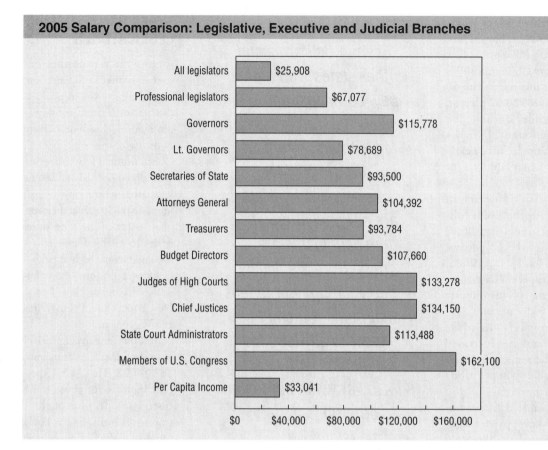

All legislators	$25,908
Professional legislators	$67,077
Governors	$115,778
Lt. Governors	$78,689
Secretaries of State	$93,500
Attorneys General	$104,392
Treasurers	$93,784
Budget Directors	$107,660
Judges of High Courts	$133,278
Chief Justices	$134,150
State Court Administrators	$113,488
Members of U.S. Congress	$162,100
Per Capita Income	$33,041

Professional Legislator Annual Salaries by State: 1975–2005 (CPI adjusted)

State	1975	1985	1995	2005	Percent change (%) 1975–2005
Professional					
California	$78,198.91	$62,437.93	$94,109.76	$110,880.00	41.79%
Illinois	74,052.00	60,157.50	55,243.74	57,619.00	−22.19
Massachusetts	46,978.59	55,530.00	60,661.58	55,569.39	18.29
Michigan	70,349.40	67,598.52	64,249.52	79,650.00	13.22
New Jersey	37,026.00	46,275.00	45,747.80	49,000.00	32.34
New York	87,011.10	79,593.00	75,157.10	79,500.00	−8.63
Ohio	64,795.50	58,600.81	55,454.18	56,260.62	−13.17
Pennsylvania	57,760.56	64,785.00	61,432.76	69,647.00	20.58
Wisconsin	58,049.36	50,350.90	49,742.24	45,569.00	−21.50
Average	63,802.38	60,592.07	62,422.07	67,077.22	5.13
w/o CA (a)	62,002.81	60,361.34	58,461.11	61,601.88	−0.65
Median	64,795.50	60,157.50	60,661.58	57,619.00	−11.08
w/o CA (a)	61,422.43	59,379.15	58,057.88	56,939.81	−7.30

Three states in the East, however, had an inflation-adjusted net decrease in pay between 1975 and 2005. Those were Maine, New Hampshire and New York.

In the Midwest, average salaries in 2005 were $30,442.82, a 14.14 percent decline from 1975 when adjusted for inflation. That decline is reflected in the fact that there were no increases in eight of the 11 Midwest state legislatures between 1975 and 2005 when pay is adjusted for inflation.

In the South, basic compensation for lawmakers between 1975 and 2005 declined in 11 of the 16 states. In Alabama and Texas, there was no change in legislative salaries between 1975 and 2005, resulting in a 73 percent decline when adjusted for inflation. The five states with increases, when adjusted for inflation, were Arkansas, Kentucky, Louisiana, Missouri and Oklahoma. Southern lawmakers earned an average of $17,957 in 2005. Overall, Southern legislatures' average pay declined 29.23 percent between 1975 and 2005 when adjusted for inflation.

In the West, legislators' average salary in 2005 was $24,222. However, remove California's salary figures and the rest of the West averaged only $17,000, below that of the South.

While average legislative pay in the West increased an inflation adjusted 8.98 percent between 1975 and 2005,

the average pay for Western legislators actually declined 3.2 percent when California's figures are not used.

OTHER COMPENSATION

The report includes tables and charts on other forms of legislative compensation, including expense allowances, per diems and retirement benefits.

"Some states are generous with their per diem expenses allowances, therefore salaries are not the only indicator of total compensation," Chi said. "Expenses, retirement and health care benefits are highlighted in the report."

Chi also uses data to compare legislative salaries with those of other elected and judicial officials. While acknowledging that most state legislators are part time, he uses for his comparison the averages of the nine professional legislatures. State high court justices, for example, earn a national average of $133,278, nearly double the salaries of the average lawmaker in professional legislatures.

Executive branch offices included for comparison . . . are governors, lieutenant governors, secretaries of state, attorneys general, treasurers, budget directors and state court administrators.

18

Texas-Style Tax Cut

Dave McNeely

Public schools and taxes
stymied the Texas legislature
for years. It took a bipartisan
commission to come up with
a solution.

From *State Legislatures,*
April 2007

After years of backing and filling, Texas lawmakers finally cut the state's overextended local property tax last year. The Texas Supreme Court made them.

In a spring special session, legislators reduced the school property tax rate by a third, and made up the difference by replacing the outmoded and often-ignored state franchise tax with a broad-based business tax.

Even then, it wasn't simple. The courts and the Legislature have haggled over the Texas school finance system for years.

After watching the Legislature go through one regular 140-day session, and four special sessions that he called, and still not come up with any solution to the property tax dilemma, Republican Governor Rick Perry did something desperate. He called on John Sharp, the former Democratic state comptroller and his former friend from student days at Texas A&M University, to chair an advisory panel called the Texas Tax Reform Commission.

The reason Sharp is described as a "former friend" is that he and Perry had squared off in the 1998 race for lieutenant governor. Perry, with the enormous help of then–Governor George W. Bush's re-election coattails, was elected.

What caused Perry to turn to his Democratic rival? Partly desperation. But Perry also realized, after a chance meeting at a skeet shoot where the two re-established their friendship, that Sharp—a legislator for eight years, member of the Texas Railroad Commission for four years, and the state's tax collector for another eight years—is one of the brightest experts on both tax policy and politics in Texas. The tax problem was tied in such a convoluted knot that it required a Houdini dealmaker—whom business folks and politicians alike respected—to untie it.

EQUALIZE SPENDING

For several years, Texas courts had ruled that public school per pupil spending should be equal, no matter whether the school district is rich or poor.

Most other states use a three-legged taxing system, collecting levies on property, sales and income. But Texas is one of a handful of states with no income tax. Even though one has been suggested from time to time, most officeholders would rather handle rattlesnakes than vote for an income tax.

In 1993, under an earlier order from the Texas Supreme Court to equalize per-student spending, legislators turned to a system that quickly was nicknamed "Robin Hood." That's because the state required richer districts, with greater property wealth, to share their funds with poorer districts.

Legislators also set a lid on the tax of $1.50 per $100 of taxable property. That worked for a while, but in recent years, more and more school districts reached the maximum. As they did, their abilities to spend what they felt was necessary for adequate education was hamstrung.

Richer districts, in particular, hated the system. A few school boards were shipping out millions of dollars to other school districts, while having to cut teachers and extra-curricular activities to keep spending per student equal.

Efforts to do away with Robin Hood always ran into a major problem: About nine-tenths of the public school students were in districts that received rather than sent out property tax money. If Robin Hood were to be banished, replacement money had to be found.

SHRINKING STATE SHARE

Over the years, the state's share of funding public schools had dropped from 80 percent in 1949, when a new financing system was established, to 38 percent by 2004. Clearly, school officials around the state thought the state isn't doing its share, and the Legislature and governor are to blame.

In 1997, then-Governor Bush sought to increase the state's contribution to school costs, and move away from dependence on property taxes to fund schools. But the alternative tax package passed by the Democrat-led House with Bush's backing was killed by the Republicans in the Senate.

Although poor districts had brought suits before that had forced the Legislature to do something, this time the rich and poor school districts banded together to sue the state. Part of the contention was that the state wasn't spending enough money to educate its children. But the more compelling and obvious argument was that Texas was, in essence, forcing a statewide property tax on local school districts. And Texas legislators and voters had passed a constitutional amendment in 1982 banning a state property tax.

The plaintiffs at the trial in the summer of 2004 argued that because more than half the school districts were at the $1.50 lid, with more joining each year, the local districts were forced to levy local property taxes, but had lost any control over the rate.

The plaintiffs were helped by Bill Ratliff, the former Republican state senator who had written the Robin Hood bill in 1993. He told the court that the bill was written under duress, and with so many districts now at the $1.50 cap, it obviously had outlived its usefulness.

In late 2004, State District Judge John Dietz ruled that school funding was inadequate and the property tax collection system unconstitutional. He gave the Legislature, which convened in regular session in January, until Oct. 1, 2005, to fix the problem.

Lieutenant Governor David Dewhurst, the presiding officer of the Senate, worked to pass a gross receipts tax that many businesses opposed. One retailer, for example, would have had to pay more than a

> *"You can pay a tax on payroll or on goods sold. You get to choose whichever is more beneficial to you, and you get to change it every year."*
>
> —John Sharp, Texas Tax Reform Commission chairman

third of its net profits in taxes. Plus, almost no businesses in Texas were allowed to even see the Dewhurst tax until it was being debated. The House killed it.

On the House side, the plan offered was a tax on businesses per employee, referred to as a "head tax." Small businesses with few employees liked it, but large employers, like retailers and airlines, didn't. It also died.

The Legislature adjourned after 140 days with no solution. A few months later, Perry turned to Sharp.

Meanwhile, the Texas Supreme Court overruled the part of Judge Dietz's ruling that said spending was inadequate, while conceding that spending needed to be raised. But the justices agreed that the collection system was indeed a state property tax, and thus unconstitutional. They gave the Legislature until June 1, 2006, to fix it.

COMMISSION GOES TO WORK

The 24-member tax commission held hearings all over the state. Sharp also worked closely with the business community to develop a new tax to replace the tattered franchise tax.

(Once, corporations paid it because it gave their executives immunity from personal liability. Partnerships escaped the tax but were subject to personal liability. A law passed later extended liability protection to partnerships. After that, large corporations like Dell converted to partnerships and quit paying the franchise tax. The result was that many companies were escaping the tax entirely.)

Originally, many commission members wanted to increase the sales tax and remove some or all exemptions. The Texas state sales tax is 6.25 cents on the dollar, and cities and metropolitan transit districts are allowed to tack on an extra two cents. The result is that the sales tax for most Texans is 8.25 percent. Sharp opposed a sales tax hike and eventually prevailed, but it wasn't easy. He credited an organized effort by the Industrial Areas Foundation, a parent group of organizations like Austin Interfaith, with helping to kill the sales tax idea. They had dozens of people at every tax commission hearing to talk about the onerousness of the sales tax on the poor.

"Some wanted just to make it a big sales tax and take out all the exemptions, including food," Sharp says. "And I knew that could never pass, because half the sales tax is paid by businesses, and they didn't want it. And consumer groups didn't want sales tax increases to pay for property tax relief, having poor folks pay for richer folks to get a tax cut. So the first thing we did was we brought in the business community, which basically as far as I could see hadn't been done. So we said that we needed them to come up with taxes."

A SOLUTION

The business tax Sharp crafted used gross revenue as a base, and then allowed businesses to deduct either the cost of goods sold, or all personnel costs, including salary and benefits, to encourage businesses not only to hire people but to give them health care. "One of the things I learned as comptroller is that you can devise a tax for big manufacturers, but it won't work for the wholesalers and retailers, and vice versa," Sharp says. "So that's where we came up with a choice, where you can pay a tax on payroll or on goods sold. You get to choose whichever is more beneficial to you, and you get to change it every year.

"By using the bifurcated rate, we were able to get a bill that the manufacturers, the wholesalers and the retailers could support. Not so much that they thought it was the best thing since sliced bread, but the alternatives had them scared to death."

The Sharp commission also proposed that wholesalers and retailers be taxed at 0.5 percent and everyone else at 1 percent, exempting small businesses with less than $300,000 in annual gross revenues. Sharp says that division is similar to the different rates used in Washington State.

One sticking point was that the proceeds of the tax shift went solely to reduce property taxes, with no new money for schools. Sharp knew that the state's school superintendents could block it. So with the help of Austin Independent School District Superintendent Pat Forgione, Sharp talked to groups of superintendents all over Texas.

"I met with maybe half of them in the state and told them I knew they weren't going to be for it because there wasn't any more money for schools," Sharp says. "And they could kill it. But I told them that there wasn't ever going to be any money for schools unless we got past this sticking point."

"The superintendents took a long-term view and agreed to say, 'Let's fix this, and let's let the process work,'" Sharp says. "And thanks mostly to Florence Shapiro [the Plano Republican chair of the Senate Education Committee], the schools eventually wound up with billions."

Turning to Old Friend Pays Off

Republican Governor Rick Perry's selection of Democrat John Sharp to head a tax study commission was a bold move.

They'd been friends at Texas A&M University, in the same unit in the Corps of Cadets, and elected to offices: Sharp as a student body president, Perry as yell leader. (Not cheer leader. Aggies yell. They don't cheer.)

After graduation, Sharp worked in Austin for five years as an examiner for the Legislative Budget Board. Perry became an Air Force pilot. In 1978, Sharp won a seat in the Texas House of Representatives. Not quite four years later, he won a special election for the Senate seat of a member who died. Perry returned from the Air Force to his family's ranch, and in 1984 was elected to a vacant House seat as a Democrat.

In 1986, Sharp was elected to the three-member Texas Railroad Commission. Three years later, Perry accepted the party-switching invitation of then-U.S. Senator Phil Gramm, a former A&M economics professor and former Democrat, and declared he was a Republican. In 1990, he narrowly upset Democratic populist Jim Hightower for Agriculture Commissioner.

Also in 1990, Sharp was elected Comptroller of Public Accounts, replacing Democrat Bob Bullock, who'd been elected lieutenant governor. Sharp and Perry were re-elected in 1994.

When Bullock said he wouldn't seek re-election in 1998, Sharp and Perry both ran for lieutenant governor, and their friendship fizzled. Perry, with Governor George W. Bush's re-election above him on the ballot, ran almost 700,000 votes behind Bush, but nonetheless beat Sharp by just under 70,000 votes—less than two percentage points.

Also in 1998, Houston multimillionaire David Dewhurst, a Republican energy tycoon spending millions of his own money, won the land commissioner job vacated by Democrat Garry Mauro, who haplessly challenged Bush. Dewhurst had considered running for lieutenant governor, but Perry backed him off.

In 2002, Sharp helped assemble the multiracial Democratic Dream Team: energy and banking multi-millionaire Tony Sanchez of Laredo for governor, African-American Dallas Mayor Ron Kirk for U.S. Senate, and Sharp again for lieutenant governor. But as part of the Dream Team, Sharp got an even lower percentage of the white vote than in 1998. Dewhurst because lieutenant governor and president of the Senate.

In 2006, Sharp toyed with running against Perry for governor. But the challenge of raising millions as a non-incumbent, plus Perry's take-charge competence after Hurricanes Katrina and Rita in contrast to the ham-handed Bush administration response squelched the idea.

So intermediaries suggested Perry draft Sharp to help solve the tax puzzle. When Perry announced the move at a press conference with Sharp by his side, it angered Dewhurst, who hadn't been consulted. But it helped solve three problems for Perry.

First, it sidelined the Democrat most likely to beat him if conditions were right.

Second, Sharp, now a tax consultant, had been a major adviser to his successor as comptroller, Republican Carole Keeton Strayhorn. The tax commission job sidelined Sharp from helping Strayhorn in her effort to unseat Perry.

And third, Sharp might actually be able to find a way out of the tax forest, and then sell it to the Legislature.

Darned if it didn't work. Sharp solved the problem, which got Perry out of a tight spot. Perry was re-elected with just 39 percent of the vote against Democrat Chris Bell and Independents Strayhorn and Kinky Friedman. Had Sharp been the Democratic nominee ... who knows?

When the commission initially took its plan to legislators, many were skeptical. Sharp and Perry boosted the persuasion process with an almost daily string of press conferences featuring business groups endorsing the plan, including the Texas Association of Business, doctors and others. Sure enough, the plan passed the House virtually intact.

The Senate was another matter. Lieutenant Governor Dewhurst had beaten Sharp in a hard-fought race for lieutenant governor in 2002, and opposed Sharp's appointment. Dewhurst said the Sharp plan gave too much

property tax relief. But several Republican senators, led by Shapiro, sweetened the pot with a few billion from the surplus for schools and helped push the bill through to an unanimous vote. The House overwhelmingly concurred with the Senate's version.

The eventual result was that the local property tax lid dropped to $1 per $100 valuation. The Legislature appropriated several billion dollars from a budget surplus to fund the tax cut in the short run. And to protect against school districts continuing to raise the property tax above that, the Legislature allowed a one-

What the Texas Tax Plan Does

- Cuts local property taxes by a third, to $1 per $100 valuation. Districts can add up to 4 cents for local programs, more if voters agree.
- Replaces Texas franchise tax, which many businesses had quit paying.
- Requires business to pay a margins tax of 1 percent, after deducting either the cost of goods purchased, or the cost of employee payroll and benefits. Retailers and wholesalers pay 0.5 percent. Sole proprietorships and general partnerships are exempt, plus companies earning less than $300,000 a year.
- Increases the tobacco tax by $1 a pack for cigarettes, to $1.41; smokeless tobacco goes from 35.2 percent to 40 percent of value.
- Taxes used-car sales at blue book value.

time increase of up to four cents. Anything beyond that would require a vote of the district's people. And if appraisals are raised, the tax rate has to be adjusted to keep the revenue flow the same.

The new business tax, plus a $1 increase per pack in the cigarette tax, came on Jan. 1, 2007. The business tax for 2007 will be due on March 15, 2008. And now, Texas will get a chance to see how the new tax system and approach works.

Sharp said while the commission was meeting that the business and cigarette tax weren't currently enough to cover the property tax cut, but predicted economic growth would boost what they will produce. However, budgeters and Lieutenant Governor Dewhurst and House Speaker Tom Craddick have already cautioned legislators not to spend all of a presumed budget surplus, since some of it will almost certainly be needed to help reduce the property tax.

Meanwhile, Sharp says he's been invited to visit about 30 states to discuss the new approach to taxing business.

"The business community likes it, and it raises some money," Sharp says. "We had about 90 percent of the businesses for it. You just can't be excluded from the tax base, and then say at the same time you support education. Either you do or you don't. You can't very well say you're for schools and not be willing to pay for them."

Governors and Executives

Governors and other state and local executives are flexing their muscles. The federal government won't address global warming? Fine. California governor Arnold Schwarzenegger is willing to push for laws in his state to address the issue. The feds regulating business with too light a hand? No problem. State attorneys general are aggressively policing all manner of business laws and regulations. Former New York attorney general Eliot Spitzer made his political reputation as a crusading protector of the average investor. He's now governor of the state. His successor in the attorney general's office, Andrew Cuomo, is carrying on the Spitzer tradition; in 2007 he pursued and exposed deceptive student loan practices.

Of late state executives have been on a roll. With a disproportionate share of the federal government's attention focused on wars in Iraq and Afghanistan, state executives have proved more than willing to occupy any vacuum on the domestic, and even global, front. The readings in this section provide a glimpse into some of their initiatives and activities as well as insight into how executive power is being deployed to spearhead such efforts.

THE ORIGINS OF ELECTED EXECUTIVES

States and localities are very different from the federal government in the number and nature of their elected executives. There is no federal executive office elected by a nationwide popular ballot. The U.S. presidency is decided in the electoral college, which is not bound by the popular vote in making its decision. In 2000, for example, George W. Bush lost the popular vote (more people voted for his opponent Al Gore), but won in the electoral college.

If the federal government has a complete absence of popularly elected executives, state and local governments have a veritable surplus of them. State and local governments do not just have elected chief executives, that is, governors and mayors. Many other executive offices also are elected. Everyone from the insurance commissioner to the head of the state's education bureaucracy to the state attorney general may be elected rather than appointed. This can create friction, since the governor is technically the head of the executive branch, but key offices may be held by people with different partisan, ideological, and personal agendas. That can make governing hard. In many states, the executive branch more resembles a collection of independent electoral fiefdoms than a hierarchical organization with the governor at the top.

How did the states end up with such a different system from the federal government? The short answer to that question is that the states, or at least their citizens, wanted it that way. Specifically, they sought to make sure to set limits on the power that could be concentrated in the hands of a single executive. The governor's office represents the oldest form of executive office in the United States, predating the founding of the country. Governors often wielded considerable power, including the ability to veto bills or dissolve colonial legislatures. Appointed by the British crown rather than elected by the people, early colonial governors were agents of the Crown rather than of the people, and they were not always popular.

Not surprising then that after the United States won its independence from Great Britain this suspicion of executives was reflected in how states organized their governments. Initially, governorships were fairly weak positions. In some states there were even plural executives, which meant that the governor's job essentially was done by a committee rather than by a single person. Most governors had no veto power, were subject to stringent term limits, and possessed little in the way of appointment or budgetary powers.

In the 1800s power was further fragmented in the executive branch with the rise of the so-called long ballot and the populist movement. The descriptively named long ballot was a reform that gave citizens the power to decide on a broad range of executive offices. This meant that everything from county sheriff to state treasurer became an elected rather than an appointed office in most states. Having many elected executives further diluted the power of governors, who had little say over who ran the key government agencies and how they ran them.[1]

This situation, basically one of weak gubernatorial powers, lasted until roughly the last half of the twentieth century. By that time it was clear that the drive to restrain and fragment the powers of the executive was interfering with effective governance. The responsibilities and expectations placed on states had increased enormously. Public education, health and welfare, law enforcement, roads and utilities—the presence and levels of the services taken more or less for granted these days would astonish a nineteenth-century governor.

And that was a key problem—the executive branch in the states (and many localities) was a nineteenth-century creation unsuited for the full-service state governments of the late twentieth century. This created a reform movement to give governors the tools to exercise true executive authority, to make them in practice the real chief executive officers of state. Included in these reforms were line-item veto and expanded budgetary powers and the authority to hire and fire people in key agency positions.[2] The movement found most of its success in the 1970s, 1980s, and 1990s, and as governors began to exercise their newly acquired powers they also emerged as increasingly important figures in the federal system. Today, governors not only wield considerable power within their states, through the National Governors Association (NGA) they collectively wield considerable influence at the national level.

RECENT TRENDS

Governors have come a long way in a hundred years. Rather than being the weaker siblings of state legislatures, they now often dominate state politics. They set the agenda, and they are not shy about using the power of the bully pulpit to advance their policy preferences.

Several readings in this section take a look at how individual governors have shaped the politics in their state and even influenced politics nationally. Alan Greenblatt's essay examines the impact of Gov. Jeb Bush on Florida politics. During his eight-year term, Governor Bush rarely wavered from a core conservative vision of what government should be: smaller, less regulatory, and more market-like. Although Bush is no longer governor of the state—terms limits prevented him seeking a third term and he left office in January 2007—he has left a considerable legacy in state politics. Bush managed to impose his conservative vision on a variety of issues and institutions that will continue to shape state politics and policy for the foreseeable future. While some disagreed with his specific policies and views, all agree that he concentrated power in the executive and exercised that power to great effect.

Josh Goodman's essay looks at a series of governors who also have sought to impose a strong executive imprint on politics and policy, but have done so while belonging to the minority political party within their respective states. Democratic executives elected in red states and Republican executives elected in blue states are not shying away from bold ideas and initiatives just because the legislature is controlled by the other party. Just the opposite, in fact: they have proven willing to use the powers of their office to lead rather than simply negotiate.

A second essay by Greenblatt focuses on a single governor and a single issue: Arnold Schwarzenegger and the environment. Schwarzenegger is in a powerful position to shape environmental issues; regulations in California have ripple effects across the country because of the state's sheer size and economic oomph. In his first term, Schwarzenegger got mostly good marks from the environmental movement. Among other things, he proved willing to step into the vacuum created by the federal government's inaction on global warming, successfully advocating for a bill limiting greenhouse-gas emissions. Schwarzenegger won a second term in 2006, and environmentalists wonder if he can keep his green momentum.

The final essay by Mary Branham Dusenberry gives an overview of the policy visions of governors across the country. In many 2007 state of the state speeches many governors expressed a willingness to follow the example of Schwarzenegger and tackle issues without waiting for the federal government. Such issues as energy use and the minimum wage long have been considered federal policy domains; governors, however, increasingly are willing to push for action if Congress and the president are unresponsive to calls for action. The powers accumulated in the state executive office in the latter part of the twentieth century are being actively employed to shape politics in the twenty-first.

Notes

1. Larry Sabato, *Goodbye to Good-Time Charlie: The American Governorship Transformed,* 2nd ed. (Washington, D.C.: CQ Press, 1983).

2. Nelson C. Demetrius, "Governors: Their Heritage and Future," in *American State and Local Politics,* ed. Ronald E. Weber and Paul Brace (New York: Chatham House, 1999), 38070.

19

Jebocracy

Alan Greenblatt

Jeb Bush's eight-year reign in Florida is almost over. Tallahassee may never be the same.

When public officials praise figures from the political past, usually what they end up doing is describing idealized versions of themselves. You could say that was the case in October, when Jeb Bush gave a speech in Tallahassee honoring one of his predecessors as Florida governor, LeRoy Collins. Bush lauded Collins, who served during the 1950s, for standing up to segregationists and sparing Florida much of the racial strife that bedeviled other Southern states during the civil rights era. "He is our greatest governor," Bush said. At the capitol, Collins' portrait hangs in a place of honor outside the governor's reception room, at Bush's insistence.

There are some obvious differences between Bush and his historical hero. Collins was a fairly liberal Democrat, for one. As his biographer, Martin Dyckman, points out, "Collins warmly believed in the power of government." Nobody would say that about Bush, who spent his eight years in office shrinking state government's influence through privatization and deregulation. But what Bush admires in Collins is his fearlessness. "Courage like his is rooted in conviction and undeterred by critics—something that all governors can take to heart," Bush said in his speech, leading him to stray from his prepared remarks. "After you've been here a while, you really don't care too much about people who disagree with you, if they're consistent about it. Once you get that taken into consideration, standing on principle's a lot easier to do."

If Bush sees something of himself in LeRoy Collins' brand of intractability, his critics are apt to think of someone else: his brother. Comparing Governor Bush with President Bush can be a dubious exercise, but one similarity worth noting is that both have

From *Governing,*
December 2006

worked hard to consolidate power in the executive office. Jeb Bush has persuaded legislators and voters to give him more control over the institutions of government than any governor in Florida's history. And he has never shied from using his authority to reward friends and make his enemies sorry. Even a few Republicans around Tallahassee have described the governor's style as "dictatorial."

If Governor Bush has been perceived as a bully by some and a champion by many others, there's one statement nobody can argue with: Bush has been a transformative figure in both state and national politics. When his term ends on January 1, he will leave behind not only a radically new Florida reshaped in his own image but also a conservative template for state governance in America. From Florida's schools to its economy to the very apparatus of government, Bush has shaken up institutions, rolled over opposing forces and centralized power in service of the most ambitious agenda of any governor in his state's history.

Bush believes that government can't do everything, and that everything it does do would work better if attuned to market signals. To that end, he contracted out numerous government functions, from child welfare to state employee services, eliminating 14,000 civil service jobs along the way. Bush injected competition into public schooling via charter schools, private-school vouchers and a mandatory testing regime that predates the federal No Child Left Behind law. He also persuaded the legislature to pass tax cuts every year he was in office—$19 billion worth in all.

The governor not only embraced big ideas but he proved to be a tireless manager and implementer of his own policy visions. He was attentive to the smallest details and disarmed opponents with his knowledge of state programs and legislation. "While I aspire to be an unrelenting critic of his policies," says Dan Gelber, the incoming Florida House Democratic leader, "I think he's honest, very hard working and does have a deep grasp of the complexities of government and the intricacies of the policies he's attempting."

Bush hasn't gotten his way on everything. He suffered setbacks in many important areas, including his signature issue of education and his desire to turn over the management of Medicaid patients to private insurers. His privatization plans have been magnets for scandal and accusations of cronyism. But where most governors are lucky to impose their will in two or three major policy areas, Bush substantively changed Florida's approach to just about everything state government takes on—tax policy, budget policy, child welfare and a list that goes on and on. "You run down the litany of what Bush has accomplished, and you have to say by any standard he's been a successful governor," says Darryl Paulson, a government professor at the University of South Florida.

It's hard to argue with the numbers. Florida enjoys a healthy general fund surplus, a triple-A bond rating and an unemployment rate that's barely more than 3 percent—well below the national average. Florida, in fact, has consistently led the nation in job growth over the past couple of years, despite a string of devastating hurricanes. Bush leaves office with approval ratings in the high 60s. His Republican successor, the newly elected Charlie Crist, ran largely on a platform of defending his legacy for another term.

STRONG GOVERNOR

In short, Bush has dominated Tallahassee in a way that no governor had before him. Some of that was luck. At the same time Florida voters elected him in 1998, they also decided to shrink the state's cabinet and place more power directly in the governor's office. What's more, Bush has had a fairly pliant legislature to work with. Not only was he the first Republican governor matched with a Republican-controlled legislature since 1874, but a stringent new term-limits law kept both houses stocked with inexperienced lawmakers. "Without any question, he was the political leader," says Curt Kiser, a former legislator who now lobbies in Tallahassee. "Lots of legislators were frankly a little bit green about what the legislature's power or actions should be. They were willing to be led."

Bush also actively sought to consolidate executive power. Voters rejected his "seamless" K-20 education system, but he nonetheless ended up with greater control of higher education by winning the right to appoint each state university's board of trustees. Similarly, Bush persuaded the legislature to give him total control over judicial nominations—a power that the governor formerly shared with the state bar association. Critics complain that Bush made ideology a more important qualification for judges than it was in the past. But the *Tampa Tribune* editorialized last year, "The truth is that while

Jeb at a Glance

Issue	What Jeb Wanted	What Florida Got
Tax Cuts	Lots of them	$19 billion in tax cuts but doubled state debt to $22.5 billion.
Affirmative Action	Colorblind college admissions and contracting	African-American enrollment at state universities dropped from 17.6 percent in 2000 to 14 percent. State business with minority contractors more than doubled.
Education	Competition and accountability	Testing is mandatory from grades 3 to 10 and influences school funding. Charter schools enroll 80,000 students. Courts ruled major voucher program unconstitutional.
Government Operations	Privatization and efficiency	14,000 fewer state workers, but scandals and snafus plagued child welfare, state personnel services and prison privatizations.
Medicaid	For-profit insurers	Acute care pilot underway in two counties; feds approved long-term-care waiver in September, but plan needs legislative signoff.
Disaster Preparedness	Emergency plans for all agencies	Quick, calm response to nine hurricanes.
Euthanasia	To keep Terry Schiavo alive	Brain-damaged patient was taken off life support despite efforts of Bush and congressional Republicans to stop it.
Politics	A red state	Florida GOP is the best-funded state party in the U.S. Republicans maintain huge majorities in the legislature, but lost one statewide office and two congressional seats in November.
Economic Development	A diversified economy	Biotech institutions in Orlando, Palm Beach County and St. Lucie County, at a cost of more than $1 billion in state and local incentives.

Source: Compiled by Heather Kleba and Alan Greenblatt.

Bush's selections naturally tend to be conservatives, they also have been, for the most part, highly qualified."

Bush's biggest power play was to assert himself into the appropriations process in unprecedented ways. Pork-barrel projects are called "turkeys" in Florida and, as in most states, they are a time-honored way for legislators to exercise some clout. But Bush robbed them of that benefit. While unveiling his first budget, he announced that he would veto any turkey that had not received a prior sign-off from his administration.

Bush was as good as his word, using his line-item veto authority to eliminate $350 million worth of projects that first year and more than $1.5 billion in total. Although legislators raised a fuss, they never tried to override him. "That is a legislature that has been emasculated," says Alan Rosenthal, an expert on state legislatures at Rutgers University. "That used to be a brawny legislature, really powerful and assertive. It's become a one-way street, with Bush calling all the shots."

The story of Alex Villalobos helps explain why. Villalobos was the Senate majority leader and in line to become Senate president when he dared to cross Bush on a pair of education votes. Villalobos was quickly stripped of his leadership post, but that, apparently, wasn't punishment enough. Bush recruited a candidate to run against Villalobos in this summer's GOP primary and helped raise a staggering $6 million for the campaign to unseat him.

Despite Bush's intervention, Villalobos managed to win the primary by a few hundred votes. Some see Villalobos' win as a possible turning point for legislative power; one hot rumor in Tallahassee is that Villalobos will stage a Senate leadership coup once Bush is gone. Whether or not that happens, it's likely that legislators will try to reassert some of their branch's authority. Marco Rubio, the incoming House speaker, has issued a broad "100 ideas" platform. Rubio has hired no fewer than 18 former Bush aides to help him try to implement it. Since most changes in the governor's power under Bush are institutional in nature, however, future inhabitants of the governor's mansion will continue to enjoy the advantage.

TESTING, TESTING

The results of Jeb Bush's governing philosophy and tactics are evident in every corner of Florida. But nowhere is Bush's imprint felt more strongly than in the schools. Bush implemented mandatory testing from grades 3 to 10. He pushed through legislation to make passing standardized tests a requirement, under certain circumstances, for third graders to advance to fourth grade and for seniors to graduate from high school. Florida also now requires local districts to tie a portion of teacher pay to student improvement on the achievement test.

All this testing has not been universally popular with parents or students. Jim Davis, the Democrat who ran unsuccessfully to replace Bush, made his complaints a central issue on the campaign trail, contending that schools had become "dreary test-taking factories." But Bush found support for his ideas among many educators and in some of Florida's most troubled schools, such as the Ivey Lane Elementary School in Orlando.

The school serves a public housing complex; all but a handful of its 400 students are poor and African American. Principal Ruth Baskerville subscribes to the idea, which Bush has promoted heavily, that standardized tests force districts to pay far more attention to students who have traditionally been neglected. "That which gets measured, gets done," she says. "It's human nature."

In 2005, Baskerville's school received a "double-F," the lowest grade possible under Bush's accountability system. Although she wasn't thrilled about it, the low score translated into extra help for Ivey Lane, including performance bonuses for teachers who raise student scores, priority for new textbooks and teachers and the introduction of math and reading coaches into the school. Most important, in Baskerville's view, Bush has created a mentoring program for schools like hers. With more than 70 volunteer mentors visiting individual kids once a week, discipline problems have declined and student scores have gone up. Ivey Lane earned itself a modest but certainly more respectable "C" for the most recent school year.

Ivey Lane's improvement was one small part of an important trend. Florida has narrowed the achievement gap between white and minority students more rapidly than any other state, save Texas. Nevertheless, the overall record of Florida's schools under Bush is mixed. Florida still scrapes the bottom of national statistics on both graduation rates and average SAT scores. Even Ruth Baskerville admits that success stories like Ivey Lane's are a matter of going from "really, really pitiful to just a little pitiful."

One surprising outcome of Bush's testing agenda is a rift with his brother over how to grade schools and what to do when they fail. Three-quarters of Florida schools receive an "A" or "B" under Governor Bush's testing regime, but more than 70 percent of them are rated as failures under President Bush's No Child Left Behind law. Jeb Bush is especially passionate about devoting more resources to flunking schools such as Ivey Lane, which the federal system punishes by draining resources and encouraging students to transfer away. "With all due respect to the federal system," Governor Bush recently told the *New York Times,* "our accountability system is really the better way to go."

BEYOND MICKEY

Just a few miles east of the Ivey Lane school, you can see a very different piece of Jeb Bush's legacy taking shape. Across the street from Orlando's NBA arena, a musty ballroom with palm-tree-and-seashell carpet is about to be refurbished into part of a graduate-level academy for video-game programmers. Orlando has become a digital media hub, the East Coast home of Electronic Arts, the company that makes the "Madden NFL" video games, as well as JetBlue's flight simulation school and the Army and Navy's model simulation purchasers. Hoping to grow this digital industry further, Bush set aside funds to fix up the underutilized conference center to get the academy up and going and charged the University of Central Florida with the job of running it.

Florida's economy has long depended on the "three-legged stool" of agriculture, tourism and the military. Perhaps Bush's single greatest push, after education, was to diversify this narrow economic base. The governor takes a personal interest in deals of any size—he loves coming in for the close—and has led numerous trade missions, notably to Latin America, where his fluency in Spanish has been a real plus. Bush's biggest coup by far was to woo three San Diego-based biotech institutes—Scripps, Burnham and Torrey Pines—into opening Florida outposts for their research. Those mega deals will cost more than $1 billion in state and local subsidies—as much as $1 million per job created—but Bush argues they'll spur high-wage clusters of biotech business.

Orlando is one of the biggest beneficiaries of Bush's economic development efforts. A scrubby dirt lot off Highway 417 is set to become the Burnham Institute's East Coast headquarters, right next door to a new medical school for UCF and a VA hospital. Meanwhile, the video-game academy is being promoted as the anchor for a new "creative village" that will bring dozens of digital and software companies to downtown Orlando.

> *"The governor gets what you have to do to be competitive in this climate in attracting high-wage jobs."*
>
> —Orlando Mayor Buddy Dyer

"We want to create the kind of jobs that aren't just popping popcorn at Disney World or sweeping streets," Orlando Mayor Buddy Dyer says. "We want the creative people, people who think for a living."

The video-game academy is the type of economic development project that Bush likes best, offering not just a boost for a single company but also the chance to encourage an entire industry to plant roots in Florida. Year-round sunshine is doubtless a major draw, but you wouldn't know it from hanging around the video-game academy, which already has taken over most of the old conference center across from the Orlando arena. Students seem to thrive on late hours and there's not a window within their ample workspaces—light would only interfere with the images on their screens. "The art in there is significant," says Krystel Guiloff, showing off the transparent stained-glass effects in a game she's been helping to create, which one of her fellow students calls "the greatest opera role-playing game in the world."

Guiloff can hardly contain her excitement about UCF's new video-game program. As an undergraduate, she expected to end up working on telecom software or something equally mundane, but she's thrilled to have the chance to work and network with notable figures in the video-game industry right in her home state. "The video-game industry is something I wanted to see grow in central Florida," she says.

She is just the sort of person Electronic Arts was hoping to recruit when it first proposed the creation of a video-game academy. The company's local studio has been growing rapidly, but it couldn't sustain its growth if it had to keep relying on California transplants. Electronic Arts executives met with local economic development and university officials, who joined with the company to deliver a pitch to Bush. The governor came through with $4 million for getting the academy started and $1 million a year to UCF for operating costs.

Mayor Dyer, who used to spar with the governor as leader of the Senate Democrats, has been around politics long enough to know that projects like this one have many fathers and mothers. But he concedes that Bush did the most to give life to Orlando's new digital and biotech dreams. "My Democratic friends don't like it when I say too many nice things about Governor Bush," Dyer says. "But I think the governor gets what you have to do to be competitive in this climate in attracting high-wage jobs. This is something that will transform the economy of central Florida for decades."

20

Against the Grain

Josh Goodman

Governors are finding success in the unlikeliest places. They're doing it by choosing boldness over caution.

If you travel the streets of Phoenix this month, it won't take you long to notice the giant yard signs with one huge name on them: JANET. They make an aggressive statement in support of Janet Napolitano, the aggressive Democratic governor whose advertising—even down to the lawn-sign level—seems to symbolize her style of management. The signs are a bold bright blue in a state that is seriously red. Arizona has voted Republican for president every time but once since 1950. The GOP has a nearly two-thirds majority in the legislature and an 8-to-2 edge in the congressional delegation.

Napolitano's own election as governor in 2002 was seen as something of a fluke. Then the state's attorney general, she won with only 46 percent of the vote against a Republican congressman who ran a poor campaign. In this context, Napolitano could have been expected to tread lightly when she took office in January 2003. She didn't.

Instead, she's spent her term taking on virtually any fight the legislature was willing to wage, be it on the budget, immigration, abortion or school vouchers. It was a risky strategy, but it seems to have worked. After nearly four years and more than 100 vetoes, most Arizonans—including those who keep electing Republicans to nearly every other office—still like her and have made her an overwhelming favorite for reelection.

Napolitano's story would be interesting if it were unusual, but it's even more interesting because something similar is going on in much of the country. At a time when Americans are constantly being told that they are more divided than ever, into conflicting red and blue political cultures, governors stand out as a giant asterisk. Twenty-one of the nation's governors come from the political party that lost the state's presidential vote in 2004.

From *Governing,*
October 2006

And while most of these governors are somewhat more centrist than the national parties they belong to, they generally aren't conciliatory in their approach to governing. From Vermont to Kansas to Arizona, they have fought contentious fights with hostile legislatures. And like Janet Napolitano, these muscular moderates have gained ground with the voters by doing so. America may, in fact, be deeply divided between red and blue, but for the most part, that color scheme does not explain gubernatorial politics.

CONSTANT CONFLICT

Napolitano's relations with her Republican legislature have been defined by conflict throughout her term. "It started out tenuous," says Ken Bennett, who has served as Senate president all four of Napolitano's years in office, "and got worse from there."

When Napolitano took office in 2003, Arizona faced one of the most severe fiscal crises in its history. The immediate problem was plugging a $300 million hole in the budget for the already half-complete 2002–03 fiscal year. Republican legislative leaders proposed cutting expenditures for health care and education to help make up the difference. Napolitano said no, the money would have to be borrowed, and she traveled the state to promote this position. She was able to bring along enough maverick Republicans to block the cuts and impose her preferred solution.

Later that year, the budget shortfall had ballooned to a billion dollars. And the scenario played out much the same, with a bloc of dissident Republican legislators balking at the plans of their leaders and Napolitano taking advantage of the GOP division to win approval of a compromise budget that once again relied heavily on borrowing and one-time revenue.

This deal might have been a step toward building goodwill between Napolitano and the legislature, but the governor had something else in mind. She line-item-vetoed 35 parts of the budget, largely to provide more funding for education and health care. Republican lawmakers took her to court, claiming she was usurping their power to appropriate money.

The relationship seemed on the mend in 2004, when Napolitano vetoed fewer bills and won approval of her signature achievement: all-day kindergarten. But that progress evaporated in 2005. After giving the governor a victory on the kindergarten issue, Republicans expected her to sign off on a tax credit for businesses that give scholarships to private school students. When she vetoed that provision, the Republicans called her a deal-breaker and liar. For her part, Napolitano said Republicans broke the deal first by not including a sunset provision in the tax credit.

The relationship between the governor and the legislature has never recovered. Stephen Tully, the House GOP leader, puts it bluntly. "There isn't really a relationship between the governor and the legislature at all," he says. "The governor's office, they just want to sit back and veto bills."

There's no question that using the veto is a key part of Napolitano's governing style. She's vetoed bills requiring parental consent and waiting periods for abortions, and a bill to protect gun owners' rights during emergencies. She angered GOP legislators in another way by signing an executive order barring discrimination based on sexual orientation in state employment. Napolitano can't be described as an out-and-out liberal—she supported a major tax cut earlier this year and has maintained generally good relations with the business community—but she's clearly chosen to fight things out in situations where one would expect a Democratic governor in hostile territory to act cautiously. She says success isn't about getting along with the legislature, which she labels "ultraconservative."

Republican legislators complain that much of Napolitano's image has been created by a sympathetic and submissive press corps. They say she claims credit for things Republicans have actually done, such as cutting taxes and strengthening the state's rainy-day fund, and that the press helps her with these deceptions.

But if those charges are valid, the Republican-leaning Arizona voters don't seem to be buying them. To all appearances, they enjoy having a Democratic governor who fights with the lawmakers they've elected. Napolitano has scored approval ratings of 60 percent or higher fairly consistently throughout her term. Part of the explanation, says Fred DuVal, a prominent Arizona Democrat, is that Napolitano's hard-nosed style fits with the state's Western ethos. In a place where any election for any office reminds some voters of a campaign for sheriff, cultivating a reputation as someone who doesn't back off from a fight is a good thing.

OFF-COLOR SUCCESSES

Western stubbornness might explain Arizona. It certainly doesn't explain Vermont, a Democratic-leaning state where Republican Governor Jim Douglas has followed a similarly headstrong path to consistent popularity since his 2002 election. George W. Bush took only 39 percent of the vote in Vermont in 2004, his third-worst showing in the nation.

The following year, Douglas faced the biggest political debate of his tenure over health care. The legislature sent him a bill that aspired to provide near-universal coverage. Douglas objected to the funding mechanisms, including a tax on the payrolls of employers that didn't offer insurance, and said it went too far in encouraging Vermonters to get their health insurance from the government. Despite Democratic legislative majorities and widespread support in the state for comprehensive health care reform, he vetoed the bill.

And, as in Napolitano's case, he got away with it. The political response from voters was muted, and this year the governor and legislature reached a compromise, creating a new program called Catamount Health that relies far more on private insurers than the one Democrats had initially pushed forward.

A similar pattern prevails in Kansas, where Governor Kathleen Sebelius presides as a Democrat in a heavily Republican state. Sebelius isn't quite as belligerent as Napolitano, but she fights, and she usually gets her way. In 2004, Sebelius wanted to increase sales, property and income taxes to comply with a state court order requiring additional funding for schools.

When legislators rejected her approach, she sent them a budget the following year with no added school funding at all, telling them that if they didn't like her recommendations, then it was up to them to deal with the situation on their own. "Probably everyone I know thought that was a mistake," says Joe Aistrup, a Kansas State University political scientist, "but that was the best thing she could have done." The legislature produced a plan she saw as inadequate; she allowed it to become law without her signature. When the judges rejected it, Sebelius finally got the larger increase in school funding she was looking for, along with the court's approval.

Sebelius hasn't shied away from causes seemingly out of the conservative Kansas mainstream. She's rejected bills to allow carrying of concealed firearms and to require annual licensing for abortion clinics. She opposed the state's constitutional amendment banning gay marriage and signed legislation giving in-state tuition rates to some illegal immigrants. None of these actions have substantially cut into her popularity. Like Napolitano in Arizona, Sebelius is a heavy reelection favorite.

So is Jodi Rell, the Republican governor in largely Democratic Connecticut. Rell is clearly a moderate Republican; she signed the first bill to allow gay civil unions that wasn't prompted by a court order. But when the Democratic legislative majority wanted to raise income taxes for the wealthiest state residents in 2005, she fought them and negotiated a budget without the tax increase. An equally strong reelection favorite is Oklahoma's Brad Henry, a Democrat who won a startling upset victory in 2002. Henry persuaded conservative voters in his state to expand gambling, create a state lottery and raise the cigarette tax through referendums in 2004. Other "mismatched" governors who seem poised for reelection include Republican Linda Lingle in Hawaii and Democrat Dave Freudenthal in Wyoming. The most muscular moderate of all, California's Arnold Schwarzenegger, seems headed for a second term as well.

Not every mismatched governor is coasting this fall. Maryland's Bob Ehrlich, a Republican in Democratic territory, is fighting for survival. GOP Governor Don Carcieri of Rhode Island, despite encouraging approval ratings, is in no position to take reelection for granted. But most of the mismatched have, like Napolitano in Arizona, enjoyed a measure of success through a combination of independence and a willingness to take on the opposing party's majority in crucial situations.

BORDER BATTLE

Len Munsil, a lawyer and conservative activist, will oppose Napolitano in November. "I think the core values of the people of Arizona," he says, "are more like my core values as a Reagan conservative than like hers." But Munsil needs an issue to crystallize his argument to the electorate. There is only one real possibility: immigration. It is a subject that has dominated public debate in Arizona all year. As Napolitano says, "it's all immigration, all the time."

As on almost every other issue, Napolitano hasn't avoided a fight. She says she favors a crackdown on illegal border crossings, but also a guest worker program and a path to citizenship for illegal immigrants. In June, when the legislature sent her a bill that would have made illegal immigrants subject to prosecution for trespassing, she vetoed it, accusing legislators of ignoring the concerns of business and placing a burden on local law enforcement.

This might have been one step too far if Napolitano hadn't insulated herself from such criticism well in advance. Last year, she and New Mexico Governor Bill Richardson, a fellow Democrat, both declared a state of emergency on the border, freeing up funds for expanded law enforcement efforts. In March, Napolitano issued an executive order expanding the National Guard's role at the border. The legislature wanted a say in the matter, and passed a bill ordering the governor to deploy the Guard. She vetoed it, saying it would undermine her prerogatives as chief executive, but the political effect of the whole confrontation was clear: Napolitano had demonstrated that, moderate stance notwithstanding, no one was going to label her as passive on immigration.

The result is that, a month before election day, most Arizona Republicans are focused more on trying to thwart Napolitano by securing veto-proof legislative majorities than on defeating her at the polls. Even that's considered a long shot. At this point, it seems highly likely that Napolitano, along with Sebelius, Douglas and virtually all the other mismatched governors, will begin a second term next January in solid political shape.

MYTH OF DIVISION?

What's the explanation? Why is it that Rhode Island has had a Republican governor for 18 of the past 22 years, or that voters in Kansas are willing to embrace a Democrat who is pro-choice and cool to gun rights? There are various theories. Some observers think that voters in Northeastern states elect Republican governors to check the power of free spending Democratic legislatures. They perceive that a governor from the opposite party can't enact much of an agenda even if he wants to, and therefore doesn't pose a serious threat to anything.

Others reflect that most of these governors represent states with relatively small populations, where retail politics can overcome traditional partisan preferences. Douglas has been using personal familiarity to win statewide campaigns in Vermont for the past quarter-century. "People don't drop over in surprise if they're standing next to

Governor Douglas in line for a movie," says Gaye Symington, Vermont's Democratic House Speaker.

But there are plenty of counter-examples. Montana's Governor Brian Schweitzer is a Democratic governor in a conservative state that voted for Bush, but voters didn't put him in office to counter-balance a GOP legislative majority: They elected a Democratic House and Senate along with him in 2004. George Pataki has won three terms as a Republican in Democratic New York, a state where it's impossible for any politician to meet more than a tiny fraction of the voters.

Stanford University political scientist Morris Fiorina has his own provocative explanation: He doesn't think America is all that polarized. In his 2004 book, *Culture Wars? The Myth of a Divided America,* Fiorina argued

Mixed Results

Democratic governors in states Bush won in 2004

State	Governor	Bush Margin
Wyoming	Dave Freudenthal	39.79%
Oklahoma	Brad Henry	31.14
Kansas	Kathleen Sebelius	25.38
Montana	Brian Schweitzer	20.50
Louisiana	Kathleen Blanco	14.51
Tennessee	Phil Bredesen	14.27
West Virginia	Joe Manchin	12.86
North Carolina	Mike Easley	12.43
Arizona	Janet Napolitano	10.47
Virginia	Tim Kaine	8.20
New Mexico	Bill Richardson	0.79
Iowa	Tom Vilsack	0.67

Republican governors in states Kerry won in 2004

State	Governor	Kerry Margin
Massachusetts	Mitt Romney	25.10%
Rhode Island	Don Carcieri	20.75
Vermont	Jim Douglas	20.14
New York	George Pataki	18.29
Maryland	Bob Ehrlich	12.98
Connecticut	Jodi Rell	10.37
California	Arnold Schwarzenegger	9.95
Hawaii	Linda Lingle	8.74
Minnesota	Tim Pawlenty	3.48

that even on the most emotional issues—abortion and gay rights, for example—public opinion data show that broad swaths of Americans favor a middle ground. This is true, he says, in the reddest of red states and the bluest of the blue.

From Fiorina's perspective, the idea that America is a country of strong partisan fault lines is a creation of journalists who see conflict between political leaders, and assume that regular folks are up in arms, too. If his theory is correct, then the presence of nearly two dozen mismatched governors shouldn't come as much of a surprise at all. When voters choose a Janet Napolitano or a Jim Douglas, they aren't crossing partisan or ideological lines; they're just oblivious to them.

If Fiorina is right, however, it raises a new puzzle. Why, if partisan polarization is largely a myth, does it seem so strong in presidential and congressional elections? Kansas voters may be comfortable with Sebelius as their governor, but they haven't elected a Democratic U.S. Senator since the 1930s, and they haven't backed a Democrat for president since 1964. No matter how well Jim Douglas does in Vermont next month, it's highly unlikely any Republican presidential candidate can carry it in 2008. When it comes to national elections, red and blue states really do exist.

Fiorina's answer is that extremists have commandeered the national political parties. He says the ideologues who run the Democratic and Republican parties don't generally allow the nomination of moderates, the kind of people who can win regardless of partisan registration. In other words, Janet Napolitano can win a nomination for governor in Arizona; she couldn't win a presidential nomination. And the kind of Democrat who does win a presidential nomination doesn't stand a chance in Arizona.

Perhaps there's some truth to that. But people on the ground in states such as Arizona, Kansas and Vermont put it a slightly different way. As they see it, voters just don't think about governors in ideological terms. The issues that dominate gubernatorial politics—economic development, education, crime, and transportation—seem to them far removed from the debates that take place in Washington. As Arizona's Fred Duval says, "you can build up a lot of credibility on the non-ideological issues." And Napolitano has done that.

Moreover, even in a state where voters don't run into the governor in a movie line, they still get to know her in a way they don't know their legislators on the federal level. Phil Lopes, the Democratic leader in the Arizona House, sees significance in those signs that just say, "JANET." They reflect, he says, a level of trust and familiarity she has been able to build up in four years of nearly constant travel and media exposure. Build a sufficient level of trust, and voters may be willing to look past red and blue. That's what they seem poised to do next month.

21

How Green
Is He Really?

Alan Greenblatt

Arnold Schwarzenegger's first term has pleased environmentalists. It's the second term they're worried about.

The environmental movement is wondering what Arnold Schwarzenegger will do for an encore. When he signed off last month on a bill to bring down California's greenhouse-gas emissions by 25 percent in 15 years, he capped a whole series of highly visible environmental initiatives that has earned him high marks from green-minded voters.

But environmental activists are a little nervous. They fear that in a second term—assuming he wins one next month—Arnold might take off his green uniform altogether. Schwarzenegger has a history of changing course abruptly on many of the state's crucial issues, and what's more, charges Bill Magavern of the Sierra Club, "he's had a pattern of making environmental promises that he does not fulfill."

That may sound a little ungenerous. Schwarzenegger has certainly compiled a stronger pro-environment record than most Republican governors. Weeks before reaching an agreement with legislators on the greenhouse-gas bill, Schwarzenegger gained international attention by announcing an accord with British Prime Minister Tony Blair to curb global warming. The implications were obvious. California was doing something about the problem, even if the feds weren't.

Schwarzenegger has aggressively pushed solar power, aiming to put panels on 1 million residential and commercial rooftops. When legislators balked at the price tag, he persuaded the Public Utilities Commission to proceed anyway. He has fought the Bush administration by opposing offshore oil drilling and road building in wilderness areas. All of these efforts earned the governor high marks in a July poll that found him leading in his reelection bid among voters who consider environmental problems important.

From *Governing*, October 2006

So why aren't activists applauding more loudly? Well, as in many areas, it's actually a mixed record. Despite the high-profile activity, Schwarzenegger has vetoed some clean air and water bills and spent much of the summer lobbying to weaken the global warming bill before finally signing off on it.

More worrisome from a green point of view, he no longer has the services of Terry Tamminen, the energy and environment adviser who came into Schwarzenegger's orbit through Kennedy family connections. Tamminen left earlier this year, and many of Schwarzenegger's other environmental appointees have been much more friendly to industry and development interests. "Terry has been our strongest ally in the administration by far," says Rico Mastrodonato, of the California League of Conservation Voters.

If Schwarzenegger wins next month, environmentalists will have to work harder to get their concerns heard. But that's only partly because Tamminen is gone. It's also because the governor has given them so much already. He may not be in a mood to go much further.

22

States Get a Head Start

Mary Branham Dusenberry

Governors outline their proposals to address the problems facing the country.

When President Bush outlined his agenda in the State of the Union address in January, he touched on many challenges individual states are already tackling. While the federal government ponders ways to address many of the challenges facing the country, governors outlined plans for their states addressing many of the same issues.

Health care, education, energy and environment are always among the major proposals for governors, but in many of their state of the state addresses given in January, the country's governors went beyond the normal rhetoric, offering innovative plans to address the needs of their residents.

HEALTH CARE

In no area was innovation more pronounced than health care reform. More than 46 million Americans are uninsured, according to the Kaiser Foundation on Medicaid and the Uninsured, and states are trying to change that.

Massachusetts and Vermont last year adopted plans that would offer universal health care to their residents. Massachusetts shifted Medicaid funding to help those who otherwise couldn't afford coverage. Bush's plan proposes allowing states to use Medicaid money currently directed to hospitals that primarily serve poor patients to help the uninsured buy coverage.

California Gov. Arnold Schwarzenegger proposed a plan that would require all residents to purchase health insurance coverage. It's similar to the plan in Massachusetts, which offers sliding scale subsidies based on income. The California plan would require all

From *State News*, March 2007

businesses with 10 or more employees to offer coverage or pay a fee of 4 percent of their payroll into a fund to help the uninsured buy health insurance. Under the plan, insurers would be forced to offer coverage to people with existing medical conditions.

Schwarzenegger also recommended expanding the state's existing program for children's health insurance to families that earn less than three times the poverty level, or $60,000 for a family of four.

California isn't the only state focusing on expanded health care coverage. Several states—Connecticut, Kansas, Minnesota, New Jersey, New Mexico, New York, Oregon and Washington—are considering proposals to cover all children or all residents. Illinois launched a program covering all children in 2006, and Pennsylvania plans to launch a similar program this year.

"I don't believe we should allow Kansans to go without health care simply because Congress cannot, or will not, act," Kansas Gov. Kathleen Sebelius said. Her plan calls for providing every Kansas child with health care from birth to age 5.

Minnesota Gov. Tim Pawlenty wants to expand coverage to all children under age 21 with a household income of $60,000 or less for a family of four. He also would like to create a program—the Minnesota Health Insurance Exchange—that he said would give uninsured residents access to health insurance and lower premium costs by about 30 percent.

New Mexico Gov. Bill Richardson, in his address, proposed two steps toward closing the uninsured gap. He suggested raising the Medicaid eligibility to 100 percent of the federal poverty level to help low income adults get health care. For those people who simply can't afford insurance, Richardson suggested expanding the state coverage program to more middle-class working adults.

Utah Gov. Jon Huntsman and Washington Gov. Christine Gregoire have proposed additional funding for the Children's Health Insurance Program to cover additional children.

> "I don't believe we should allow Kansans to go without health care simply because Congress cannot, or will not, act."
>
> —Kansas Gov. Kathleen Sebelius

K–12 EDUCATION

The president is encouraging Congress to reauthorize No Child Left Behind, his education initiative. Education Secretary Margaret Spellings, who began her campaign to gain support for the administration's plans in January, said Bush's budget includes substantial increases for education.

Governors are tackling the education issue by proposing expansion of some programs, improvements to infrastructure and changes in some requirements. Funding is a major issue, and several governors have proposed increases in the amount of money that goes into education.

Arizona Gov. Janet Napolitano, for instance, wants her state to install a minimum starting salary for teachers at $33,000, with raises beyond that and incentive pay for teachers in areas of special need in the state. Her initiative also offers financial incentives "to find, train and keep teachers who can successfully create a cutting-edge learning environment for their pupils."

Georgia, which Gov. Sonny Perdue says has the highest paid teachers in the Southeast, will provide another 3 percent pay raise for teachers. Huntsman not only has proposed a 9 percent pay hike, he's also calling for $25 million for a one-time bonus for Utah's classroom teachers.

Increased funding isn't just targeted for faculty pay, however. Several governors have included new money for expansion of all-day kindergarten and preschool programs.

Huntsman included $7.5 million in his proposed budget for extended day kindergarten in every Utah school district; and Delaware Gov. Ruth Ann Minner included funding for full-day kindergarten in 11 school districts and eight charter schools.

Minner also proposed financial incentives for early child care centers. Gov. Mike Beebe has proposed an additional $40 million for the Arkansas Better Chance program to provide voluntary, top-quality preschool classes to all children whose families earn up to 200 percent of the poverty level. Minnesota also is looking at aiding at-risk students with preschool help. Pawlenty proposed an early childhood scholarship program to provide up to $4,000 per child for at-risk students to attend a certified kindergarten readiness program.

New Hampshire Gov. John Lynch wants to increase the education budget, but says the money should be targeted to areas most in need. "… Directing education aid to the communities with the greatest need will help ensure fair opportunities for all of our students," he said. "We can lift up the communities that are struggling to provide a quality education and ease the burden of property taxes in communities that struggle the most."

Gov. Tim Kaine proposed pilot projects to expand the Virginia Preschool Initiative by including "high quality private preschool programs, including church programs, in our efforts to expand early learning."

Building or renovating schools is on the agenda in some states. California, for instance, approved bonds in November to build 10,000 new classrooms and renovate 38,000 more. Schwarzenegger asked in his state of the state address that the legislature providing funding for construction of 15,000 more new classrooms and renovation of 40,000 more.

Gov. Michael Rounds said the South Dakota Classroom Connections laptop project has been a success in the pilot sites, and he wants to double the number of laptops in his state's schools to 10,000 next year.

Not all the governors' proposals deal with funding. Lynch, for instance, encouraged the compulsory attendance age in New Hampshire be increased from 16 to 18.

"Half a high school education is no longer enough," he said.

Arizona also proposed increasing the mandatory attendance age to 18, while Georgia is addressing the dropout problem through the expansion of the graduation coach program in high schools to the state's middle schools.

> *"… Directing education aid to the communities with the greatest need will help ensure fair opportunities for all of our students. We can lift up the communities that are struggling to provide a quality education and ease the burden of property taxes in communities that struggle the most."*
>
> —New Hampshire Gov. John Lynch

Kaine also stated a goal of recruiting 750 new math and science teachers by offering college scholarships, loan forgiveness and recruiting teachers from the private sector. He proposed reducing math and science class sizes to the 25 students.

Sebelius launched Kansas Mentors, a statewide effort to provide adult role models to children. "Every Kansas parent deserves help pushing back popular culture so she can instill in her children the values that lead to a good life," Sebelius said. "Every Kansas child deserves someone he can look up to."

HIGHER EDUCATION

Increased funding for higher education is also on the agenda for several governors.

"Young people with the talent and the ability to pursue higher education in Arkansas should not be hindered by a lack of resources," Beebe said. He proposed a $1,000 state scholarship for students whose families earn less than $25,000 a year.

Gov. Mitch Daniels proposed Indiana convert its lottery from a state bureaucracy to a franchised, regulated utility. The state could create Hoosier Hope Scholarships for Indiana students to attend college in the state, he said. In New Mexico, Richardson also proposed expanding a scholarship program, and suggested the state "get a grip on the out-of-control tuition hikes that put college out of reach for many New Mexicans."

Idaho Gov. C.L. "Butch" Otter recommended a bigger appropriation for higher education, including $12.9 million to make salaries more competitive. And in Minnesota, Pawlenty suggested increases in not only tuition aid and general college and university funding, but also $50 million for performance bonuses for higher education institutions that achieve "clearly defined and obtained strategic goals."

ENERGY

Oklahoma Gov. Brad Henry, CSG's 2007 president, believes the growing energy crisis demands attention now. He's selected sustainable energy as his President's Initiative during the coming year.

It appears other governors agree there needs to be some focus on the current energy situation in the United States. Several mentioned energy—some in conjunction with economic development—in their State of the State addresses.

Alaska Gov. Sarah Palin said the state's primary focus for long-term energy is the natural gas pipeline. "The gas line is critical not just for our future, but for the nation's future," she said. "It's also an essential component for our nation's energy policy."

Other states are looking at developing or expanding renewable energy forms. New Mexico, North Dakota and Colorado, for instance, are looking at solar and wind among other types of renewable energy sources. Biofuels is a big topic in the states as well.

"Energy is today's version of the space race of the '60s and the technology race of the '80s and '90s," said Colorado Gov. Bill Ritter.

Like other governors, Ritter wants to make changes in energy usage. He suggested converting Colorado's vehicle fleets to hybrid or flex-fuels as they are replaced, and he would like to renovate state buildings to comply with higher energy-efficiency standards.

Richardson suggested transforming New Mexico's schools into "green buildings" to save energy costs and protect the environment.

Schwarzenegger, in California, encouraged the legislature to fund the global warming legislation that caps greenhouse gas emissions. He also proposed California "be the first in the world to develop a low carbon fuel standard that leads us away from fossil fuels."

OTHER PRIORITIES

As Congress wrestles with whether to increase the federal minimum wage, proposals are on the floor in Iowa, New Hampshire, New Mexico, South Dakota, Kentucky and Virginia to increase those states' minimum wages.

"Today's minimum wage means that some Virginians work 40 hours a week, 52 weeks a year and earn less than $11,000," said Kaine. "That is not enough to take care of a family, not enough to buy a home, not enough to afford health insurance."

Other states have proposed tax reform measures. Perdue, for instance, proposed that Georgia cut taxes on retirement fund income, and Otter asked the Idaho legislature to review the state's personal property tax laws and proposed an increase in the grocery tax credit for lower-income Idahoans to $90 per person.

Gov. Jon Corzine proposed a direct credit reducing the property tax bills of New Jersey residents by 10 percent to 20 percent of taxes owed. And Kaine proposed increasing the threshold for Virginia state income tax from $7,000 to $12,000 for an individual and from $14,000 to $24,000 for a married couple, a change that would eliminate income tax liability for around 147,000 Virginians.

Governors in Alaska, New Mexico, New York and Utah proposed ethics reform for state officials. "Holding the highest ethical standards is not a privilege," said New Mexico's Richardson, "but our responsibility as public servants. It's also the best, and only way, we can protect the public's faith in our democracy."

Courts

I t's not easy being a judge. There are the challenges of knowing and interpreting the law, applying the right precedents, making sure juries get the right instructions, and responding to lawyers' briefs and arguments. But everyone who dons a black robe knows, perhaps even relishes, those sorts of challenges.

Yet there is a lot more than that going on in state courtrooms these days. Courts are facing challenges that they don't teach you about in law school and that you don't see on the courtroom dramas on TV. Courts are formulating plans of action to follow in case of a terrorist attack or some similar emergency. They are trying to accommodate new technology (Perry Mason never made a Power-Point presentation to a jury, let alone arraigned somebody by video conference). They are dealing with demands for easier access to records and information via the Web, yet are under pressure to ensure that privacy rights are upheld. Courts also are being pressed to quantify their workload and success by creating measurable benchmarks that other branches of the government and the general public can use to make them accountable. And like the other branches of state government, they are dealing with budget issues (and like the other branches, the big issue is too much to do with too little money).

The readings in this section introduce the reader to some of these trends and also explore the important role that courts and criminal justice agencies play in the broader federal political system.

THE STRUCTURE OF STATE COURTS AND THE SELECTION OF JUDGES

The United States is unusual in that it has a dual judicial system. This parallel, two-track system is a by-product of federalism. The federal system, at least in theory, makes state governments and the federal government co-equal partners. Just as a governor is not subordinate to the president, neither are state courts subordinate to federal courts. Broadly speaking, the federal courts deal with issues of federal law and the U.S. Constitution, whereas state courts deal with state law and state constitutions. The only real point of overlap is at the very top. Sitting at the head of both systems is the U.S. Supreme Court, which has final say on what both levels of government are empowered to do under the U.S. Constitution.

State courts thus constitute an independent system with their own jurisdictions. State criminal justices systems are structured by state constitutions and state law. The latter covers most criminal law and a good deal of civil law. State courts handle everything from traffic tickets to murder, gay marriage to divorce. That all adds up to a lot of work: there are roughly one hundred million cases filed in state courts every year.[1]

Most state court systems are organized into a basic three-level hierarchy. At the bottom are trial courts, or courts of first instance. This is where a case is initially heard, meaning it is where the parties involved make arguments and present evidence to a judge (and often to a jury). The judge and jury decide what the facts of the case are and which side the law favors. These are the most numerous type of state court. Roughly thirty thousand people work for state trial courts nationwide, a figure that includes judges, magistrates, and other court officers.[2]

Above trial courts are courts of appeal. The basic job of an appeals court is to examine whether the law and proper procedures were followed by trial courts. An appeals court does not provide a "do over" for the losing party in a trial court; these courts exist to hear claims that some legal or procedural error in a lower court damaged the loser's chances of winning the case.

At the top of most state court systems is a state supreme court. This constitutes the highest legal authority within a state. The only place to appeal the decision of a state supreme court is the U.S. Supreme Court. To do so requires making a federal case of a dispute through a credible argument that some element of the state court process or state law violates the U.S. Constitution. This is usually a tough argument to prove, and relatively few cases jump from state supreme courts to the U.S. Supreme Court.

Although this basic three-level system serves as a generic example of state court systems, there is a lot of variation. Some states have courts that specialize in criminal or civil cases, others have specialized courts for juvenile offenders or for drug cases. Some states have no trial courts at all. If you're interested in how a particular state organizes its courts you can go to the Web site for the National Center for State Courts, which includes an interactive page on the organization of state courts: www.ncsconline.org/D_Research/Ct_Struct/Index.html.

Just as the structure and organization of courts vary from state to state, so do methods of selecting judges to preside over these courts. The process of selecting judges is important because it must reconcile two conflicting values. Most people want an independent judiciary, judges who make decisions based on an honest reading of the facts free from any partisan or political interests. It is generally reckoned that judges are less likely to respond to such partisan and political interests if they can make decisions without worrying whether their choices will cost them during the next election or prompt the legislature to remove them from the bench. Judicial independence, then, argues for insulating judges from the ballot box and from the other branches of government. This is what is done in the federal courts; a federal judge is appointed for life and does not worry about winning elections or staying in the good graces of an executive or a legislature.

Yet this approach, some argue, raises a problem of accountability, because paradoxically, while we want judges to make independent decisions free of outside influence, we also want them held accountable to outside forces for the choices they do make. Thus some argue that judges should be elected, and if they make unpopular decisions voters should have the opportunity to remove them from the bench. While electing judges makes them accountable to the voters, it obviously makes them less independent. Remember, we wanted judges to make decisions based on the law, not on what will get them the most votes.

There's no objective way to decide whether independence or accountability should take precedence when it comes to selecting judges. Independence wins out at the federal level, with judges appointed for life. At the state level accountability is given a greater role, with states electing rather than appointing judges. Indeed, roughly half the states use some form of popular election to select at least some of their judges. Many of these are non-partisan elections, but a few states still use partisan ballots for judicial elections. Most of the remaining states use some form of appointment system, although only a handful use a pure appointment system in which the governor or the legislature has the sole power to select judicial nominees. Many states use a hybrid system called "merit selection" in which a nominating committee, typically a nonpartisan group that includes representatives from the court system and the legal profession, draws up a list of candidates highly qualified to serve as judges. The governor (usually) or the legislature (less often) picks judges from this list.[3]

Even judges in appointive or merit systems still may have to face voters. Judges, regardless of how they are selected to serve on the bench, often have to run in retention elections. In such elections they run uncontested; voters are asked simply to vote whether or not they want to retain a judge in office.

RECENT TRENDS

The first reading in this section, by a team at the National Center for State Courts (NCSC), provides a comprehensive overview of key issues courts are facing today. These include a wide variety of concerns not typically considered in discussions of the courts, including cultural diversity, the impact of an aging population, and the impact of technology.

The essay by Mark Thompson takes a closer look at drug courts, something mentioned in the NCSC report. Drug courts have specialized jurisdictions and purposes. They were created to provide an alternative to incarceration for drug offences, and they have become increasingly popular in the states. Thompson's essay examines their impact and successes.

Lastly, Daniel Weintraub's essay provides an example of the U.S. Supreme Court's unique role at the head of the nation's dual judicial system. When the Court strikes down a state law it often has impacts far beyond the state that passed the law. Weintraub's essay takes a look at Vermont's law limiting campaign contributions. The Court invalidated this law in 2006, but it left unclear to what extent states could regulate campaign contributions. While Vermont's law did not meet with the Court's approval, do similar laws in other states pass constitutional muster or not? What that question means, among other things, is that the issue will end up back in court.

Notes

1. National Center for State Courts, *Examining the Work of State Courts 2005*. www.ncsconline.org/D_Research/csp/2005_files/1-EWFront%20Matter_final_1.pdf.

2. Ibid.

3. David Rottman et al., "Courts and Judges," in *State Court Organization 1998* (Washington D.C.: Bureau of Justice Statistics, 2000).

23

Ten Trends Impacting State Courts

NCSC

New trends, such as an aging population and new information technology, create challenges for state court systems.

From the National Center for State Courts

EMERGENCY PREPAREDNESS IN THE STATE COURTS

Historical Basis

Since September 11, 2001, federal and state governments have taken steps to ensure the continuity of government, at all levels, in the event of a disaster. While the judicial branch is not generally required to comply with executive-branch policies, many of the policies, programs, and approaches to emergency management and preparedness can be very helpful to courts. The enduring effects of Hurricane Katrina underscored the necessity of every court to have a plan to ensure that its essential functions can continue when faced with a broad array of disruptions.

In 2005 breaches of security at court facilities, and attacks on court staff, judicial officers, and even their families, compelled courts to revisit and enhance critical incident response and security procedures to protect court assets: people, facilities, and records.

Present Conditions

Disruption of court operations can result from natural events, such as hurricanes, floods, earthquakes, and fires, as well as man-made events, such as terrorism caused by conventional, biological, and chemical weapons. Courts should concentrate resources on planning for the possibility that at any time the courts can be adversely impacted or destroyed. Planning for the unthinkable can ensure resiliency, continue essential functions with minimal delay, and save lives, property, and vital records. Few courts actually have comprehensive continuity of operations plans, or COOPs.

A COOP is a document prepared to ensure that a viable capability exists to continue essential court functions when faced with a broad array of disruptions. The plan should address:

- continuous performance of essential functions and operations
- protection of court facilities, equipment, records, and other assets
- reduction or mitigation of disruptions to operations
- identification and designation of principals and support staff to be relocated to alternate facilities, or assigned to the primary facility to perform essential functions
- facilitation of decision-making processes
- recovery and resumption of normal operations

A COOP provides a strategic framework for judicial officers and court managers to use during conditions that require the relocation of leadership and essential staff to alternate work sites geographically removed from the courthouse or affected court facilities. It establishes a reliable response capability with effective processes and procedures to quickly deploy predesignated personnel, equipment, vital records, and supporting hardware and software to an alternate site to sustain the court's essential operations for up to and perhaps more than 30 days.

The COOP establishes an emergency response team usually composed of a chief justice/judge, key court leaders from each court office, and technology and subject-matter experts who will perform the essential functions and establish technological capabilities to access essential records and databases.

Probable Future

The future may see court systems embrace emergency management as a routine function of court operations, similar to case filings, trials, and judicial proceedings, and weave it into the fabric of the court culture. Enhanced technologies will continue to play a significant role in the protection and accessibility of court vital records, information systems, and databases—and electronic case filings and case management systems may become the standard protocol. First-responder volunteer teams composed of subject-matter experts, such as IT, finance and budget, human resources, and case management, might be deployed to court systems impacted by a disaster.

11 Key Components of a COOP

1. Alert and Notification Procedures
2. Essential Functions
3. Order of Succession
4. Delegations of Authority
5. Alternate Facilities
6. Communications
7. Interoperable Communications
8. Vital Records, Databases, and Information Systems
9. Human Capital
10. Devolution
11. Recovery/Reconstitution

Innovative Practices

- The Administrative Office of the U.S. Courts deployed a Special Assessment Team to the Gulf States in the wake of Hurricane Katrina. The College of William & Mary's Courtroom 21 Project is developing a concept of operations for a national state court corps of first responders.
- Electronic filing in courts will help ensure smooth operation in the event of future emergencies. Back-up files can be sent to alternate sites for protection.
- Remote access to a court's intranet data communication network (DCN) via private broadband Internet and dial-up services is critical for all essential functions. The more laptops the court has available in emergencies, the better.
- The Communications Center for Displaced Attorneys facilitated direct e-communications for relocated lawyers with Internet access during Hurricanes Rita and Katrina. Representatives from the local Federal and Louisiana Bar associations provided lawyers with information regarding where to contact court officials, what special orders were in place, how to seek extensions or continuances, and other tasks.
- Communications for judges, court executives, and essential staff have been enhanced through the use of an enterprise Blackberry network and cellular phones or wireless personal digital assistant devices.

Resources

National Center for State Courts. "Protecting Court Staff: Recognizing Judicial Security Needs." *Future Trends in State Courts 2006.* http://www.ncsconline.org/D_KIS/Trends/index.html

Carolyn E. Ortwein. "A Road Map for Design and Implementation of a State Court Emergency-Management Program." *Future Trends in State Courts 2006.* http://www.ncsconline.org/D_KIS/Trends/index.html

J. Douglas Walker. "Intelligent Video Technologies Enhance Court Operations and Security." *Future Trends in State Courts 2006.* http://www.ncsconline.org/D_KIS/Trends/index.html

American University and State Justice Institute Court Security and Disaster Preparedness Project. *Planning for Emergencies: Immediate Events and Their Aftermath—A Guide for Local Courts.* http://spa.american.edu/justice/csdp.php

Best Practices Institute, National Center for State Courts. *Emergency Management for Courts Best Practices.* www.ncsconline.org

Joan Cochet. "Emergency Preparedness Bibliography." Knowledge and Information Services, National Center for State Courts, 2006.

George B. Huff, Jr. "Planning for Disasters: Emergency Preparedness, Continuity Planning, and the Federal Judiciary." *Judges' Journal* (Winter 2006): 6–17.

THE IMPACT OF TECHNOLOGY

Historical Basis

Advances in technology have always found a ready market in the private sector, where the need to be efficient and competitive are major driving forces. On the other hand, courts—saddled with the necessary burden of precedence, due process, and deliberation—have not been early adopters of technology. Over time, nevertheless, they have come to embrace its benefits wholeheartedly and today are as technology dependent as the rest of society.

Perhaps word-processing systems can be credited with initially moving courts from the traditional paper, pen, and (later) typewriter, introducing the concept of electronic documents, and paving the way for computerized case management systems (CMS). The resulting evolution of effective CMSs dominated the court technology scene for more than two decades. During this period, courts also began slowly incorporating video technology, beginning with closed-circuit television for security and limited court appearances; electronic document transmission, beginning with fax machines; and the Internet, beginning with e-mail and rudimentary court Web sites. Adapting their operations to use each new tool or technique required revising rules, procedures, and sometimes statutes, as well as changing attitudes within the legal culture.

Present Condition

Courts now routinely employ multiple technology products and solutions to conduct their operations. Electronic files are considered the official court record in most courts of any size, although paper copies usually coexist for utility and backup. Many courts have at least one courtroom equipped for video arraignment and other appearances, and a growing number of courts around the country boast impressive high-tech exhibit-presentation capabilities for today's multimedia-conditioned jurors. Biometric technologies—especially fingerprint, iris, and face recognition systems—are materializing in a few courthouses to improve positive identification of defendants and control of access to facilities and information systems.

Although less flashy than the products and systems themselves, one of the most encouraging milestones is that, for the first time in the history of justice, usable national court technology standards are emerging. Draft versions of standards now exist for consolidated CMS functions, electronic filing of court documents, and the electronic exchange of common forms and documents between courts, law enforcement, and other justice partners. Providing the basis for practical information exchanges nationwide is the groundbreaking development of the Global Justice XML Data Model (GJXDM). The GJXDM enables organizations using disparate computer systems and databases to share information via uniform data semantics and structure. The Department of Justice and Department of Homeland Security are jointly sponsoring development of the National Information Exchange Model (NIEM), an outgrowth of the GJXDM that includes non-justice

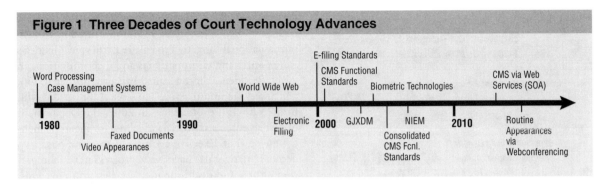

Figure 1 Three Decades of Court Technology Advances

agencies and will help courts exchange information with all of their partners.

Arguably, the Internet has had the most profound overall impact on how courts currently operate and interact with the public. In addition to directly benefiting judges and court staff through enhanced availability of information and electronic communication, the Web has opened courts to the public as never before, making court information more accessible and improving public service. Nearly every court now has a Web presence, and many offer an astonishing range of interactive services along with video webcasts of trials and hearings. While reducing the burden on court staff and facilities, Internet technology also has elevated public expectations and spotlighted significant issues of privacy vs. public access, as well as data security concerns.

Probable Future

Continued development and application of national standards will enable a quantum leap in the effectiveness of many technology solutions, especially when combined with the Internet's potential to leverage and synergize a wide range of technology applications. CMS

> *"Courts are more than criminal justice partners. The NIEM will also help courts exchange information effectively with agencies in areas like health and transportation."*
>
> —Thomas Clarke, PhD.,
> Vice President of Research
> and Technology, NCSC Chair,
> Global Infrastructure/Standards
> Working Group

vendors not only will produce more cost-effective and flexible systems, but will be capable of delivering standardized components via Web services (see "Understanding Web Services"), allowing courts to obtain the functionality they need with neither a data center nor dependency on a single vendor.

Moreover, these "mix-and-match" systems inherently will be able to exchange data with other justice and non-justice partners through compliance with the NIEM.

Electronic filing will become more widespread as vendors adopt improved e-filing standards while advances in screen resolutions and portability will

Available National Court Technology Standards
(may be unapproved draft versions)

Consolidated CMS Functional Standards (V0.20)
Electronic Court Filing Standards (V3.0)
Information Exchange Package Documentations (IEPDs)
Global Justice XML Data Model (V3.0.X)
National Information Exchange Model (V1.0 beta)

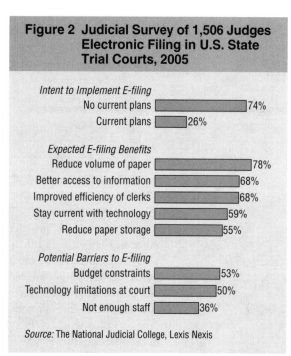

Figure 2 Judicial Survey of 1,506 Judges Electronic Filing in U.S. State Trial Courts, 2005

Intent to Implement E-filing
No current plans 74%
Current plans 26%

Expected E-filing Benefits
Reduce volume of paper 78%
Better access to information 68%
Improved efficiency of clerks 68%
Stay current with technology 59%
Reduce paper storage 55%

Potential Barriers to E-filing
Budget constraints 53%
Technology limitations at court 50%
Not enough staff 36%

Source: The National Judicial College, Lexis Nexis

increase the utility of electronic documents and records. Meanwhile, in addition to transportation costs, the inconvenience of travel and courthouse access due to security concerns will increase demand for conducting court business—including conferences and hearings—via the Internet, pushing the "virtual courthouse" a step closer to reality.

Resources

National Center for State Courts. www.ncsconline.org/D_Tech/

United States Department of Justice. http://it.ojp.gov/index.jsp

"Understanding Web Services." Webopedia. http://www.webopedia.com/DidYouKnow/Computer_Science/2005/web_services.asp

CULTURAL DIVERSITY: THE USE OF COURT INTERPRETERS

Historical Basis

In the late 1980s, the Conference of State Court Administrators (COSCA) and the Conference of Chief Justices (CCJ) recognized the need for every state to establish a task force to address bias and discrimination in the state courts. COSCA adopted a resolution in 2006 to support a national campaign to ensure fairness in America's state courts and eliminate bias and discrimination. In 2000, President Clinton signed Executive Order 13166, which seeks to improve access to services for persons with limited English proficiency. In 2002, the Department of Justice published official guidelines for the implementation of that Executive Order. Over the past two decades, many states have made progress in the elimination of bias and discrimination in their court systems, but the steadily increasing population of non-English-speaking individuals in the United States strains resources and presents ever-changing challenges. The threat of discrimination and bias is real in every office in the courthouse. If the party or defendant in a case cannot understand what is being said in the courtroom, equal access to justice is an unfulfilled promise.

Present Conditions

There is a substantial and steady increase in the percentage of the population in the United States who speak languages other than English at home and who do not speak English "very well." The U.S. Census reveals a 60 percent increase in those that do not speak English "very well" from 1990 to 2000. The increase in limited-English-proficient individuals, coupled with the increase in the number of different languages being spoken, presents difficult challenges for the nation's courts. The judiciary cannot concern itself with arguments about language rights and "English-only" rules, regulations, and ordinances. Instead, it is challenged to uphold the constitutional pledge of equal justice, without regard to race, color, or national origin.

For the courts, the most effective method for making a non-English speaker "present" during court proceedings is to provide a qualified court interpreter, allowing the limited-English-proficient individual to hear and understand what is transpiring and providing the opportunity to speak and communicate with the court and the bar. Five major programs offer oral performance examinations to identify individuals who possess the minimally required knowledge, skills, and abilities to interpret in the courts. The Federal Court Interpreter Certification Examination program was established in 1980 and continues today to test and certify Spanish interpreters for the federal courts. The Consortium for State Court Interpreter Certification, founded in 1995, and currently consisting of 36 member

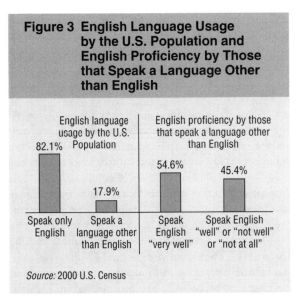

Figure 3 English Language Usage by the U.S. Population and English Proficiency by Those that Speak a Language Other than English

English language usage by the U.S. Population

82.1% Speak only English

17.9% Speak a language other than English

English proficiency by those that speak a language other than English

54.6% Speak English "very well"

45.4% Speak English "well" or "not well" or "not at all"

Source: 2000 U.S. Census

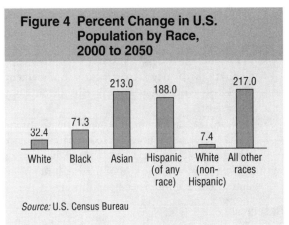

Figure 4 Percent Change in U.S. Population by Race, 2000 to 2050

32.4 White
71.3 Black
213.0 Asian
188.0 Hispanic (of any race)
7.4 White (non-Hispanic)
217.0 All other races

Source: U.S. Census Bureau

states, develops and shares test instruments in twelve languages to certify state court interpreters. The National Association of Judiciary Interpreters and Translators (NAJIT) developed a Spanish performance examination in 2001.

Despite the growth in interpreter-testing opportunities, state courts continue to lack qualified interpreters, especially in languages other than Spanish. Some states have implemented training programs to increase the skills of borderline candidates, others have stepped up the recruitment process, and all are interested in increasing the number of qualified interpreters available to interpret in the courts.

Probable Future

The courts will continue to experience a dearth in the number of qualified interpreters (especially in languages other than Spanish) and will continue their efforts to recruit

"This extremely important and fundamental issue [court interpretation] has been allowed to become a 'stepchild' of the justice system: understudied, underfunded, and in terms of its ultimate impact, little understood."

—Minnesota Supreme Court Task Force on Racial and Ethnic Bias in the Judicial System

potential individuals and offer training to those who show promise. The judiciary will build institutional capacity by hiring staff with bilingual skills for services provided outside the courtroom and manage its calendars for better utilization of qualified interpreters inside the courtroom. Together, the courts and other agencies and organizations can coordinate available resources for meeting the needs of the diverse communities they serve.

The higher demand for interpreters in recent years is expected to continue and contribute to growth in the number of jobs for interpreters.

Innovative Practices

- As a result of Executive Order 13166, the judiciary is facing the challenge of translating public-service documents, signs, and court forms into languages other than English when the population of foreign-language speakers reaches a prescribed level within the jurisdiction. In Massachusetts, the Reinventing Justice Project has helped to develop brochures that have been translated into the languages of the communities that the courts serve.

- In Washington, the Standing Committee on Public Trust and Confidence helps to ensure that the courts demographically reflect the communities they serve.
- In Oregon, the Access to Justice Committee helps facilitate the Justice Department's commitment to address various issues of diversity throughout the system.
- In New York, the Eighth Judicial District Committee has developed a program to educate minority communities about the importance of jury-service participation, with the goal of making juries more representative of the general population.

Resources

U.S. Census Bureau. *Census 2000,* Summary File 3, Table P19 (2003).

U.S. Census Bureau. Table 4, "Language Spoken at Home and Ability to Speak English for the Population 5 Years and Over by State: 2000." www.lep.gov.

Conference of State Court Administrators (COSCA). Resolution 06-A-3 and policy statement adopted November 30, 2001.

Wanda Romberger and William E. Hewitt. "Wanted: Career Paths for Court Interpreters." *Future Trends in State Courts 2006.* http://www.ncsconline.org/D_KIS/Trends/index.html

THE IMPACT OF AN AGING POPULATION

Historical Basis

Two facts are shaping America's future. First, baby boomers (those born between 1946 and 1964) began turning 60 this year and are rapidly approaching retirement age. By 2030, the number of people older than 65 in the United States will exceed 71 million—double the number in the year 2000. Second, our concept of aging is changing. In the not-so-distant past, "old age" and retirement were considered a time when persons withdrew from society. Today's older Americans are healthier, more educated, more financially secure, and more active than previous generations.

Yet governments have not adequately addressed this demographic shift. A survey of more than 1,790 towns, counties, and other municipalities (carried out by the National Association of Area Agencies on Aging) found that fewer than half of all communities are looking at strategies to deal with an aging population. Nationally, a crisis of increased spending on Social Security, Medicare, and Medicaid is on the horizon. Cutbacks in traditional pension plans and rising health-care costs are reasons why financial security and health care continue to top the list of seniors' concerns.

Present Conditions

Americans are living longer and having fewer children. At the turn of the century, the life expectancy was 46 years; today it is approximately 76 years. In the 1990s alone, the number of centenarians in the United States nearly doubled (from 37,000 to 70,000). Analysts at the Census Bureau suggest that this per-decade doubling trend may continue, with the centenarian population possibly reaching 834,000 by the middle of the next century.

The gentrification of society varies by gender. In 2000 there were 20.6 million women aged 65 and over compared with only 14.4 million men. In fact, a woman retiring at 65 today has a one-in-three shot of living to 90, and the odds for future retirees will be even better.

Probable Future

The aging of American society will impact every sector of the nation, including the courts. State legislatures and courts are already beginning to reform laws and practices on guardianships and conservatorships. Cases involving elder abuse, domestic violence, and family violence affecting older persons are increasingly finding their way into the nation's courts. Probate courts are especially likely to be strained in the near future. Courthouse renovations and new facilities will have to be built with a focus on accommodating the needs of disabled and older persons. The courts will be increasingly challenged to deliver efficient justice if the demographic shift is not taken into account in strategic planning for the future.

The United States Bureau of the Census paints the following picture of the future of American society:

- The number of people older than 65 will more than double between 2000 and 2050, and the population over age 85 will quadruple.
- Approximately 114,000 Americans will be centenarians in 2010, a number expected to swell to 241,000 by 2020.
- By 2050, 40 percent of the population will be older than 50. This means that for the first time in history, seniors will outnumber children and youth.
- There are currently nearly five people of working age for each older person. In the near future, this

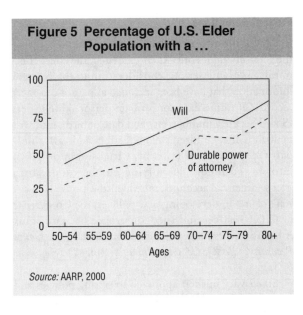

Figure 5 Percentage of U.S. Elder Population with a ...

Will

Durable power of attorney

Ages

Source: AARP, 2000

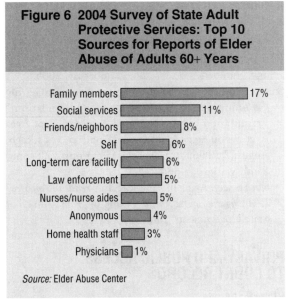

Figure 6 2004 Survey of State Adult Protective Services: Top 10 Sources for Reports of Elder Abuse of Adults 60+ Years

Family members	17%
Social services	11%
Friends/neighbors	8%
Self	6%
Long-term care facility	6%
Law enforcement	5%
Nurses/nurse aides	5%
Anonymous	4%
Home health staff	3%
Physicians	1%

Source: Elder Abuse Center

ratio will drop to fewer than three workers for each older person.

The aging of America will exert great pressure on health-care costs, forcing difficult choices. Caretaking options will remain challenging, especially for middle-aged adults who become the primary caretaker for both children and parents. On the economic front, elderly workers may play a larger role in the economy to minimize the impact of workforce shortages. Finally, communities will become more aware of the needs of their older citizens, ideally developing programs and facilities that improve the quality of life of an aging population.

Innovative Practices

In April 2006 the National Center for State Courts, with support from the Archstone Foundation, held the first meeting of the Elder Abuse and the Courts Working Group, which brought together national experts to discuss effective strategies courts can use to improve their response to elder abuse and neglect, including outlining a training program for judges and court staff and identifying components of effective court responses. Members of a "special courts session" of the working group drafted a benchcard on elder abuse to provide a reference point for judges.

The Working Group also discussed promising court programs, including:

- an overview of a model courtroom designed to accommodate the needs of older persons;
- the Elder Abuse Protection Court in Alameda County Superior Court, California, which is the only court in the country that coordinates civil and criminal elder abuse cases in a single department; and
- the Elder Justice Center in Florida's 13th Judicial Circuit Court in Tampa.

Key Components of an Effective Court Response to Elder Abuse and Neglect

1. Training judges, judicial officers, and court staff
2. Judicial leadership
3. Data collection and evaluation
4. Coordinated community responses
5. Improving access to the courts
6. Regular monitoring and docket management
7. Use of an advocacy model
8. Increased awareness of the problem
9. Developing a customer service orientation
10. Providing community outreach

Source: Brenda Uekert, Denise Dancy, Tracy Peters, and Madelynn Herman. "Policy Paper: A Report from the First National Meeting of the Elder Abuse and the Courts Working Group Meeting." National Center for State Courts, June 12, 2006.

Resources

"Age: 2000." *Census 2000 Brief,* U.S. Census Bureau, October 2001.

Kathleen Fackelmann. "Centenarians Increase in Age and Numbers." *USA Today,* October 23, 2005.

Sandy Markwood. "The Maturing of America: Getting Communities on Track for an Aging Population." Presentation for the National Association of Area Agencies on Aging (n4a) Annual Conference, Chicago, August 7, 2006. http://www.n4a.org/ppt/2006conf_SandyMarkwood.ppt#294,1

"Silver Society: Aging of America." In *Trends in America: Charting the Course Ahead.* Lexington, KY: Council of State Governments, June 2005.

PRIVACY AND PUBLIC ACCESS TO COURT RECORDS

Historical Basis

Since pre-constitutional times, the concepts of open trials and open court records have been the cornerstone of judicial integrity. While the right of access to court records is not "absolute" and such acts as the Freedom of Information Act and the Privacy Act do not apply to court records, there is a recognized common-law right to inspect and copy judicial records, as well as a common-law right to privacy. Courts have long been challenged to use their own discretion in the delicate balance between the harm that may be rendered by the disclosure of certain sensitive information contained in the court record and a "fully open" court record. Examples of court discretion are illustrated by adoption records, medical records, and juvenile proceedings. The responsibility of the courts dramatically changes as the court record slowly migrates from paper form to electronic form where it may be disseminated in bulk, accessed over the Internet, or both.

Driven by overcrowded courthouses and understaffing, courts welcomed the idea of placing their court records online. It is now commonplace to find court Web sites offering access to their records. Whereas open access to manual court records was naturally limited (practical obscurity) by such elements as the location of the courthouse, staff availability, document-retrieval time, and reproduction costs, electronic court documents can be easily obtained with the click of a computer mouse.

Present Conditions

In light of the increased exposure of the court record and the intensifying identity-theft epidemic, the court community is giving serious consideration to the types of information that have been included as part of the court record. Of immediate concern are personal identifiers (Social Security number, city and date of birth, mother's maiden name, children's names, street address); third-party identifications (victims, witnesses, informants, jurors); and unique identifying numbers (operator's license, financial accounts, state identification). To assist state courts in developing new policies, the Conference of Chief Justices and the Conference of State court Administrators have published *Public Access to Court Records: CCJ/COSCA Guidelines for Policy Development by State Courts.*

States vary in their approach to setting policies and procedures for public access to court records. Most state guidelines fall somewhere between the Ohio county that placed entire divorce records on the Internet and the state of Florida that temporarily removed all their records from the Internet while developing new policies. Some states are making identifiers less personal by, among other precautions, using only the last four digits of the Social Security number; referring to only the year of birth; recognizing minors by initials; and identifying only city, state, and zip code in addresses. Some states are creating two records—a public record and private record for sensitive information. Still others are redacting this information. Efforts to mask harmful information from the online record so far have turned into a criminal's

Figure 7 How an Identity-Theft Victim's Information Is Misused

Credit-card fraud	26%
Phone or utilities fraud	18%
Bank fraud	17%
Employment-related fraud	12%
Government documents fraud	9%
Loan fraud	5%
Other identity theft	25%

Source: Federal Trade Commission, 2005 Data

delight. Identity theft is one of the fastest growing crimes in the United States. The Internet is a rich source of information for thieves looking for unique personal identifiers (Social Security numbers, etc.) to enable them to assume someone else's identity. The accountability for the information contained in the court record is shifting to the parties involved. Parties, especially in family-court cases, need to be educated to exercise care in what is revealed in the public court record.

Probable Future

In the past decade the court community has made significant progress toward the paperless or paper-on-demand court. Paper files are on their way to obscurity. Just as technology has created many of the privacy dilemmas facing the courts today, technology remedies will emerge to solve them. For instance, in the future parties will be required to identify sensitive information during the electronic and manual filing processes. This information will be screened out of the public court record. Vendors are already successfully testing more reliable redaction software. Authentication processes (see McMillan, 2005) are being developed that will ensure that electronic documents are legitimately filed and tamper-proof. Electronically filed documents will be held to a much higher privacy standard than manual files. In the meantime, court leaders continue to work diligently to keep judicial integrity intact.

Figure 8 Annual Identity Thefts Reported to the Federal Trade Commission

215,177   246,847   255,565

2003   2004   2005

Source: Federal Trade Commission, 2005 Data

Innovative Practices

The Supreme Court of Florida issued a report, *Privacy, Access, and the Court Record,* in August 2005. This report addresses policies to regulate electronic court records by identifying sensitive information that is unnecessary and making this information exempt from the right of access (see http://www.flcourts.org/gen_public/stratplan/privacy.shtml).

Resources

Federal Trade Commission. "Identity Theft Victim Complaint Data: Figures and Trends." January 1–December 31, 2005. http://www.consumer.gov/idtheft/pdf/clearinghouse_2005.pdf

Susan M. Jennen. *Privacy and Public Access to Electronic Court Information: A Guide to Policy Decisions for State Courts.* Williamsburg, VA: National Center for State Courts, 1995

Susan M. Jennen Larson. "Court Record Access Policies: Under Pressure from State Security Breach Laws?" *Future Trends in State Courts 2006.* http://www.ncsconline.org/D_KIS/Trends/index.html

James E. McMillan. "Digital Rights Management (DRM) Technology Will Change the Way Courts Work." *Future Trends in State Courts 2005.* http://www.ncsconline.org/WC/Publications/Trends/2005/DocManDigitalRightsTrends2005.pdf

JUDICIAL INDEPENDENCE AND SELECTION

Historical Basis

The U.S. Constitution established three separate and independent branches of government to check and balance one another and to ensure that no single branch dominates over the others. Judicial review of the constitutionality of the actions of other branches established in *Marbury vs. Madison* in 1803—is central to those purposes. Fair and impartial justice hinges on the judicial branch's ability—as individual judges and as an institution—to render decisions independent of political interference, public intimidation, or intrusion by the other branches into the authority given the courts.

The vast majority of states still elect judges. For years, judicial codes of conduct ensured that judicial candidates campaigned differently from other elected officials to preserve fair and impartial justice and public trust in the judiciary. The U.S. Supreme Court's *White* decision in 2002 struck down prohibitions on judicial candidates announcing their views on disputed political and legal issues. Subsequent federal court decisions removed even more of the traditional barriers that kept courts fair and impartial. The 2000 presidential election controversy, the *Schiavo* decision, and the struggle against terrorism, however, may have contributed to a new level of dissatisfaction and more concerted efforts to constrain the courts.

Present Conditions

Third-party and special-interest group involvement, campaign spending, negative advertising, and slanted judicial candidate questionnaires are becoming commonplace nationwide. Lawsuits challenging codes of judicial conduct and campaign activities have been successful in more than a half dozen states. In the wake, judicial candidates struggle with ethical questions on what and what not to say, and at what cost. Judicial campaign oversight committees ask candidates to agree to adhere to voluntary standards for campaigning.

> *"I think I ought to be very clear about what judicial independence is not. It is not immunity from criticism.... They're [the courts' decisions] there for all to see, and informed criticism is certainly welcome.... But it should not degenerate into attack on individual judges for the decision as a means of intimidation, and it should not take the form of institutional retribution, action against the judiciary as a whole that might inhibit the judges from performing their vital function."*
>
> —Chief Justice John G. Roberts, Jr., U.S. Supreme Court

State ballot initiatives and legislation aimed at limiting the independence of the judiciary are other approaches. Seven states have such initiatives on the 2006 ballot. A Colorado initiative would impose term limits for all appellate judges, removing the majority of current judges over the next two years. "JAIL4Judges" in South Dakota would eradicate judicial immunity and empower a special grand jury to fine judges, indict them, or remove them from the bench. A less virulent but similar Montana initiative broadens the basis for recall of judges. Other state initiatives would limit judicial authority on property rights and eminent domain, as well as in family-law cases. A recent Pennsylvania Supreme Court decision on judicial salary increases (as well as other public officials' salary increases) provoked new proposed legislation reducing judicial terms and rescinding the salary increase.

Probable Future

Judicial elections across the country are likely to become even more politicized. Merit selection states may also see increased special-interest-group activity in their retention elections. Continued demands for public accountability may prompt more attempts to change current forms of judicial selection. Recent news from two states highlighting the failure of judges to recuse themselves due to campaign contributions may increase calls for public financing of judicial campaigns, more stringent recusal procedures, and sanctions for failure to do so. Candidate questionnaires and challenges to state codes of

In addition to attempts to further politicize judicial selection, efforts to limit or "strip" courts of jurisdiction over certain types of cases are increasing. Recent federal legislation and executive actions have aimed to limit or deny judicial review of cases related to the Pledge of Allegiance, military tribunals, Guantanamo prison detainees, and individuals (illegal immigrants) facing deportation.

Figure 9 Views of Court Officials, Missouri Municipal Courts, 2004

Source: *Court Review*, Summer 2004

conduct may grow in sophistication and frequency. Judicial campaign oversight committees, voluntary codes of conduct, and campaign conduct agreements will increase. Judicial performance evaluations, already used in a number of states with retention elections, may increase in use.

The current tug-of-war over constitutional powers and attempts to constrain the courts will likely continue. New or revised versions of state ballot initiatives are also likely. More state legislation to strip courts of jurisdiction, cut their budgets, limit judicial pay or terms, and politicize judicial selection processes seems likely.

Innovative Practices

- The new *Kansas Commission on Judicial Performance* will conduct nonpartisan, qualification-based judicial performance evaluations based on court-user survey information to support a more informed electorate about judicial candidates.

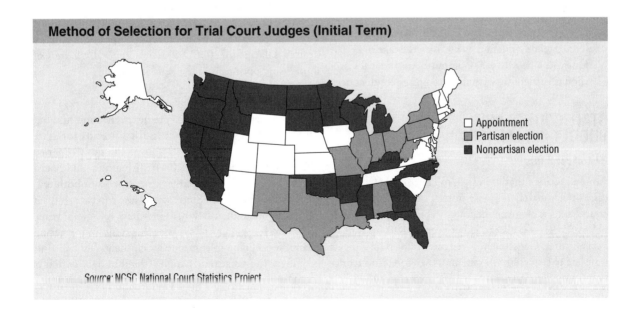

Method of Selection for Trial Court Judges (Initial Term)

- Appointment
- Partisan election
- Nonpartisan election

Source: NCSC National Court Statistics Project

- The *Iowa Judicial Compensation Commission* and the *Missouri Citizen's Commission on Compensation for Elected Officials* are independent commissions with constitutional or statutory authority to make binding recommendations regarding judicial salaries.
- Campaign oversight committees, such as the *Maryland Judicial Campaign Conduct Committee,* exist in 15 states, and are committed to enhancing the quality of judicial campaigns and candidate behavior.
- The U.S. Administrative Office of the Courts' Courts to Classes is one of many court-based, public-education outreach efforts to increase public understanding and confidence in the courts.
- Broad-based organizations are being created, such as Arizona's *Justice for All* and the *Missouri Legal Institute,* to provide support to state courts when under attack and to educate voters about the role of the judicial branch.

Resources

Conference of Chief Justices, "Resolution 7: In Support of Action to Improve Judicial Selection and Improve Public Confidence in the Judiciary," August 2, 2006. http://ccj.ncsc.dni.us/JudicialSelectionResolutions/resol7JudicialSelection.html.

Davison M. Douglas. "Election Law: What State Courts Should Expect." *Future Trends in State Courts 2006.* http://www.ncsconline.org/D_KIS/ Trends/index.html

Justice at Stake Campaign. www.justiceatstake.org.

National Ad Hoc Advisory Committee on Judicial Campaign Oversight. www.judicialcampaignconduct.org.

STATE COURTS AND BUDGET CHALLENGES

Historical Basis

Any reductions that are made to court budgets have a disproportionately negative impact on services because court budgets are overwhelmingly composed of personnel expenses—levels range between 70–90 percent of expenditures. Consequently, reductions in court budgets translate to reductions in staff and, therefore, into reductions in service. State courts have addressed prior funding crisis by cutting spending, increasing court revenue, and increasing efficiency.

Spending reductions include cutbacks in out-of-state travel, hiring, pay raises, and court hours. Long-term budget cuts hit areas such as the education/training budgets, performance management, maintenance, and IT investment. On the revenue side, a measure used during fiscal shortfalls is an increase in fines and fees. Experts have challenged the value of this approach by suggesting that high fine and fee increases restrict access to justice and that the increases are temporary unless collection rates and methods improve simultaneously. Increasing efficiency often requires increasing investment in long-term programs such as PC/software upgrades, which can streamline operations, save man power, and increase fine and fee collection rates.

Present Conditions

Most states have seen widespread gains in the level of overall revenues during 2005–06 as a result of strong tax collections at the state level. The budgetary outlooks for most states as a whole are better than they have been since before the 2001 recession. However, the general improvement in revenues does not necessarily carry into judicial budgets. The tendency in many states is that once a court program is cut during a budget crisis, it is rarely restored to full funding. Additionally, state budgets are under increasing pressure to help provide funding for the soaring expenditures on Medicare and Medicaid. A majority of states have begun raising judicial salaries again after a multiyear lull (37 out of the 50 have raised salaries in 2006), which is generally a sign of increasing optimism in the legislatures.

Probable Future

State budgets are difficult to predict in the long run, but there are two very foreboding fiscal trends for state courts. One, as mentioned above, the government's increasing liabilities for Medicare, Medicaid, and Social Security are making up larger components of both federal and state budgets. Since health-care costs are rising at a rate higher than inflation, as they have for several years, it would be prudent to say that this trend in increasing liabilities is going to continue indefinitely.

Two, the persistently high federal budget deficit is forcing the states to fund a greater proportion of tradi-

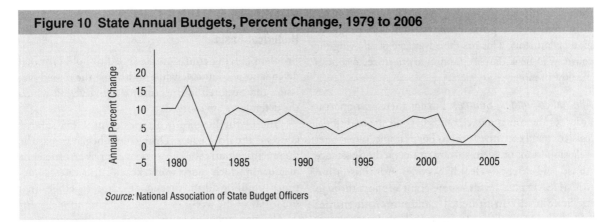

Figure 10 State Annual Budgets, Percent Change, 1979 to 2006

Source: National Association of State Budget Officers

tionally federal government services. Without continual increases in tax revenues, sooner or later the federal government will have to reduce spending to balance the budget. The federal government has already begun shifting fiscal burdens to the states: Beginning in 2005, states noticed decreased federal grants and support to justice programs, transportation, and education. The many states with balanced-budget amendments will feel this pressure even more acutely. This trend, if it continues, will certainly put a great deal of strain on state coffers; by FY 2008, at least 19 states expect structural deficits.

Innovative Practices

While the trends discussed above do not seem very hopeful, the picture is not entirely bleak; there are a few measures that the courts and legislatures can take together to help protect judicial budgets from these fiscal problems.

A Change in Tactics. One of the principal problems faced by the judicial system is the relationship with the state legislature. Several states are trying to improve the flow of information between the two branches to ensure that a strong case for the judicial budget is made and the need to be seen as an independent branch of government is reinforced. Several states have judicial councils composed of legislators, judges, and administrators, which make recommendations to the legislatures. A number of states also feature programs designed to familiarize new legislators with the courts and individual judges; these can range

from having legislators "ride-along" (sit in during court proceedings) to holding "meet-and-greet" affairs where legislators and judges can discuss the issues of government and become more aware of each other's work.

Moving Toward General Funds. Another idea to ensure that priority areas get funding is for the courts to work with legislators and state executives to get more control over their own budgets. Rather than asking for increasing appropriations, some courts have compromised to increase

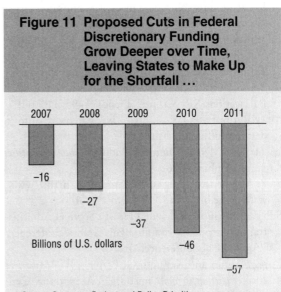

Figure 11 Proposed Cuts in Federal Discretionary Funding Grow Deeper over Time, Leaving States to Make Up for the Shortfall …

Billions of U.S. dollars

Source: Center on Budget and Policy Priorities

their discretionary power over their budgets, asking for disbursement into general funds rather than programmatic allotments. This has the advantage of allowing the courts, who are in the best position to prioritize, to control the flow of money.

Alternative Funding Sources. Finally, there are opportunities for the courts to seek funds beyond the traditional legislative and executive sources. For example, some states seek support for problem-solving courts via the Substance Abuse and Mental Health Services Administration (SAMHSA). There is also some grant support through the State Justice Institute (SJI) and nonprofit entities such as the Mary Byron Foundation and the Wachovia Foundation.

Resources

Katherine Barrett and Richard Greene. "Bad-News Budgeting." *Governing* (November 2001).

Editorial Staff. "Statestats." *State Legislatures* 32, no. 2 (February 2006).

Milt Freudenheim. "Health Care Costs Rise Twice the Rate of Inflation." *New York Times* (September 27, 2006). Online edition.

Daniel J. Hall, Robert W. Tobin, and Kenneth G. Pankey, Jr. "Balancing Judicial Independence and Fiscal Accountability in Times of Economic Crisis." *Judges' Journal* 43, no. 3 (Summer 2004).

Information Services Staff. "Financial Resources and Interbranch Relations." *Report on Trends in the State Courts,* 1994–95. Williamsburg, VA: National Center for State Courts, 1995. http://www.ncsconline.org/WC/Publications/KIS_CtFutu_Trends94–95_Pub.pdf

Mary Byron Foundation. http://www.marybyronfoundation.org/funding.html

Nicole Casal Moore. "Ominous Outlook." *State Legislatures* 32, no. 6 (June 2006).

State Justice Institute. *Grant Guideline.* http://www.statejustice.org/pdf/07-SJI-FedReg.pdf

Substance Abuse and Mental Health Services Administration. http://www.samhsa.gov/Grants/conference/PA_06_001_Conference.aspx

Robert Tobin and Kenneth G. Pankey, Jr. *Managing Budget Cutbacks.* Williamsburg, VA: National Center for State Courts, 1994.

Wachovia Foundation. http://wachovia.ask.com/wachovia/match.asp?ask=grants&origin=5

PROBLEM-SOLVING COURTS

Historical Basis

Problem-solving courts are designed to hold criminal defendants accountable while addressing the underlying issues that resulted in the criminal activity with which the defendants are charged.

One of the best-known types of problem-solving courts is the drug court. Drug courts began not as the therapeutic courts we know today, but as an efficiency measure in which courts would hear all drug cases, sometimes bundling all the defendant's cases together, on a single day of the week.

The more attention courts paid to these cases, the more it became clear that defendants required more than quick case processing. Treatment, sometimes difficult to obtain, and even more difficult to follow through with, was also in order. Courts used the drug dockets to solve a variety of related community problems. Thus, therapeutic drug courts provide an early example of a problem-solving court.

The therapeutic jurisprudence movement views courts as conduits by which defendants, and indeed society, can better themselves. Problem-solving courts spread to other areas—DUI, quality-of-life crimes, and mental health, among others.

Key elements of problem-solving courts have been identified:

- focus on outcomes
- nontraditional roles
- system change
- screening and assessment
- judicial involvement
- early identification of potential candidates
- collaboration

Present Conditions

Long-term success and continued existence are two issues faced by problem-solving courts today.

Funding is an issue for many problem-solving courts. Early drug courts began with seed money from the federal government. After these funds lapsed, states and localities were forced to pick up the slack. The long-term survival of these courts depends on a creative and multifaceted approach to funding.

Measuring success is another hurdle faced by problem-solving courts. Problem-solving courts cannot be compared to traditional courts. The investment of judicial time, col-

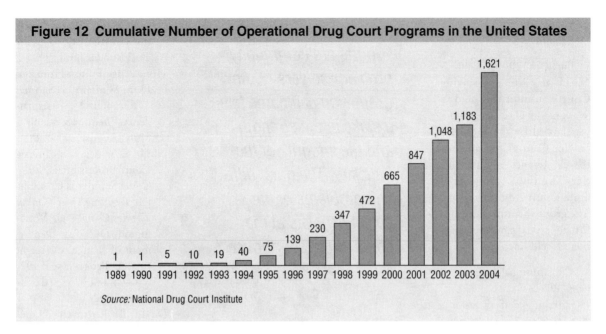

Figure 12 Cumulative Number of Operational Drug Court Programs in the United States

Source: National Drug Court Institute

laboration with entities such as probation and treatment providers, and holistic view of the issues prohibit problem-solving courts from being measured in the same way as other courts. The ability of problem-solving courts to get to the root of the matter means that recidivism and the long-term health of the defendant will be factors demonstrating success or failure. Short-term failures, such as "falling off the wagon," are part of the process. This challenge will likely continue as courts struggle for funding.

Probable Future

Problem-solving courts may well spread to other subjects. However, not all "specialty courts" are of a problem-solving nature.

One goal identified by those in the field is to integrate the principles of therapeutic jurisprudence into the court system as a whole. Thus, traditional courts would use the lessons learned from problem-solving courts.

The funding and performance measurement challenges discussed above will continue to present challenges to problem-solving courts. Best practices with regard to both issues should emerge in the future.

Innovative Practices

The National Center for State Courts has created a data base (www.ncsconline.org/D_Research/ProbSC/) by

which one may search state-by-state for the following types of problem-solving courts:

- community
- mental health
- domestic violence
- reentry
- drug

Some Problem-Solving Courts

DWI Court	**Drug Court**
Family Dependency	Adult Drug Court
Treatment Court	Campus Drug Court
Gambling Court	Juvenile Drug Court
Gun Court	Reentry Drug Court
Homeless Court	
Mental Health Court	
Teen Court	
Tribal Healing to	
Wellness Court	
Truancy Court	

Source: C. West Huddleston III et al. *Painting the Current Picture: A National Report Card on Drug Courts and Other Problem Solving Court Programs in the United States,* Volume 1, no. 2 (May 2005)

- other
- family

Early in 2006, the first National Problem-Solving Courts Summit was held in Washington, D.C. The summit was hosted by the Problem-Solving Courts Committee of the Conference of Chief Justices and the Conference of State Court Administrators. The group identified areas for future study and development, including:

- institutionalization
- advocacy
- training and education
- research and evaluation

Another innovation in this area can be seen in law schools. Although they have traditionally aimed to produce adversarial lawyers, law schools are teaching and fostering therapeutic jurisprudence. Students at the Marshall-Wythe Law School at the College of William & Mary (Virginia) formed the Therapeutic Jurisprudence (TJ) Society, which "seeks to further [therapeutic jurisprudence] goals and views through the promotion of academic study, scholarship, research, community involvement, and collaboration with other organizations." The infusion of therapeutic jurisprudence into law-school education will create a new generation of lawyers who think and work differently.

> *"Courts are community problem-solvers.... Any group you can name has a stake in the strength and the integrity of the judiciary. The most difficult problems of our society are laid at the steps of the courthouse."*
>
> —Paul J. De Muniz,
> Chief Justice of Oregon

Resources

Daniel Becker and Maura D. Corrigan. "Moving Problem-Solving Courts into the Mainstream: A Report Card from the CCJ-COSCA Problem-Solving Courts Committee." *Court Manager* 18, no. 1 (2003): 6.

Donald J. Farole, Jr., Nora Puffett, Michael Rempel, and Francine Byrne. "Applying Problem-Solving Principles in Mainstream Courts: Lessons for State Courts." *Justice System Journal* 26 (2005): 57

Victor E. Flango and Carol R. Flango. "What's Happening with DWI Courts?" *Future Trends in State Courts 2006.* http://www.ncsconline.org/D_KIS/Trends/index.html

Hon. Peggy Fulton Hora and Hon. William G. Schma. "Therapeutic Jurisprudence." *Judicature* 82, no. 1 (July–August 1998): 8.

National Association of Drug Court Professionals, Drug Court Standards Committee. *Defining Drug Courts: The Key Components.* Washington, DC: U.S. Department of Justice, Office of Justice Programs, 1997. www.nadcp.org/docs/dkeypdf.pdf.

David B. Rottman. "Does Effective Therapeutic Jurisprudence Require Special Courts (and Do Specialized Courts Imply Specialist Judges)?" *Court Review* 37, no. 1 (Spring 2000): 22.

David B. Rottman and Chantal G. Bromage. "Problem-Solving Courts: Is the General Public Buying-In?" *NASJE News Quarterly 21,* no. 1 (Winter 2006). http://nasje.org/news/newsletter0601/resources_04.htm.

David B. Rottman and Pamela Casey. *Problem-Solving Courts: Models and Trends.* Williamsburg, VA: National Center for State Courts, 2003. www.ncsconline.org/WC/Publications/COMM_ProSolProbSolvCtsPub.pdf.

David B. Wexler and Bruce J. Winick, eds. *Law in a Therapeutic Key: Developments in Therapeutic Jurisprudence.* Durham, NC: Carolina Academic Press, 1996.

ACCESS TO JUSTICE: THE SELF-REPRESENTED LITIGANT

Historical Basis

In the last few years, a growing number of court professionals have come to realize that self-represented litigants are not just a minor, peripheral source of irritation for court administrators and judges. Rather, they see that self-represented litigants provide a large and important percentage of the courts' customer base, and innovations in access for the self-represented will significantly improve the functioning and reputation of courts. Attention to self-represented litigation issues serves the interests of all court users and staff, not just the self-represented litigants. Expanding assistance to self-represented litigants is an integral part of providing all Americans with equal access to justice.

Courts agree that the numbers of self-represented litigants have been increasing over the last ten years. This increase has placed a burden on judges, court staff, and court processes and is expected to continue. Self-represented litigants are most likely to appear without counsel in domestic-relations matters such as divorce, custody and child support, small claims, landlord/tenant, probate, protective orders, and other civil matters. Studies from several states have shown that while significant majorities of the self-represented come to court without lawyers because they cannot afford to obtain one, they are not limited to the poor. The self-represented include a broad range of income and educational levels. In many courts and parts of the system they may represent 50 to 80 percent of the caseload.

Present Conditions

A survey by the American Judicature Society in 2005 found, "eleven states have established reasonably comprehensive programs in support of self-represented litigant access, nineteen states have partially integrated programs, fourteen states were described as 'emerging.'" The courts, the bar and legal aid have cooperated to establish many of these programs.

Many states have set up task forces, commissions, or committees to study the number of self-represented litigants in their states, and ways to address their needs. Current assistance for self-represented litigants include: self-help centers, one-on-one assistance, court-sponsored legal information assistance, Internet technologies, and various collaborative approaches (workshops, clinics, videos, telephone assistance, mobile service centers, lawyer-for-a-day programs). In addition to the courts, legal-service providers and libraries play a role in providing assistance to self-represented litigants.

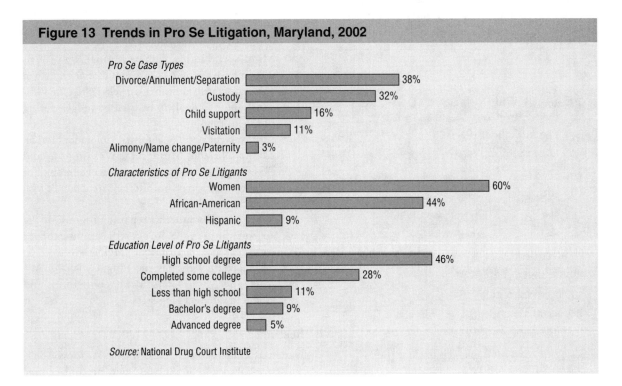

Figure 13 Trends in Pro Se Litigation, Maryland, 2002

Pro Se Case Types
- Divorce/Annulment/Separation — 38%
- Custody — 32%
- Child support — 16%
- Visitation — 11%
- Alimony/Name change/Paternity — 3%

Characteristics of Pro Se Litigants
- Women — 60%
- African-American — 44%
- Hispanic — 9%

Education Level of Pro Se Litigants
- High school degree — 46%
- Completed some college — 28%
- Less than high school — 11%
- Bachelor's degree — 9%
- Advanced degree — 5%

Source: National Drug Court Institute

Many courts have developed Web sites geared toward self-represented litigants that provide information such as online forms, instructions, and guides. Some courts have case coordinators to assist self-represented parties. In Washington State, facilitators refer parties to legal, social-service, and ADR resources; assist in the selection, completion, and distribution of forms; explain legal terms; provide information on basic court procedures; and preview pro se pleadings to ensure procedural requirements have been met. Several courts are adopting protocols for judges to use during hearings involving self-represented litigants, as well as changing court rules to allow court staff to provide assistance to self-represented litigants.

Probable Future

Every indication is that courts will become more user-friendly to those choosing self-representation. Technology will continue to play an increasing role. Web-based document-preparation tools, interactive forms, and electronic filing will become more commonplace. Courts will use videoconferencing workshops and clinics to assist self-represented litigants. Courts will consider systematic change to make access more user-friendly for this growing population. Innovations will include enhanced education for judges, dedicated calendars for self-represented litigants, formalized services, judicial support such as bench books, compliance support programs, and collaborations. This will be a major cultural change for many courts. Once courts realize that programs to assist self-represented litigants can save the court time, they will embrace these changes.

Innovative Practices

- Maryland provides statewide assistance to self-represented litigants with Family Law Self-Help Center programs in nearly all circuit court jurisdictions.
- A statewide project between the Supreme Court of Idaho, Idaho Legal Aid Services, and the Idaho Pro Se Project is underway to convert 300 court forms to an online format that has a document-assembly component.
- A live chat component of the Montana LawHelp Web site allows users to obtain information related to self-representation.
- Rural counties in California participate in SHARP (Self-Help Assistance and Referral Program) video-conferencing workshops.
- Minnesota, Florida, California, Idaho, and Wisconsin have adopted court rules that clarify when and how court staff can assist self-represented litigants and protocols to be used by judges during pro se hearings.
- At least eight states (California, Colorado, Florida, Maine, Nevada, Minnesota, Washington, and Wyoming) have amended their rules of ethics and/or civil procedures to permit attorneys to unbundle legal services.
- The Legal Document Preparer Program of the Arizona Supreme Court certifies non-attorney legal-document preparation providers.
- Several court Web sites, including California, Arizona, and Minnesota, provide court forms and guides in different languages.

Resources

National Center for State Courts, Trends Articles on Self-Representation, 2006. http://www.ncsconline.org/wcds/Pubs/pubs1. asp?search_value=53

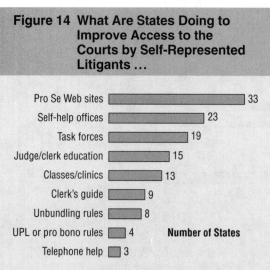

Figure 14 What Are States Doing to Improve Access to the Courts by Self-Represented Litigants ...

	Number of States
Pro Se Web sites	33
Self-help offices	23
Task forces	19
Judge/clerk education	15
Classes/clinics	13
Clerk's guide	9
Unbundling rules	8
UPL or pro bono rules	4
Telephone help	3

Source: Survey Results, Summit on the Future of Self-Represented Litigation, 2005

Selfhelpsupport.org. This Web site serves as a national clearinghouse of information on self-representation. http://www.selfhelpsupport.org.

The Future of Self-Representation: Report from the March 2005 Summit. National Center for State Courts, 2005.

John M. Greacen. "Legal Information vs. Legal Advice—Developments During the Last Five Years." *Judicature* 84 (January–February 2001): 198. http://www.ajs.org/prose/pro_greacen.asp.

Madelynn Herman. *Pro Se Statistics.* National Center for State Courts, Knowledge and Information Services Memorandum, September 25, 2006. http://www.ncsconline.org/WC/Publications/Memos/ProSeStatsMemo.htm.

Richard Zorza. *The Self-Help Friendly Court: Designed from the Ground Up to Work for People Without Lawyers.* Williamsburg, VA: National Center for State Courts, 2002. http://www.ncsconline.org/WC/Publications/Res_ProSe_SelfHelpCtPub.pdf.

> "… chart a course for every endeavor that we take the people's money for, see how well we are progressing, tell the public how we are doing, stop the things that don't work, and never stop improving the things that we think are worth investing in."
>
> —President William J. Clinton, on signing the Government Performance and Results Act of 1993

MEASURING COURT PERFORMANCE

Historical Basis

In the private sector, the principal measure of successful performance is profitability. A number of performance measure strategies, including six-sigma quality, TQM, and Quality Circles, emerged over the past several decades to help guide and manage the world's largest private-sector enterprises. Public agencies, on the other hand, have no such universal and widely accepted performance measure of success. For state courts, success can be more abstract; concepts such as equality, fairness, and liberty are difficult to measure.

All high-performing organizations, whether public or private, must be interested in developing and deploying effective performance measurement and management systems. Success is often viewed from the distinct perspectives of various court constituents such as legislators, regulators, vendors and suppliers, the general public, and other governmental bodies. Therefore, it is important that court performance measures be created, implemented, and monitored by all of these stakeholders.

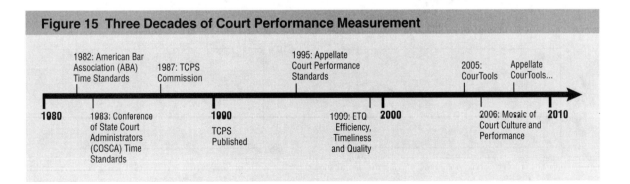

Figure 15 Three Decades of Court Performance Measurement

Present Conditions

Courts are increasingly under pressure to improve their operations and deliver products and services more efficiently, and at the lowest cost to taxpayers. Performance measurement is a useful tool in this regard, since it formalizes the process of tracking progress toward established goals and provides objective justifications for organizational and management decisions. State courts currently use a variety of individual non-standardized performance measures, not typically integrated under a comprehensive and easily comparable system.

The NCSC is currently initiating the CourTools project, which blends successful public- and private-sector performance ideals. This balanced set of court performance measures provides the judiciary with the tools to demonstrate effective stewardship of public resources. Being responsive and accountable is critical to maintaining the independence courts need

"With CourTools, state courts now have a balanced and focused set of performance measures. The key, of course, is actually using performance information to improve the work of the courts. Over the next decade, the biggest challenges will be sustaining these efforts and creating effective ways for courts to show they are delivering quality and value to the public."

—Brian J. Ostrom, Ph.D., CourTools Project Director

to deliver fair and equal justice to the public.

Probable Future

The future of court performance measurement is assessing how effectively courts can adopt and tailor CourTools to their individual organizations. With CourTools performance indicators in place, judges and court managers will gauge how well courts are achieving basic goals, such as access and fairness, timeliness, and managerial effectiveness.

Not everyone will see and accept the purported benefits of court performance measurement. Skeptical reactions will range from "performance measurement won't tell us anything we don't already know" to "we're happy with the way things get done now" to "we just don't have the time and money to even try this." These types of reactions show the need for a discussion of why the bench and court managers should devote

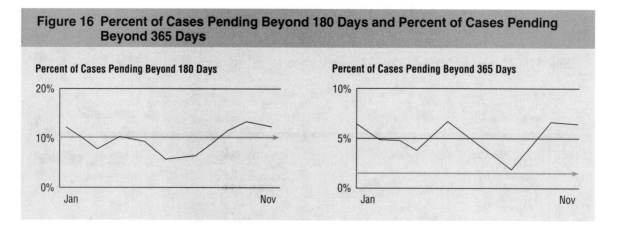

Figure 16 Percent of Cases Pending Beyond 180 Days and Percent of Cases Pending Beyond 365 Days

List of CourTools Measures

1. Access and Fairness
2. Clearance Rates
3. Time to Disposition
4. Age of Active Pending Caseload
5. Trial Date Certainty
6. Reliability and Integrity of Case Files
7. Collection of Monetary Penalties
8. Effective Use of Jurors
9. Court Employee Satisfaction
10. Cost per Case

energy to the systematic and ongoing task of performance measurement.

Courts are just now beginning to examine the concepts of more formal performance measurement.

Resources

National Center for State Courts. *CourTools.* http://www.courtools.org

National Partnership for Reinventing Government. *Serving the American People: Best Practices in Performance Measurement,* United States Government. http://govinfo.library.unt.edu/npr/library/papers/benchmrk/nprbook.html#executive

24

Hug-a-Thug Pays Off

Mark Thompson

Drug offenses are a big reason prisons are so crowded. Drug courts seek alternatives to incarceration for offenders.

From *State Legislatures*, September 2006

Drug courts have joined the ranks of motherhood and apple pie as causes embraced by legislators, judging from votes on appropriations measures in a diverse array of states over the last several years.

Lawmakers from New Jersey and California to Oklahoma and Idaho have endorsed drug courts, which impose intensive, judicially monitored treatment in lieu of incarceration on criminal offenders with drug problems. Appropriation bills have sailed through those legislatures unanimously.

There are now more than 1,600 drug courts nationwide, up from about 100 a decade ago. There was only one in 1989, when officials in Miami opened the nation's first drug court at the height of the crack cocaine epidemic. Many drug courts were launched as pilot programs with three-year federal grants that started to run out about five years ago, leaving their fate in the hands of states and counties. According to the latest tally released by the National Drug Court Institute, legislatures in 35 states have appropriated funds to help fill the void.

State legislative support wasn't always there for the drug-court concept. At first, the treatment programs, which allow drug-addicted criminals to avoid spending time behind bars, were considered a touchy-feely social experiment that could easily label their backers "soft on crime."

"There was skepticism all the way up," says Judge Keith Starrett, formerly a state circuit judge in Mississippi who is now on the federal bench. "Law enforcement was skeptical and the legislature was skeptical. Lawmakers didn't trust anything that appeared soft on crime."

That misconception has been put to rest, says Starrett, echoing comments from officials in other states. Referring addicted offenders to drug courts is as effective and much cheaper than sending them to prison, they say.

WINNING HEARTS—AND FUNDING

Judges, looking for ways to stop the revolving door for drug offenders, tested the alternative in their own courts and discovered how effective the approach could be. "A lot of people were calling it a hug-a-thug program," recalls Joseph Craft, drug court project manager with the Mississippi Administrative Office of the Courts. But drug courts, which require participants to attend counseling sessions and submit to frequent random drug tests, under the threat of stints behind bars for any backsliding, "are a lot tougher than traditional probation," says Craft.

A report released by the Mississippi state auditor in 2003 pointed out that if 500 offenders were sent to drug court instead of prison, the state could save $5.4 million a year. The Legislature responded that year with a bill authorizing a statewide network of drugs courts and the following year with an appropriations measure funding them—to the tune of about $5 million for FY 2006.

The money for Mississippi's drug courts comes from a special $10 assessment on an array of felony crimes and misdemeanors, from driving under the influence to litter law infractions. The payments are funneled into a state fund from which a state advisory board makes allocations to county drug courts.

In Idaho, it was the prospect of a costly new prison to house a steadily growing number of inmates addicted to methamphetamine that put the Legislature in a receptive frame of mind in 2000.

"Judges had started drug courts pretty much on their own, working after hours," recalls Senator Brent Hill. "When we saw those judges going the extra mile, actually donating their own time, and coming in and sharing success stories with us, that is what got the Legislature motivated."

The Idaho Drug Court Act, along with nearly $1.6 million in funding, passed unanimously in both houses. The legislation imposes a wholesale tax on liquor sales to fund the courts. Since then, legislators have boosted funding when. It's up to $3.5 million for FY 2006. The act has

also been amended to include mental health treatment. It now authorizes the courts to extend the same treatment-oriented approach to criminal offenders with underlying mental illnesses.

DO DRUG COURTS WORK?

The national Drug Court Clearinghouse, a project of the Bureau of Justice Assistance housed at American University in Washington, D.C., has collected 66 studies published since 2000 that attempt to quantify the cost-effectiveness of drug courts. The widely varying results, almost without exception, demonstrate that drug courts are helpful even though they are not a panacea. A 2003 study in six counties in New York, for example, found that the reconviction rate among 2,135 defendants who participated in a drug court program was, on average, 29 percent lower over three years than for the same types of offenders who did not enter the drug court. A Las Vegas study published in 2003 found that 65 percent of drug court participants were rearrested within three years of leaving the program. Still, that was better than the 79 percent rearrest rate for members of the control group.

"Previously, we presented the Legislature with a report showing gains in employment, reductions in general assistance payments and medical costs," explains Judge Stephen Manley, a drug court judge in San Jose and president of the California Association of Drug Court Professionals. "But now, the only savings that the Legislature looks at is savings in prison bed days, which does not include savings from lower recidivism," he says.

By that measure, according to a 2005 report, California saved $1.31 for every $1 spent on drug courts, Manley says. The Legislature's contribution to drug courts, which number more than 200 and have about 10,000 participants at any given time, comes to $20 million in FY 2006.

PRAGMATISM ON THE GREAT PLAINS

Wyoming, which has one-seventieth the population of California and about 400 drug court participants, appropriated $4.5 million for drug courts for FY 2006, the highest per capita state contribution.

The Wyoming Survey & Analysis Center at the University of Wyoming, which is under contract to assess the drug courts' performance, found that in FY 2005, 90.1 percent of the 32,029 drug tests conducted were clean. The average period of sobriety between "dirty" tests was 182 days. And the in-program recidivism rate was 8.2 percent. Costs are less: $22 per person per day in drug court vs. $115 per day in the men's penitentiary and $135 in the state prison for women.

"We know we're not going to solve the problem, but we can ameliorate it a little bit," says Representative Doug Oshorn, who sponsored the 2001 bill that launched Wyoming's drug courts. "What we were doing before was just having a revolving door in prison, which is hugely expensive. Even though drug courts are fairly expensive, it is way less than sending [addicts] to prison, when they're going to be at least as bad when you take them out as when they went in.

25

Contribution Limit Liability

Daniel Weintraub

The U.S. Supreme Court sits at the head of all state court systems; its decisions affect them all.

A U.S. Supreme Court decision striking down Vermont's limits on campaign contributions soon could have a ripple effect across the country.

That wave might be felt first in California, where voters this fall will consider wide-ranging campaign finance reform that could run afoul of the high court's evolving stand on the issue.

But other states from Arizona to Maine, Colorado, Florida and elsewhere might soon see their contribution limits come under challenge as well.

The legal question at issue, as it has been for 30 years, is when do limits on campaign contributions become so low that they represent an unconstitutional infringement on free speech?

Vermont's law, adopted in 1997, was the strictest in the nation. Enacted in tandem with public financing of campaigns and campaign spending limits, the law capped contributions to candidates for governor at $400 for a two-year election cycle, including a primary and a general election. It limited donations to state Senate candidates to $300 and to $200 for legislative candidates.

The public financing provisions of Vermont's law were never challenged. The spending limits were, and the Supreme Court, in its opinion, quickly dispatched them. The Court has held all campaign spending limits unconstitutional since 1976 and saw nothing in the Vermont law to make it reconsider.

MUDDY AND MURKY

But the case law on contribution limits has always been murkier, and the Court did little to clarify it in this case.

From *State Legislatures,*
October/November 2006

The right of states and the federal government to regulate campaign contributions rests on a landmark 1976 case known as *Buckley v. Valeo.* In *Buckley,* the Court held that the government's interest in preventing corruption and the "appearance of corruption" outweighed the First Amendment interests of contributors to use their money to communicate with fellow voters through a politician's campaign. The Court ruled that the $1,000 federal limit at issue in that case, and others like it, could be permitted as long as they were "closely drawn" to fight corruption and the perception that money influenced lawmakers' decisions.

The Court also acknowledged that it might be difficult to determine exactly when a contribution limit crossed the line and began to impinge on free speech. But the Court said it would largely defer to legislators on that question, saying it had "no scalpel to probe" such distinctions.

That disclaimer, and the Court's later rulings in cases upholding Missouri's contribution limits and the McCain-Feingold federal campaign finance law, gave observers reason to believe that the justices might never overturn a contribution limit. Then came Vermont.

After the Green Mountain State adopted its limits, they were challenged by the ACLU and, separately, the Vermont Republican Party. Both plaintiffs contended that the limits were so low that they effectively cut off free speech.

"It is not the government's role to tell candidates how much they can speak and to tell voters how much information they need to receive during an election campaign," said Mitchell L. Pearl, an ACLU attorney involved in the case, known as *Randall v. Sorrell.*

The plaintiffs ultimately prevailed, but the Court's decision was far from unanimous. The 6-3 opinion was written by Justice Stephen Breyer and joined in full by only one other justice—Chief Justice John Roberts.

Breyer's opinion, seeking to define a standard for how low is too low when it comes to contribution limits, was in some ways reminiscent of the late Justice Potter Stewart's famous observation about obscenity: "I know it when I see it." But Breyer did try to offer some concrete guidance for legislators and lower courts to follow.

First, he asked, are there "danger signs" that suggest the limits will decrease political competition?

Second, did the legislators who adopted the limit provide a record to show that the measure was "closely drawn" to achieve its anticorruption objective?

In the Vermont case, the plurality opinion first found that the danger signs did exist—the limits were the lowest in the nation and far lower than any the court had previously upheld—and then found that the measure was not closely drawn.

To make that determination, Breyer relied on five factors:

- Expert testimony in the case suggested that the limits would restrict the amount of funding available for challengers to mount competitive campaigns.
- The same limits that applied to individual contributors applied to political parties, undermining the right of citizens to associate with like-minded people to take political action.
- The law counted volunteers' out-of-pocket expenses as contributions, meaning campaign workers could easily exceed the limit by simply driving to events across the state or hosting coffees for their neighbors to meet the candidates.
- The limits were not adjusted for inflation, unlike the Missouri limits the high court had previously upheld.
- The Vermont legislature did not provide a record demonstrating that its exceptionally low limits were necessary to fight corruption.

Four other justices agreed with Breyer and Roberts that the Vermont limits were unconstitutional, but they felt the need to speak for themselves on exactly why they believed the limits crossed the line, and what that might mean for future cases.

Justice Samuel Alito said he thought Breyer went too far in implying that the *Buckley* case should be upheld. Alito said the Vermont matter could be resolved without addressing that question.

Justice Anthony Kennedy, meanwhile, also agreed that the Vermont limits were unconstitutionally low, but he said he thought the *Buckley* precedent should at least be reviewed in this case so that the Court could decide whether its logic still held.

Justice Clarence Thomas, joined by Antonin Scalia, said clearly that they would reverse *Buckley,* probably prohibit all contribution caps as unacceptable limits on speech, and leave it to voters to decide whether or not the candidates are corrupted by money.

On the other side, Justice John Paul Stevens said he thought Vermont's limits were constitutional, and David

Souter and Ruth Bader Ginsburg, in a separate dissent, said not only would they let the caps stand, but the Court should rule that limits on campaign spending are allowable as well.

That means that four of the nine current justices are at least open to the idea of getting the government out of the business of regulating campaign donations, while perhaps three want the government freed to regulate even more. If one of the liberals is replaced by another justice who questions the *Buckley* precedent, the Court could one day wipe out all state limits on contributions.

QUESTIONS REMAIN

In the meantime, states are left to wonder whether their limits would pass muster if challenged under the new standard the Court created in this case.

According to NCSL, eight states have limits of exactly $1,000 in statewide races. Another six states have limits below that—Arizona, Colorado, Florida, Maine, Massachusetts and Montana.

But others think the lower limits will survive as long as they don't have the same defects that hobbled Vermont's law in the view of the justices. States might have to adjust their limits annually for inflation, and make sure that parties are allowed to contribute more than individuals. Volunteers' incidental expenses should be largely exempt from the limits.

The California proposal, known as Proposition 89, would prohibit contributions to candidates who accept public funding (except for a small amount of seed money) and place new limits on privately funded candidates who refuse the subsidy. In statewide races, contributions from individuals would be limited to $1,000. The measure also seeks to limit campaigning through independent expenditures and limits party spending in governor's races to $750,000, less than the cost of one week's worth of statewide television advertising.

In an analysis written for the sponsors of the measure (the California Nurses Association), election law expert Rick Hasen, a professor at Loyola Law School in Los Angeles, said he thought the measure would withstand Court scrutiny. He noted that the limits are much higher than Vermont's, they are adjusted for inflation, and they permit parties to contribute far more than individuals.

Contribution Limits in Statewide Races

States with limits of $1,000 in statewide races:
Alaska
Arkansas
Kentucky
New Hampshire
Rhode Island
South Dakota
West Virginia
Wyoming

States with other limits
Arizona ($760)
Colorado ($500)
Florida ($500)
Maine ($500)
Massachusetts ($500)
Montana ($500)

The limits, Hasen concluded, "are very likely to be upheld as constitutional in the event they are challenged after the proposition's passage."

But James Bopp, an Indiana lawyer who represented the Vermont Republican Party, noted that the $1,000 limit on contributions to statewide candidates is less than half of what is now allowed under federal law, and the political parties, which can and do spend millions of dollars in U.S. Senate races, would be far more limited in state campaigns.

"A limit of $1,000 in California would be too low," said Bopp, who has represented plaintiffs in many such cases around the country. "They are talking about something that's a lot lower than the federal limits."

In the short term, states can probably expect case-by-case scrutiny of their limits, with California, if it passes Proposition 89, perhaps the first in line. But if the make-up of the Court moves further to the right, another landmark decision could be in the offing, overturning the precedent set in *Buckley* and striking down all contribution limits, no matter how high they are.

"It's possible," Bopp said. "There's nothing in this decision that would preclude any of the justices who joined it from joining a future Scalia or Thomas opinion striking down all contribution limits."

Bureaucracy

Bureaucracy is possibly the least loved branch of government. Its popular image is almost entirely negative, as it is generally equated with red tape and inefficiency. Yet here's the paradox of bureaucracy: as much as we claim to hate it, we seem to be incapable of getting along without it. State and local government certainly could not function without it.

Collectively, state and local public agencies employ roughly eighteen million people. And despite the popular image, most professional students of the bureaucracy agree that most of the time those bureaucrats do a pretty good job.[1] Actually, most citizens think so too. Ask them if they like government bureaucracy and the answer is likely to be a firm negative. Ask them about teachers in the local schools, the local librarian, the cop on the beat, or the crew down at the firehouse and you're likely to get a much more positive evaluation.

The funny thing is that public agencies such as schools, libraries, and police and fire departments *are* bureaucracies. Those who work for them, technically speaking, are bureaucrats. Governments rely on public agencies—what generally are called "the bureaucracy"—to get things done. It's not legislators or executives who enforce laws or actually implement and manage the programs they pass. The job of translating the intent expressed in budgets, bills, and executive mandates into action is turned over to the bureaucracy. A reading program might be required by a state legislature, for example, but somewhere along the line it's a teacher who actually has to make that program a reality. We seem to like teachers and what they're doing, even if we do not like the idea of "bureaucracy."

The paradox of not liking the notion of bureaucracy, but actually being pretty positive about the reality of it, helps explain the most notable trend in bureaucracy: reform. This is not a recent trend, but more of a permanent part of the American political system. For as long as the public sector has had an extensive, professional civil service arm—and that's been more than a century—people have been criticizing it for being too big, too slow, and too inefficient.[2] In other words, people have been convinced there must be a better way to run the administrative side of government basically since there has been an administrative side of government. We like the things bureaucracy does for us, we just want them done better. The past few years have been no different.

The readings in this section highlight the role of the bureaucracy in doing what might be termed the "dirty work" of government—the detail-oriented labor that makes the expressed wishes of representative institutions reality. They also highlight the people who run and staff the bureaucracy and the challenges public agencies face in carrying out the specific wishes of state and federal legislatures.

WHAT BUREAUCRACY IS AND WHAT BUREAUCRACY DOES

Broadly speaking, bureaucracy can be thought of as all public agencies and the programs and services they implement and manage. Most of these agencies are housed in the executive branches of state and local governments and run the gamut from police departments to schools, state health and welfare departments to public universities.

These agencies exist to implement and manage public programs and policies. In effect, bureaucracy is the "doer" of government. When a legislature passes a law to, say, set maximum speed limits on state highways, it expresses the will of the state. The law, however, does not catch speeders zipping down the highway. A traffic cop does. To translate the will of the state into concrete action requires some mechanism to enforce that will, such as the state highway patrol in the case of speeders on state highways. Virtually every course of action that state and local governments decide to pursue requires a similar enforcement or management mechanism. Collectively these are public agencies and the people who work for them—the police, fire, and parks departments; the schools; the welfare agencies; the libraries; and the road crews. In short the bureaucracy.

The bureaucracy is not just an agent of policy. In many cases bureaucracies and bureaucrats make policy. Public universities, for example, have broad leeway to set the required courses for their degree programs. Such policies affect the day-to-day lives of millions of college students, determining where they will be on certain days of the week and what they will be doing (maybe even studying state and local politics!).

The actions of public agencies do not just shape the lives of college undergraduates—they affect everyone who lives within the jurisdiction of a state or local government. Consider, for example, the role of state regulatory agencies, which, among other things, are responsible for licensing a broad variety of professional occupations. If you intend to be a doctor or a lawyer, or a barber or a bartender, you may require a state license. To get that license means that at some point—and probably on an ongoing basis—you have to complete and meet the steps required and monitored by the relevant agency as prerequisites to licensure.

Bureaucracies are thus heavily involved in rules and regulations; it's just the nature of what they do. And this goes a long way toward explaining why they have such a negative reputation. Few people relish filling out forms at the Department of Motor Vehicles, dealing with building inspectors, or getting a speeding ticket. Yet bureaucracies do not have much choice. Laws and public programs require rules, and the job of bureaucracy is to make sure these rules are enforced. This does not always make them popular, and there is a constant search to find a better way for the bureaucracy to do its job.

RECENT TRENDS

This section's readings provide a variety of perspectives on bureaucracy. The essay by Jonathan Walters takes a look at the challenge of recruiting top-level talent to manage and run state and local bureaucracies. Running public agencies and programs is often a demanding job, and putting together a high-quality management team in the public sector can be a huge challenge. State and local governments, as Walters details, are meeting that challenge by casting broad recruiting nets and pursuing talented people who may not have the traditional public sector background.

Patrick Yoest's essay takes a sympathetic look at the most unsympathetic of bureaucracies: departments of motor vehicles (DMVs). State DMVs stereotypically are the butt of bureaucracy jokes that involve long lines and even longer forms. Yet, as Yoest points out, DMVs are being asked to carry out a pretty thankless task. Yoest is looking specifically at the REAL ID Act, a law passed by Congress designed to impose a set of federal standards on driver's licenses. While this sounds good from the federal perspective—it makes it harder for potential terrorists to fraudulently obtain identification documents—it is going to be an administrative nightmare to implement. It is a new set of rules and regulations that will require redoing state requirements, dealing with mounting privacy concerns, and carrying it all out on a shoestring (Congress has underfunded the project). It's also a massive political hot potato; several states as of this writing were furiously lobbying Congress to revise or repeal the law. In the meantime, DMVs have a deadline to meet: the law was supposed to be implemented by 2008, although that has since been extended to 2009.

Anya Sostek's essay takes a peek into what bureaucracy is thinking about that you'd rather not. Hurricane Katrina and 9/11 are high-profile examples of what happens when natural or intentional disasters strike: local and state governments are the first responders. Part of the job for emergency agencies is thinking the unthinkable

so they are better prepared. Former Federal Emergency Management Agency director James Lee Witt made a name for himself as a consummate manager of a first responder agency at the federal level. He's now lending his expertise to state and local agencies, including those in Philadelphia, Pennsylvania.

In the final essay, Christopher Swope revisits utility deregulation. Deregulating public utilities, especially electric utilities, was a big reform movement for roughly a decade. The idea was to get energy out from under the control of fussy public bureaucracies with their rules and regulations and put it into the hands of the market. Competition would mean lower prices and better service. Except that it hasn't; prices have gone up, and some states have traded public monopolies for private ones. This is a cautionary tale for those who want to reform bureaucracies: be careful what you ask for—you just might get it.

Notes

1. Kenneth J. Meier, *Politics and the Bureaucracy: Policymaking in the Fourth Branch of Government,* 3rd ed. (Pacific Grove, Calif: Brooks/Cole, 1993).

2. Charles T. Goodsell, *The Case for Bureaucracy* (Chatham, N.J.: Chatham House, 1994).

26

Courting Talent

Jonathan Walters

High-level public jobs are getting harder to fill—and recruiters are venturing into some unlikely places to fill them.

From *Governing,*
March 2007

Last year, the City of Boston needed help, and a lot of it. Its top management team was suddenly full of holes. In the space of a few months, the city had to find a public works and transportation commissioner, a fire commissioner, a director of information technology, and someone to head up its office of intergovernmental affairs.

Just a few years ago, this would have been a painful but relatively simple problem. The mayor would have checked the roster of available candidates from within, placed a few discreet calls to friends in other cities, and made the best choice he could from the list he had.

What Boston did last year was nothing like that. Chief hiring coordinator Pat Canavan looked at the inside candidates, but she tried a host of other things as well. She advertised in general-interest magazines and on the Internet. She lit up local networks of experts and enlisted them to hunt for talent. She contracted with professional headhunting firms. She checked in with professional associations representing the specialists she was after. And she did what cities often do these days: She wandered far off the beaten path.

In the end, the four new vacancies were filled from every corner of the public-employment spectrum. The intergovernmental affairs job was handled more or less the old-fashioned way, by promoting a candidate from inside city government (although from a different agency). The new CIO came out of the private sector, a technology manager for a hotel chain who was interested in a civic-minded career switch. The public works commissioner came from Denver, where he'd helped build everything from transit systems to stadiums. And then, most intriguingly, there was the new fire commissioner— a hire straight out of the ranks of the U.S. military.

That's a story worth telling. In casting around earlier for someone to fill the public works job, Canavan had noticed that one of the strongest candidates was an ex-military officer. The city didn't hire him, but it got Canavan thinking: What other skills do retired military have that might be brought to bear on municipal government?

So Canavan popped an ad for fire commissioner on the Web site of the Military Officers Association of America, the main association serving officer-level military retirees. That turned up Roderick Fraser, who had finished his military career training Iraqis on off-shore oil rigs and U.S. sailors in terrorism prevention and fire fighting. "I'd called seven or eight big-city fire departments asking for advice," says Canavan. "We advertised in every fire-fighting publication and Web site. And then I advertised on this Web site for people coming out of the military, and that's what worked."

Boston found its managers in a relatively short time. But the city's experience offers some lessons to any jurisdiction looking for help. One is that the hunt for high-level public-sector talent is getting more complicated. Cities such as Boston are feeling the need to cast their net wider and wider to find good people.

There are several reasons for this. One is that, in an age of Internet communication, it's less trouble to think broadly than it was before. But equally important is something simple and disturbing: the increased difficulty of finding top-quality candidates who are willing to take the job.

All over the country, municipalities are widely reporting that it's hard to recruit city managers, technology directors, engineers and people with expertise in the fields of accounting and finance. States seem to be having a little easier time of it right now, especially if they are in the heady throes of gubernatorial transition. In Massachusetts and New York, during these past couple of months, private-sector experts in areas ranging from public health to homeland security have been enticed to lend a hand to ambitious new governors, even though it has meant putting another career on hold and taking a huge hit in salary.

But those stories represent the exception rather than the rule. In most states and the vast majority of cities and counties, hiring is a much tougher job than it was even five years ago. And that, in turn, has led to the rapid emergence of broad-based and unconventional strategies for turning up the people that governments think they need.

"I don't know that it's necessarily directly related, but it began around the time of the World Trade Center attack," says Bob Slavin, a Georgia-based consultant who has been a public-sector headhunter since the 1970s. "When I first got into this business, everyone's goal was to be city manager of Dallas [which at the time was the largest manager-run city in the country]. That's just not the case today. I'm hearing more and more that people are satisfied to stay in a medium-sized city, that they're focused as much on their family life as their career." Kids in school, spouses working in their own satisfying jobs, a comfort level with the home community—all of these were issues a decade ago, but now, in many cases, they are deal-breakers.

Frank Fairbanks of Phoenix, widely considered to be the dean of the city manager corps nationwide, sees exactly the same phenomenon. "Seven or eight years ago," he says, "we'd advertise for an upper-level management job, and we'd get 50 résumés. We had a good reputation as a place to work, and so finding people to come here wasn't that difficult. But things are changing. We're getting to the point where we're seeing huge turnover and fewer people willing to move." Fairbanks says an analysis of the 80 positions in Phoenix city government classified as "executive" level showed a 25 percent turnover in 2006 alone.

Spikes in turnover existed in the old days, too, of course, timed to changes in the national economy and the overall employment picture, but back then, it wasn't especially difficult for a city to turn inward for

> *"When I first got into this business, everyone wanted to be city manager of Dallas. Now people are satisfied to stay in a medium-sized city."*
>
> —Headhunter Bob Slavin

top talent to fill upper-supervisory and executive-level openings. Now that generally isn't an answer. "We work hard at developing our own people, but we're depleted there as well," Fairbanks says. "Among the 250 middle managers in Phoenix, people in top technical and supervisory positions who are ready to move into executive management, many of them are now retiring."

At the state level, the situation isn't quite as dire, says Boston headhunter John Isaacson. He says states are still finding decent pools of talent in health and higher education. But he acknowledges they are having trouble in human services and corrections. "Nobody ever grew up wanting to be a prison warden," Isaacson says. And nowadays, it's more difficult for a state to come up with the inducement that might overcome the initial reluctance.

INTERNET STRATEGY

One way to broaden the pool of applicants is to move the most important part of the process to the Internet. That's what Deval Patrick did as he prepared to take office as governor of Massachusetts in January. He set up a widely publicized one-stop electronic résumé drop for anyone wanting to get into state service. In one respect, it worked well. The volume of applicants for the jobs was much higher than could have been achieved any other way. But the experiment created serious administrative problems of its own.

Candidates who chose to go the electronic-application route uniformly reported a "black hole" experience, in which inquiries and résumés seemed to take a fast track to nowhere. One reviewer who screened the electronic applications reports that highly qualified aspirants were frequently bypassed by inexperienced gatekeepers, who simply weren't tuned in to the applicant's reputation. "There were a bunch of campaign volunteers managing that whole thing," says Polly Price, the former director of human resources at Harvard University who supervised headhunting for Patrick during his transition. "They culled through résumés and came up with pages and pages of people they perceived to have cabinet-level potential. The whole thing turned out to be overly paper-driven and inefficient," says Price. And she can think of nobody who was hired as a direct result of the Web-based campaign.

There's little question, though, that the electronic talent hunt is an important part of the future in government hiring, for states and local jurisdictions alike. It's an inevitable response to the increased difficulty in finding talent the traditional way.

When Antonio Villaraigosa became mayor of Los Angeles in 2005, his headhunters required all potential high-level aspirants to apply online, says his transition chief and now chief of staff, Robin Kramer. In the end, Villaraigosa ended up filling most of his top jobs the tried-and-true way: He approached people who were known to him or his top staff or who were referred by some other trusted source. Still, Kramer argues that the Web-based approach is the wave of the future. First, she says, the Web-based application process helped define a universe of talent so that the transition team could more confidently pick and choose those who were willing and ready to work for the mayor. And while Kramer agrees that the personal touch will always be important in hiring, she argues that future public executives will grow increasingly used to electronic job seeking rather than "calling or putting pen to paper."

This helps explain the increasing popularity of Web sites that list jobs in specific disciplines, such as the one maintained by the American Public Works Association. The APWA's Web site has a heavily trafficked "Work-Zone" page devoted exclusively to job openings in the highly competitive world of public works and civil engineering. At any given time, WorkZone has upwards of 100 to 150 jobs listed. The listings have proved to be a popular and effective avenue for connecting jobs and applicants, says APWA executive director Peter King.

Still, King acknowledges that for high-profile jobs in larger cities, he often gets a phone call. "Maybe once a month I get a call from a municipality, or a firm that's been retained by a municipality, wanting to have an informal discussion about candidates who might fit their criteria." In other words, the Web plays its role, but few governments are comfortable using it as the decisive instrument, even in situations where the need is urgent and the supply of candidates is limited.

NON-TRADITIONAL CANDIDATES

One reason the Web is still viewed with a bit of skepticism among government headhunters is that they are looking harder than ever for generalized management ability, not just technical skill. A city might need a finance director with experience in cleaning up fiscal messes or a public works director who understands the politics of snow removal.

Overall management skills and the right temperament for the job in question are always going to be hard to ferret out electronically. Dennis Royer, the Denver official hired away by Boston to be Public Works and Transportation commissioner, found himself working his way through nine separate interviews with Boston officials, only half of which focused on his technical knowledge. The rest aimed at his temperament as a manager and how he might fit in with Mayor Thomas Menino's top team.

The emphasis on management skill is gradually taking hold in every area of public hiring. Joey Rodger, a long-time urban library official and now a professional headhunter for libraries, says it took her profession a while to figure out that finding technically proficient librarians wasn't much help to the larger cause of generating executives who could function in the broader—and highly political—world of advocating for public library budgets and priorities.

Because of that, libraries have begun to work harder on broadening librarians' skill sets to include managerial, financial and political competence. And increasingly, that is leading to hires that would have been considered eccentric, even outlandish, not too long ago. Rodger cites the case of Herb Elish, a retired steel company executive, who in 1999 was selected as the library director in Pittsburgh and proved to be a success.

Governors and mayors increasingly are adopting the same attitude. Specifically, they are looking for retired private-sector executives to take cabinet-level positions. "There's a very clear strategy among governors these days to expand their search beyond traditional areas," says Ray Scheppach, executive director of the National Governors Association. "They are trying to reach out to smart people who've had successful careers, people who are 60 or 61, who are willing to take the salary hit, and pull them in for four years."

The key to attracting that kind of help, of course, is the willingness to ask. In seeking agency heads for Los Angeles, Villaraigosa made an explicit pitch to both late-career and well-situated public- and private-sector executives: "Come here, work hard, sweat a lot, and change the world and for not a lot of money." The strategy lured top executives out of high-paying jobs and drew public-sector high-fliers from as far away as Washington, D.C.

Juliette Kayyem says a significant part of her decision to become Patrick's top homeland security adviser in Massachusetts was simply that he issued a personal invitation. "You have governors like Patrick and [New York's Eliot] Spitzer pulling in a vast array of people who wouldn't have been considered for state jobs, or who wouldn't have considered working in state government," says Kayyem, who quit two jobs to go into state service, one as a lecturer at Harvard, the other doing terrorism analysis for NBC News.

THE OUTSIDE IMPERATIVE

Of course, relying on the personal pitch is one thing for high-profile governors such as Patrick and Spitzer,

The Big Churn

Eligibility for retirement of classified state employees in selected states, as of 2004

	% eligible in 5 years	% in 10 years
Tennessee	40.0%	58.0%
Maine	37.2	59.4
Nebraska	37.0	53.0
Delaware	35.0	50.0
Washington	34.2	63.7
Pennsylvania	33.0	54.0
Michigan	28.8	55.9
Rhode Island	28.3	41.3
Oklahoma	27.9	49.4
Alabama	27.0	50.0
Montana	27.0	47.0
Ohio	26.1	45.5
Mississippi	25.3	42.8
W. Virginia	25.0	42.0
Alaska	25.0	42.0
Georgia	24.7	47.3
Louisiana	24.1	46.3

Source: Government Performance Project

A Wide Net

Selected appointments by Governor Eliot Spitzer of New York and Deval Patrick of Massachusetts

Spitzer Appointees	Previous Employer*
Gladys Carrión, Commissioner of the Office of Children and Family Services	United Way of New York City
Brian Fischer, Commissioner of the Department of Correctional Services	New York State Department of Correctional Services
Kumiki Gibson, Commissioner of the Division of Human Rights	National Urban League
Michael F. Hogan, Commissioner of the Office of Mental Health	Ohio Department of Mental Health
Lorraine Cortés-Vázquez, Secretary of State	Cablevision Systems Corporation
Paul Francis, Budget Director	Cedar Street Group
Elliot "Lee" Sander, Executive Director of the Metropolitan Transit Authority	DMJM Harris

Patrick Appointees	
JudyAnn Bigby, Secretary of Health and Human Services	Harvard Medical School Center of Excellence in Women's Health
Kevin M. Burke, Secretary of Public Safety	Burke & Mawn Consultants, LLC
Suzanne Bump, Secretary of Labor and Workforce Development	McDevitt & Bump, P.C.
Dana Mohler-Faria, Special Adviser for Education	Bridgewater State College
Richard Chacón, Director of Policy and Cabinet Affairs	*Boston Globe*
Nancy Fernandez Mills, Director of Communications	Boomer Media Properties
Mike Morris, Director of Governmental Affairs	Massachusetts State Treasurer

* Previous employers exclude positions on political campaigns

Sources: New York Office of the Governor, Massachusetts Office of the Governor

sweeping in anew and promising to transform government. They can call on a vast network of friends and acquaintances who might be amenable to dropping other, much more lucrative jobs for public service—in fact, Kayyem worked with Patrick when they were both in the Clinton Justice Department.

In the less-lofty reaches of government, however, the search for top talent is still going to boil down to hard work, unconventional approaches and, more frequently than ever, outside help. Just a few years ago, Fairbanks of Phoenix used headhunters in only about one-third or one-half of his searches for top talent. Now the city uses them all the time.

Bob O'Neill, executive director of the International City/County Management Association, can rattle off a short list of top municipal headhunters without even consulting his Rolodex, and agrees that their role in matching up cities and talent is on the rise. There are still "marquee" locations, says O'Neill, cities that maintain reputations as top of their class and so have a bit less trouble recruiting. But for the most part, municipalities are accepting the fact that there is no alternative to the "wider net" strategy.

Which is where people like Bob Slavin come in. Slavin, who specializes in recruiting city managers, fire chiefs and police chiefs, says one of his more interesting recent talent hunts kicked off in the fall of 2004, when the citizens of Topeka, Kansas, voted for dramatic change.

"The city was going from about the strongest mayor-council form of government you'd find to the strongest council-manager form," says Slavin. Under the new system, the city council chooses the city manager, but the city manager gets to make every other top municipal appointment after that. And so Topeka had to get the best manager it could find, and quickly. But it didn't need just a manager, it needed someone with experience in wholesale culture change. The new job required an executive who possessed the skills, temperament and confidence to work with a council and a corps of employees used to an entirely different political and administrative structure.

Not too many years ago, that might have meant expanding the search a little bit beyond Kansas and Missouri, looking to managers in cities of comparable size around the Midwest. But in the changed world of headhunting, it meant looking as far as both coasts, which led Slavin to the unlikely destination of Plainfield, New Jersey, and to its city manager, Norton Bonaparte. In 2000, Bonaparte had been asked by New Jersey's governor to go to corruption-plagued Camden and do something to clean it up. He was met by a vow from the mayor that if Bonaparte tried to set foot in city hall, he would be arrested as a trespasser.

Bonaparte went in to Camden anyway, and spent the next two and half years restoring its government to reasonable functionality. Then he moved on to Plainfield, a smaller but also troubled New Jersey city, and had some tangible successes there. All in all, it was a record that con-

vinced the Topeka city council that he was the man for the job. But the city and the manager would never have found each other if a headhunter hadn't been brought in to spin the search nationwide—something that almost certainly wouldn't have happened a decade ago.

In the end, however, even the most carefully cast nets often aren't enough to catch—and hold—prize talent. While Boston's mayor had good luck last summer filling his four vacant posts, right now he's stewing over the one that got away—a prime example of how hard it can be for an entrenched administration to compete with a new regime that can promise job prospects they'll be on the leading edge of sweeping change.

Menino spent an entire year looking for a new school superintendent, and by the end of 2006, he was so convinced he had a prize hire that his coup was reported in the local papers. Manuel J. Rivera, superintendent of schools in Rochester, New York, and one of the recognized all-stars in the field, would be heading to Boston.

It was with a great deal of chagrin—and not a little anger—that Menino discovered in January that Rivera wasn't coming after all. He had been lured away to be Spitzer's top education adviser in New York. Spitzer's promise that he owed Menino "two draft choices" didn't do much to assuage the mayor. For Spitzer, it was another hiring triumph. For Boston, it was back to the now-familiar grind of casting the big net for big-time help.

27

Card Games

Patrick Yoest

From REAL ID to PASS cards, states will have their hands full making sure their constituents are who they say they are.

As the legislative director for California's Department of Motor Vehicles, Bill Cather markets the massive department's agenda. That's not always an easy sell—think testy constituents, rising fees and impatient legislators.

But now Cather faces an unprecedented challenge, one that will stretch his agency's budget and likely raise the frustration level of California drivers. The REAL ID Act, which was passed by Congress last year, promises to change the face of state identification cards and driver's license—all in the name of homeland security.

Like DMVs in all 50 states, Cather's agency will have to gather "breeder" documents, such as birth certificates, from issuing agencies to verify that drivers are who they say they are. In addition, it will have to deploy technology to store the digital images of these breeder documents and train employees in fraudulent-document recognition.

The cost will be high. California alone will have to invest close to $500 million to make the necessarily improvements to its DMV, without much help coming from the feds. And time will be as short as money. DMVs will have less than two years to get the job done. The statutory deadline is May 11, 2008. "We all feel that that's an extremely ambitious deadline," Cather says.

No one in the states or their DMVs denies that changes in driver's licenses and other identity cards need to be made. The 19 terrorists responsible for the 9/11 attacks carried a total of 13 state driver's licenses and 21 state-issued ID cards. But like many state and local officials, business executives and members of Congress, Cather simply wishes that the legislation had taken a different course and that the Homeland Security Department's regulatory process had more clarity.

From *Governing,*
October 2006

TIME AND MONEY

REAL ID legislation was enacted last year with the idea of harmonizing all 50 state driver's licenses to federal standards. With the states' varied licensing rules unified, it would then be more difficult for a terrorist—or anyone else bent on criminal activity—to obtain a legitimate card fraudulently. The cards issued by the state in accordance with federal standards would then be recognized by the federal government and used by the card holder for a variety of identification purposes—from boarding airplanes to receiving benefits.

The problem is not so much with the goal as with the process and the legislation that came out of that process. REAL ID wasn't a law unto itself but part of a tsunami relief package. As such, it saw very little debate in Congress. And that lack of deliberation has had negative consequences down the line.

Almost immediately, the federal government had difficulty implementing the new requirements. The Homeland Security Department, which has had little experience in promulgating regulations, was assigned to the job—and faced the attenuated 2008 deadline and very, very nervous states. A study by the National Governors Association, the National Conference of State Legislatures and the American Association of Motor Vehicle Administrators called the deadline "unreasonable, costly and potentially impossible to meet."

In terms of meeting those costs, Congress was not exactly full of largess. It allocated a total of only $40 million last year, but states say they will need a lot more money to handle costs—and soon. For fiscal year 2007, President Bush and Congress have shown no inclination to increase that amount, and in fact, the administration included no new money for REAL ID in its budget request. "We can't wait until the next fiscal year to see if the feds are going to help us with the funding," Cather says.

As to the rules for implementation—guidance to the states on how to manufacture REAL ID-compliant driver's licenses and identification cards—no one seemed to know when they had to be available. "There was no real formal deadline that we had," says Jonathan Frankel, director of law enforcement policy at the Homeland Security Department. "We wanted to make it as early as we could, because we recognize that states need time to comply. We were always walking a tightrope between

doing as thorough a job as we could and giving states time to comply with it."

Many state officials say that if rulemaking had been negotiated—which would require input from states—then things might have run more smoothly. But that simply wasn't required in the law.

The expectation is that Homeland Security will finish up rulemaking this fall.

THE SNOOP FACTOR

Time and cost are not the only factors affecting Homeland Security's ability to draw up the new cards. Privacy advocates of all stripes—from traditional opponents of national identification, such as the American Civil Liberties Union, to less-expected coalitions of evangelical Christians—have expressed reservations.

The concerns, as they see them, are twofold. First, REAL ID-enabled driver's licenses would adhere to national standards, and eventually put all identification information into a common database. While each state would still have individual credentialing processes, the shared standard and shared database could create a brave new world of driver's licenses. DMV employees—and perhaps law enforcement officials as well—could access databases of breeder documents from around the country.

"You create one super-powerful database, where information flows from the State Department, to various elements of the Homeland Security Department, to states, locals, all sorts of intelligence agencies," said Tim Sparapani, a legislative counsel from the American Civil Liberties Union who has served on the Homeland Security Department's REAL ID Working Group. "From a privacy perspective, the convergence of databases that looks like a mass tracking system is the biggest concern."

Anxiety that REAL ID would, in effect, turn into something more ominous was behind New Hampshire's revolt over the card. Neal Kurk, a Republican state representative in New Hampshire, led his fellow lawmakers in the state House to vote 217 to 84 not to implement REAL ID driver's licenses and identification cards. While the measure appears to be bottled up in the state Senate, the message was clear: Many citizens believe the new cards constituted national IDs.

"I can't think of any difference between a national identification card and this one, except that every state will have its own name on it," Kurk says. "All of the information has to be available to law enforcement through a federal database, and that database will be available to federal authorities."

States could simply choose not to comply with the law. "There's the misperception that what we're doing through these regulations affects every driver's license in the United States," HLS's Frankel says. "It will affect every license a state issues that intends to comply with this law."

U.S. Senator Judd Gregg, a New Hampshire Republican who chairs the Senate's Homeland Security Appropriations panel, secured $3 million for New Hampshire to become one of the first two states to pilot a REAL ID system, but that money remains unspent. It could remain so if Democratic Governor John Lynch fulfills a pledge to sign the legislation barring REAL ID in New Hampshire. But any such measure, according to Kurk, would not likely come to Lynch's desk until 2007.

Such a rejection could prohibit New Hampshire citizens from participating in activities that require a federally certified identification, such as boarding an airplane.

At the very least, it would force a high-profile standoff on REAL ID, which the program's detractors would likely relish.

FEAR OF SKIMMING

The second concern comes from the technology to be deployed in the new cards. By law, the REAL ID card needs to be machine readable, and radio frequency identification technology, or RFID, would fulfill that requirement. One advantage of RFID is its familiarity: RFID tags are now inserted in a variety of "smart cards"—from passes that allow drivers to bypass cash-based tollbooths to tiny credit cards that work by contacting a sensor rather than by swiping.

The Homeland Security Department has not, at this point, mandated RFID for the cards, and Frankel has signaled in the past that the department would not require RFID. But it is a very likely answer to the tech-

> *"I can't think of any difference between a national identification card and this one, except that every state will have its own name on it."*
>
> —Neal Kurk, New Hampshire State Representative

nology issue, and the ACLU's Tim Sparapani, among others, warns that the allure of RFID could seduce individual states into using the technology. And the possibility of RFID in the cards raises the privacy anxiety level. Specifically, the concern with the technology comes from the prospect of intruders "skimming" information transferred through RFID technology.

The Homeland Security Department's Data Privacy and Integrity Advisory Committee, comprising privacy and technology experts from across the country, released a draft paper panning the potential use of the technology and calling attention to the risk of skimming. "The silent, unnoticeable operation of radio waves," the paper says, "means that individuals will always have difficulty knowing when they are being identified and what information is being communicated, leaving them vulnerable to increased security risks such as skimming and eavesdropping."

FORWARD PASS

While there may be no mandate to use RFID in the REAL ID card, RFID is likely to be part of a new border-crossing card—called PASS for People Access Security Service. The PASS card would be a high-tech version of a passport, and it would help citizens comply with a new federal law requiring a passport to cross any U.S. land border. The passport requirement was part of the Western Hemisphere Travel Initiative, which Congress passed in 2004 to tighten border security by limiting the number of documents U.S. Customs agents can accept. The PASS card would be less expensive to obtain than a passport and would be machine-readable, thereby speeding up border crossings. The passport requirement is due to go into effect in 2008.

Unlike the REAL ID driver's licenses, which state motor vehicle bureaus will issue to anyone lawfully admitted to the United States, the PASS card will be issued only to citizens and legal permanent residents.

While the two cards have two very different functions, the public policy process involved in their creation followed a similar path: Congress created requirements for the cards but did not give much guidance for actual implementation. A lack of public communications bred public antipathy for perceived threats to privacy and sovereignty. States and localities have been resisting the changes, with some refusing to comply with the new and, as yet, undefined, rules.

This has direct implications and ramifications for agencies and businesses that deal with citizens who have to use the card. Darryl Brian, for instance, runs a ferry service that serves Whatcom County, Washington, and Victoria, British Columbia, as well as Seattle. Concerned about the passport requirements, he did a customer study, and found that 17 percent of his passengers simply would no longer use the service if they needed to acquire a passport. While the deadline is still a year off, the law already has taken its toll on his business. Many people believe the deadline has already passed and are avoiding travel to Canada altogether. Some have deferred future trips because of uncertainty over the requirements. And he expects that smaller ferry operators, which may serve more day trippers than vacationers, may face an even larger impact.

While businesses with interests in border communities will have to become intimate with the details of the PASS card, and state and local governments will have to help citizens navigate the process to gain the new cards, the PASS system remains more a vision than a reality. The Homeland Security Department has suggested that it could be a puzzle piece that links together disparate "trusted-traveler" programs, such as NEXUS and FAST, which are used primarily by truckers.

"We want to create a global enrollment network that will unify all of these individual programs into a single comprehensive system that will be the overall PASS system," Homeland Security Secretary Michael Chertoff said this past April, adding that "the idea is also to build the kind of biometric card and reader that will allow people to use the same card in multiple different ways to deal with their access requirements and their security requirements."

Sparapani worries that the PASS card could become linked with REAL ID-enabled driver's licenses, creating identification cards that contain RFID components, which would allow the government to monitor movement of the cards. "That," he says, "turns the driver's license into a tracking device."

For Terri Lynn Land, Michigan's secretary of state, the unification of PASS with REAL ID would be a boon and a benefit. She has lobbied the U.S. State Department to allow her to include a PASS option for driver's licenses and state identification cards. She argues that a single card would prove easier and cheaper for frequent border crossers. In her own state, trucks use the Ambassador Bridge to cross into Canada on a regular basis.

Paul Rosenzweig, a senior policy official at the Homeland Security Department, opened the door for a combined card at a June hearing before the House Judiciary Subcommittee on Immigration, Border Security and Claims. A combined card, he noted, "is an attractive option that we would like to consider." But, he added, "it is also one that poses some substantial operational difficulties, not the least of which would be how a state driver's license issuance agency would be enabled to adjudge U.S. citizenship."

Rosenzweig's latter comment—that state DMVs might not be equipped to certify passport equivalents, a task traditionally given to federal entities, such as post offices—resonates at the U.S. State Department, which expressed disapproval for any plan that would effectively outsource passport services. But Homeland Security and the State Department may differ on the type of card to use. While the State Department reportedly prefers "vicinity" readers for RFID, rather than shorter-range "proximity" readers, Homeland Security officials have expressed a preference for "proximity" readers, which are comparatively less secure than the "vicinity" readers but able to read RFID tags from a greater distance.

All of those things could combine to force a delay of implementation dates for the Western Hemisphere Travel Initiative. For state and local officials, the best news would be an extension of the deadlines—any breathing space at all, really—for both cards.

28

Master of Disaster

Anya Sostek

Philadelphia asks an outsider to expose its innermost weak spots.

W hen James Lee Witt travels, he doesn't return empty-handed. His Washington, D.C., office is crammed with neatly arranged plaques, trinkets and crafts—among them a certificate naming him an honorary citizen of California, a hand-carved miniature wooden boat from Thailand and a full-length Choctaw headdress from Oklahoma.

The items are mainly gifts to Witt from communities experiencing some of the darkest moments in their histories, from earthquakes to tsunamis to bombings. Taken together, the collection in his office is a catalog of tragedy over the past 15 years—at least as much of it as can be viewed in one room.

For eight years, Witt served as President Bill Clinton's director of the Federal Emergency Management Agency. Dubbed the "master of disaster," Witt hop-scotched the country from flood to fire to hurricane to tornado, in the process building FEMA's reputation from crummy to competent.

Earlier this year, as a private citizen with all that federal disaster experience on his résumé, he spent a considerable amount of time in Philadelphia—not because the city had weathered a disaster but because it hadn't. Last summer, as Philadelphia Mayor John Street watched the events of Hurricane Katrina unfold—and saw the heaps of criticism fall on local officials for their lack of disaster planning—he wondered how his city would fare under similar circumstances. To find out, he hired Witt, to the tune of $1 million, to assess every aspect of the city's readiness for emergencies.

"This was about us seeking out to know what we didn't know," says Pedro Ramos, the city's managing director and co-chair of the mayor's Emergency Preparedness Review Committee. "We wanted

From *Governing,*
October 2006

to get the most candid assessment possible on how ready we are."

Witt, who founded a consulting business shortly after Clinton left office, had, among other jobs in the public sector, helped oversee recovery efforts for the University of Houston after Hurricane Allison and investigated a fatal fire in the Cook County Administration Building for the state of Illinois. But he had never taken on a client such as Philadelphia, which wanted to know every single little thing it could do to better prepare for an emergency.

> *Disaster preparedness and mitigation need "a sustained marketing campaign, the way you might sell Gap khakis or Nike shoes."*
>
> —James Lee Witt

Cities are vulnerable. Terrorist attacks can strike anywhere, as can natural or other man-made disasters. Although cities have received some money from the U.S. Department of Homeland Security, emergency preparedness must sometimes compete against more visible funding needs, such as schools and services. While cities are moving forward with overall emergency plans, from a political standpoint, a "warts and all" outside policy review can be a risky business: It might give ammunition to opponents in future campaigns.

FEMA Reformer

Quite literally, James Lee Witt was born and bred for disaster management. "I was born during a blizzard," he jokes. "When I was a kid, one of our houses got hit by a tornado. When I was 12 or 13, our house burned down to the ground."

Witt grew up in Dardenelle, Arkansas, the son of a sharecropper and a housekeeper. His mother made clothes for him and his four siblings out of flour sacks, he started driving a tractor at age six and the family didn't have indoor plumbing until he was in his teens. Witt says that when problems arose growing up, he and his family had no choice but to fix them themselves—an experience that lent itself to resourcefulness and self-reliance.

As an adult, Witt ran a small construction company and was elected county judge for Yell County—a job that did not require a college degree nor a law degree (Witt had neither) but did involve oversight of road construction and maintenance. During several floods in the county, Witt worked with then-Governor Bill Clinton, who called Witt a man of "uncommon common sense" when he appointed him to head FEMA.

As county judge, Witt had been mystified by FEMA's shortsightedness in the wake of flooding. When 33 wooden bridges were washed out, for example, FEMA would only pay to replace them with bridges also made of wood—not stronger ones made of steel and concrete that had a better chance of surviving future storms.

Witt was hardly the only person skeptical of FEMA. The agency, which had originally been created to prepare for nuclear war, was widely viewed as a bureaucratic backwater. Assessing the agency's response to 1989's Hurricane Hugo, then-U.S. Senator Fritz Hollings of South Carolina called FEMA workers "the sorriest bunch of bureaucratic jackasses I've ever known."

As newly installed head of FEMA, Witt's first disaster to address was FEMA itself. He concentrated on improving morale by keeping his office door open for visitors, having brown bag lunches with random employees and switching around the jobs of high-level employees to get them out of old ruts. The fixes took root. When Hurricane Emily hit the North Carolina coast in 1993, for instance, FEMA deployed supplies such as generators, cots and chainsaws to the state before the storm made land rather than waiting until after the disaster to respond.

Witt also prioritized preventative measures, such as encouraging people to move away from flood plains, retrofitting homes to protect them from earthquakes and installing hurricane shutters. "He is the one who raised the issue of mitigation, implemented the mitigation programs at FEMA and got Congress to fund them," says Trina Sheets, executive director of the National Emergency Management Association. "He really emphasized doing these things before the event strikes."

MARKETING THE STORM

In many ways, Philadelphia doesn't stack up badly against other cities. The city has proved many times in the past that it could mobilize its resources fairly quickly to deal with major events. In 2005, the city came together in just 32 days to host—with no major incident—a million people who attended a Live Aid concert. The city also hosted the Republican National Convention in 2000, which went smoothly.

But there are differences between events that you know are coming—even with short notice—and those, such as terrorist attacks and tornados, that strike essentially without warning. The challenge was to find "the gaps"—what the city wasn't already doing that it needed to be.

The review process involved the city's 40-plus-member emergency preparedness committee, as well as city staff and employees from Witt's office. After Witt's hiring became public, one councilman suggested that $1 million was a lot to spend on something that the city could feasibly do by itself. But those closest to the process say that without an outside perspective, the report would not have been nearly as complete.

"We could have done it by ourselves," says Harvey Rubin, a professor of medicine at the University of Pennsylvania and the other co-chair of the Emergency Preparedness Review Committee, of the review process. "But the report is better for having James Lee and his team give their insights. He thinks deeply about these things."

Some of Witt's recommendations were startlingly obvious but had never occurred to anyone inside the city. Philadelphia's 911 call center, for example, is located on a busy street. If a car or truck slammed into the building, the city's emergency operations could be instantly crippled. "We put a jersey barrier up right away," says Ramos. "A lot of people drive by there every day, but I don't think anybody had thought of it that way. It took a fresh pair of eyes to see it."

Other problems were well known, but essentially unsolvable with the city's own resources. Philadelphia's subway tunnels, for example, are not equipped for radio communications—a problem that will cost about $23 million to fix. Noting that the report analyzing the response to last year's London subway bombings specifically identified communications as a major problem, the Emergency Preparedness Review Committee Report urges the city to find a funding solution for communications in the tunnels, saying it should be "among the highest priorities."

Preparedness committee members are hoping that the emergency preparedness report will add credibility to the city's requests for grants from the federal Department of Homeland Security to equip the tunnels with communications infrastructure. Those requests have not been granted in the past.

One of the points Witt drilled home to city officials is the need to take actions in advance of a disaster. "The bottom line is that you can't begin to prepare during a disaster—you're either ready or you're not," says Ramos, who is also charged with implementing Witt's recommendations. "We intend during the next year to really hammer that message home."

In September, the city held its first "Emergency Preparedness Month," complete with signs, brochures, and print, radio and television ads telling people what they should have "in their hearts, in their heads and in their homes" to prepare for an emergency—anything from storing a few extra gallons of water to arranging a meeting spot in case a family gets separated.

It's a concept that Witt devised about halfway through his time as FEMA director. "It dawned on me that we had to introduce the idea of disaster preparedness and mitigation through a sustained marketing campaign, the way you might sell Gap khakis or Nike shoes," Witt wrote in his 2002 book, *Stronger in the Broken Places*. "We had to market the storm."

In Philadelphia, Witt recommended reaching out not only to the general public but also to businesses large and small. Ramos recalls watching a room full of business people go silent as Witt told them that historically, only 30 to 40 percent of small businesses returned to operation following a major disaster. The statistic, Ramos says, grabbed their attention and focused it toward preparedness efforts.

To focus on larger businesses, Witt took members of the mayor's Emergency Preparedness Review Committee on field trips to New York, Washington, D.C., and Chicago to look at other emergency management operations and their work with the business community. In Chicago, for example, the city's top financial services companies formed a group called ChicagoFIRST, which has partnered with emergency management agencies to plan for emergencies.

CONTINUING TO OPERATE

Witt's final report also points out the large and small gaps in the city's current operating procedures. It strongly recommends, for instance, major changes to the Office of Emergency Management, including hiring an emergency management director, who would report directly to the city's managing director, and staffing the office 24 hours a day, seven days a week.

Many city agencies also hadn't given much thought to how they would operate if an emergency took some of their equipment, facilities or people out of commission. The prisons had not identified an evacuation site, for example, and the department that handles payroll hadn't made any formal emergency plans. And some city departments had made plans to use emergency generators but not to acquire fuel to run them.

The report recommended things such as designating and training alternate "mission critical" employees, in case the primary employees couldn't be reached. It also praised some redundancies that the city already had, like the fact that computer systems for the schools and libraries were separate from the city's systems.

Those types of recommendations, formally called "continuity of government" and "continuity of operations" planning, struck such a chord with the emergency planning committee that departments were instructed to start implementing plans before the report was even released. "Who are your essential people? Do you know where you can set up an alternative site? When your city hall burns down, what are the first three things that you do?" says Rubin. "Once we realized that that wasn't in effect, we started doing it right away." The city also started updating its succession laws, most of which were written to respond to civil unrest instead of natural or man-made disasters.

Witt also sees the planning process itself as generating measurable change within city government. "These people had never even met each other," he says of many of the public and private-sector people interviewed by his firm. "They are better prepared today than yesterday just because they know each other. That, in itself, has been a huge plus for them."

In making partnerships, with businesses, hospitals and other government agencies, the report advocates amassing as many resources as possible in the event of an emergency. Those resources are needed in part to carry the community when the federal government, and specifically the agency that Witt once headed, might not be able to.

"When you have an event, basically it is up to local governments and state governments," he says. "It's

Are We Ready Yet?	
Responses to security questions by mayors in 183 cities in 38 states	
On a scale of 1 (for lowest) to 10 (highest):	
How much has your city's level of disaster preparedness improved since 9/11?	**6.3**
What is your level of confidence that FEMA will respond quickly in the event of a major disaster?	**5.2**
What is your level of confidence that you could survive on your own for up to 72 hours following a disaster?	**6.9**

Source: U.S. Conference of Mayors. Entire survey as well as six previous surveys is on line at www.usmayors.org

important to have these plans in place and to have training done. The federal government isn't and cannot be the fix for everything." The preparedness report says that state and local governments should be able to be fully self-sufficient for at least the first 72 hours after a disaster occurs—a lesson brought home most keenly by Hurricane Katrina.

HEAVY WEATHER

There are many ways that emergency planning has been impacted by the events of Hurricane Katrina. Philadelphia's emergency report identified the top three scenarios that might result in a full-scale disaster for the city: an ice storm that causes power outages that last two weeks, a large chemical spill or explosion and an incident that forces Philadelphia to shelter 100,000 people. The last example puts Philadelphia in the position of planning not just to be New Orleans during Hurricane Katrina but also to be Houston.

The legacy of Katrina is also evident in evacuation planning. The report recommended that Philadelphia not only beef up its efforts in designing and publicizing evacuation routes but also step up planning for the "special needs" population that may not evacuate as planned. It isn't enough for the city just to say that it will shelter people in schools—the city must equip schools with

The Big Uneasy

James Lee Witt knows the lessons of Hurricane Katrina well, in part because his firm is also assisting the state of Louisiana. As Governor Kathleen Babineaux Blanco squared off in the blame game against Bush administration officials and New Orleans Mayor Ray Nagin, she sought out Witt's firm to help her navigate FEMA's bureaucracy.

The contract brought much more media attention than James Lee Witt Associates had been accustomed to in its first few years of operation. Newspapers including the *New York Times* and *USA Today* ran articles questioning Witt's lobbying ties to clients such as Allstate Insurance and AmeriCold Logistics, which also had business interests in Louisiana's disaster recovery.

Witt's spokespeople argued that less than 5 percent of the firm's work comes from lobbying. Shortly after the issue was raised, Witt recused himself from lobbying for Allstate until after he finished his work in Louisiana.

Witt isn't the only former FEMA director running a firm: Both Joe Allbaugh, Bush's first FEMA director, and Michael Brown, who resigned in the wake of Hurricane Katrina, started their own firms, although they handle proportionately more corporate clients than Witt does.

For his part, Witt admits that disaster planning is an odd way to make a living. But there's no doubt that his firm has made a significant amount of money helping governments and private companies prepare for and recover from disasters. The firm grossed $11.5 million in 2005 before it was bought out by Global Options Group in January.

---

back-up generators capable of running ventilators or refrigerators for medications. Also, the report recommended that the city accommodate the pets of those who ended up in shelters, to avoid the situation in Hurricane Katrina where people refused to evacuate and leave their animals behind.

"Katrina brought things to the forefront that they hadn't really thought of," says Witt. "There will be people with no identification, no papers, nothing. Those are the kind of things you have to plan for."

It was actions like those, and the public awareness messages going out to the community, that made Rubin confident of the value of the emergency preparedness review, even if the city never has an emergency that ranks anywhere close to its top three scenarios. "Whatever we do will just improve the daily life," says Rubin. "You don't have to have a Katrina. You could have a flood in your basement, or the carpool doesn't work that day."

Since the publication of the report, Ramos said that he has been contacted by numerous other cities eager to hear more about Philadelphia's experience. Was it worth spending $1 million to find out all the things Philadelphia was doing wrong, or wasn't doing at all? "I'm glad we did it," said Ramos, who now devotes hours every week to implementing the report's recommendations. "I think it can only benefit."

29

Static on the Grid

Christopher Swope

States that deregulated are trying to make competition work better for consumers and the state's power supply.

A decade after deregulation swept through the electricity industry, few argue that the restructuring experiment went as planned. Residential prices went up rather than down; there's been less competition for customers than expected.

In the 17 states that stuck it out, even through California's famous meltdown, the question now is what a post-deregulation world looks like. Reverting back to the old regulatory system is impractical, as most of the states required or encouraged utilities to divest their power plants. Instead, states seem intent on tweaking market flaws or coming up with hybrid regulatory models that incorporate bits of old and new.

Even Texas, once considered a model for retail competition, is looking at reworking its system. The reason goes back to the 2005 hurricane season, when natural gas prices shot up. Power prices also rose, since much of Texas' electricity is generated using natural gas. But when gas prices collapsed in 2006, power prices stayed stuck at inflated levels. Customers are now even more exposed since a state-set rate cap was lifted on January 1.

Legislators are looking at several options for stimulating competition and protecting consumers. Some want to bring back the rate cap, with new mechanisms to encourage power prices to go down as well as up. Another idea is to force customers who have been reluctant to shop around to switch utilities. Even though one-third of residential customers in Texas have switched to a competitive power supplier—far more than in any other state—the Public Utility Commission is concerned that the largest power companies enjoy too much market share.

From Governing
March 2007

Rising retail prices aren't the only concern in re-structured states. Under deregulation, utilities aren't building enough power plants to keep up with demand. Connecticut fears that if new generation doesn't come online soon, rolling blackouts may become the norm in the summer. Last month, Governor Jodi Rell proposed creating a state agency charged with making sure that doesn't happen. She also ordered a study of the state's options for generating electricity itself or buying power at bulk and reselling it to utilities.

Dominion Virginia Power, the state's major utility, is pushing "re-regulation"—a hybrid of old and new. Dominion says Virginia's restructuring law, which the company had supported, is now a hindrance to erecting new power plants. Dominion wants the predictability of old-fashioned rate-setting in order to get favorable financing for mega-projects, such as a zero-carbon nuclear plant the company proposes to build.

Consumer advocates in Virginia, who agree that deregulation is troubled, don't like Dominion's cure. They think the company is trying to lock in big profits that in the old days would have been negotiated with the traditional regulators, the State Corporation Commission.

"They're trying to get the legislature to outline what the SCC can and can't do," says Irene Leech, president of the Virginia Citizens Consumer Council, "and to legislate that no matter what happens, they'll be guaranteed to get above-average returns."

Local Government

It is hard to make generalities about local governments in the United States. For one thing, there are so many of them—roughly ninety thousand according to the U.S. Census Bureau.[1] For another, they are so different: power, responsibilities, and governance structures vary wildly across governments at the substate level. Consider: lumped under the umbrella of local government are megacities such as New York and Los Angeles, but also the Allegheny County Hospital Development Authority (in the Pittsburgh, Pennsylvania, metropolitan area), and the Plains Independent School District (in rural West Texas). What do such disparate local authorities have in common? Well, not much.

Filling potholes, maintaining health care infrastructure, and teaching math are indeed pretty different sorts of activities. And that pretty much sums up local government: different. In doing a lot of different things in lots of different ways, however, local government does a lot to make life as we know it possible. Local governments provide many of the basic services that society has come to take for granted: law enforcement, public schools, fire protection, and libraries, as well as such basic infrastructure operations as water, sewer, and local road systems.

The breadth of differences makes it tough to cover the range of recent trends, challenges, and issues facing local government. To provide a representative sample of such things would require an encyclopedia-like volume. Instead, this section's readings are designed to provide a small taste of some of the politics that go along with all those differences, and how the key issues facing local governments are being addressed.

WHAT LOCAL GOVERNMENTS ARE

Local governments come in three basic forms: counties, municipalities, and special districts. Counties originated as, and to a considerable extent still are, local outposts of state government. For governing purposes, states subdivided themselves into smaller political jurisdictions called counties, and proceeded to turn over to these smaller entities such basic local functions as road maintenance and law enforcement.

Municipalities are public corporations created to provide basic governance to defined geographic jurisdictions. They include familiar political entities such as towns, villages, and cities. They differ from counties in that they tend to be more compact geographically, are more urban, and legally exist as independent corporations rather as local offices of state government.

Special districts are something of a miscellaneous category that includes everything else, and when it comes to local government there is a lot of everything else. The most obvious difference among counties, municipalities, and special districts is that the former two are general governance units. They provide a broad range of programs and services. Special districts, on the other hand, are created to provide a specific program or service. School districts are the most common form of special district—they exist solely to provide public education. Other examples include water treatment and sewage management districts.

That said, it should be kept in mind that these definitions are fairly loose. For example, what constitutes a town or a village or a city is governed by state law, and the powers and policy responsibilities of these different categories of municipality may vary considerably. Municipalities, counties, and special districts are not even clearly separated by geography, but instead are piled on top of each other, which can be confusing to citizens and create coordination and control problems for public officials. A county may be almost completely covered by a municipality or a series of municipalities. There may be several school districts crossing over county and city boundaries. Fitted across these jurisdictions may be still other special districts. Local governments fit together like some sort of three-dimensional jigsaw puzzle with some pieces missing. Given this, it should not be surprising that local governments sometimes get into arguments about who should be doing what.

Although local governments can seem to be something of a confusing jumble from a big picture perspective, there is a fairly clear difference between the vast majority of local governments and state governments. Generally speaking, state governments are sovereign governments and local governments are not. What this means is that state governments get their powers and legal authority directly from citizens—this power and authority is codified in the state constitution.

Most local governments, however, get their power from state government, not directly from citizens. Their powers and legal authority are mostly set by state law, which is to say the state legislature. And what the legislature gives, it can take away. So unlike the relationship between the federal government and state governments, which at least in theory is a relationship of equals, the relationship between state governments and local governments is legally a superior-subordinate relationship. Some states grant local governments broad powers, others reserve much of these powers for themselves and delegate comparatively little. Even in the states that grant local governments considerable independence, the state technically is still the sovereign government.

This hierarchy is codified legally in what is known as Dillon's Rule, which is the legal principle that says that local governments can exercise only the powers granted to them by a state's government. The independence and power of local governments thus varies enormously not just from state to state but also from locality to locality within states. Some municipalities are virtually city-states, powerful political jurisdictions with a high degree of self-rule. Others are little more than local extensions of state governments.

RECENT TRENDS

Regardless of limited formal allocation of power, however, local government is the level of government that is typically the most visible to the average citizen and the most relevant to daily life. Local governments maintain roads, run schools, and have primary responsibility for such health and welfare functions as law enforcement, fire protection, and ambulance service. They also do the most to shape our immediate environments by controlling land use through zoning powers and having a large say in how communities develop.

Governing the disparate functions (dealing with differences) of local government and guiding development are two prominent themes running through this section's readings. The first essay by Rob Gurwitt provides a profile of Los Angeles mayor Antonio Villaraigosa, chief executive of Southern California's iconic, sprawling metropolis. Although mostly identified with left-leaning politics, Villaraigosa has made a point of governing from the middle, dealing with a challenging range of issues in a forceful and pragmatic manner that is earning praise from unexpected quarters.

Alan Ehrenhalt's essay examines a paradox of development faced by local governments: people do not like urban sprawl, but they have been reluctant to embrace high-density developments. Using Northern Virginia's Fairfax County as an example, Ehrenhalt shows that at least some local governments are stepping away from trying to square this circle and are signaling a new willingness to back high-density projects.

Christopher Swope's essay and the essay by Zach Patton that follows take a look at one of the familiar downsides of urban growth and a potential solution to the problem. Swope discusses the development of what amounts to constant rush hour traffic in highly urbanized areas and the difficulties local governments face in managing 24/7 commuters. Patton reveals how cities are trying to encourage people to use bicycles rather than cars to commute. More bicycles mean less gridlock, less pollution, and healthier citizens, but a bicycle-friendly system also requires a delicate balance of infrastructure redevelopment and public education.

The final essay is also by Christopher Swope, and rather than looking at the problems local governments face in dealing with growth, it explores how local governments are dealing with decline. Industrial-era cites, such as Youngstown, Ohio, have been leaking population for decades. The standard response to this pattern has been to seek ways to reverse this trend, to attract businesses and residents back to the levels of a previous era. Youngstown, however, has decided to take a different approach. It is accepting that the city is not going to enjoy a population boom, and subsequently, it is systematically seeking to "rightsize" itself. This presents a unique set of challenges very different from those of local governments dealing with explosive growth.

Note

1. Census Bureau, "Census Bureau Reports Number of Local Governments Nears 88,000," 2003. www .census.gov/Press-Release/www/2003/cb03-10.html.

30

Mayor in the Middle

Rob Gurwitt

LA's mayor grew up in
politics as a left-wing
activist. But he's governing
from the center. He doesn't
have much choice.

D uring the first week of December 2006, about a dozen Los
Angeles hotel workers set up a week-long fast outside the
Westin LAX hotel, not far from the city's huge international airport. The fast, along with its attendant vigils and protest
gatherings, was designed to pressure 13 hotels near the airport to stop
trying to block a new living-wage ordinance for their employees.

Los Angeles is home to one of the best-organized and most politically sophisticated labor movements in the nation, and the ordinance,
calling for a wage floor of $9.39 per hour with health insurance or
$10.64 without it, had easily passed the city council the month
before. It had the public backing of Mayor Antonio Villaraigosa,
himself a former union leader. The hotel owners had launched a
drive to overturn it by referendum, arguing that the city had no
business imposing a living-wage requirement on companies that
weren't directly doing business with local government.

On the last afternoon of the protest, Villaraigosa put in an
appearance with the workers, to express his support and hand out
grape juice as they broke their fast. "The idea that we would honor
work and honor the people who do work is as American as apple
pie," he declared. "When the tide rises, all boats should rise with
that tide."

What was most interesting, however, was what the mayor did
not do. He did not call the hotel owners' scheme "disgraceful," as
did his friend and ally, state Assembly Speaker Fabian Núñez. In
fact, he didn't criticize the owners at all. He simply suggested that
the various players sit down with him and hash things out. A few
days earlier, Villaraigosa had laid the groundwork for just such a
move by assuring business leaders that the living-wage expansion

From *Governing,*
February 2007

would stop with the airport hotels. "That was a tough decision for him to make," says Bruce Ackerman, president of the Economic Alliance of the San Fernando Valley, a leading business-development group in the city. "But he understands that you've got to create coalitions."

What made the decision tough was that Villaraigosa came into office as a partisan, a leader of the city's political left, with a background as a union official, immigrant-rights activist and prominent member of the Latino-labor alliance that remade Los Angeles' political environment in the late 1990s. Restricting the reach of a living-wage law wasn't anything Villaraigosa's loyal supporters put him in office to do.

But his move shouldn't have come as a surprise to them, either. The realities of governing a big city pull almost any mayor to the center. In recent years this has been most obvious with Republican mayors—New York's Rudy Giuliani and Michael Bloomberg, and Los Angeles' Richard Riordan—who have found that the demands placed on them left little room for the extremes of partisanship and ideology that national politics encourages.

While the hallmarks of Giuliani's administration included taming New York City's streets and cutting city government's reach into the economy, he showed little patience for the social conservatism that was increasingly coming to characterize the national GOP. Riordan, while clearly more solicitous of business than his Democratic predecessor, staffed his office with Democrats and ran a markedly non-ideological administration, which is one reason he fared so poorly when he tried to win California's Republican gubernatorial nomination. Bloomberg, a businessman who has presided over New York's economic resurgence, has been perhaps the least ideological of all.

Now, in Villaraigosa, Los Angeles offers the equally intriguing prospect of a mayor steeped in the values of the left but forced to grapple with the cross-cutting demands generated by a complex and fast-changing city. Villaraigosa hasn't by any means turned into a free-marketeer or a business cheerleader, but he is taking pains to court unlikely allies in the interest of moving the city in his direction on key issues.

"The powers of an L.A. city mayor are limited overall," he says, "but that can't prevent us from using the office with the purpose of building a consensus around what we need to do."

Most notably, the 53-year-old mayor is laboring to convince each of the diverse segments of this famously fractious city—black and brown, Asian and Anglo, labor and management, homeless advocates and downtown developers, environmentalists and business executives—that he takes them seriously. He is casting himself as the city's moderator and chaperone, the champion of its common ground—and the delineator of where that ground might lie. "He will take an issue and lead from the center," says Larry Frank, one of his aides. "But he'll also do everything in his power to redefine the center."

FORCEFUL START

Villaraigosa started executing that strategy in the summer of 2005, even before he took the oath of office. For the previous year, Los Angeles hotel owners and the city's rambunctious hotel-workers' union had been locked in fruitless wage negotiations. With the summer tourism season getting underway and no resolution in sight, the workers were setting up pickets and the hotel owners were preparing a lockout—steps that would have been disastrous to a key sector of Los Angeles' economy.

And so, even as he was preparing to take over the mayoralty from James Hahn, the man he'd beaten in the election the month before, Villaraigosa called both sides into city hall, stashed them in different offices, and spent two sleepless nights shuttling back and forth hammering out an agreement. "This is a great day for Los Angeles," he said when he emerged at 5:30 on a Saturday morning to announce the deal. "What I hope now is that we all work together to bring tourists back to Los Angeles."

It was a stroke that established Villaraigosa's reputation as a problem-solver and demonstrated that an era of staid and somewhat removed mayoral leadership was over. The alternative *LA Weekly*, noting that Villaraigosa had been an uninspiring member of the city council before he

> *The mayor expressed his support for striking hotel workers—but he didn't denounce their bosses.*

ran an unremarkable campaign for mayor, declared in astonishment that "it was as if a mild-mannered business-as-usual politician had ducked into a phone booth to rip off his street clothes and reveal the superhero hiding inside."

That early move made an equally strong impression on the city's somewhat nervous business community, which had come to see Villaraigosa as an arm of the labor movement. They had reason to see him that way. Starting out in politics as an immigrant-rights activist, Villaraigosa went on to become a field organizer for the United Teachers of Los Angeles, then president of the local chapter of the American Civil Liberties Union and of the L.A. local of the American Federation of Government Employees. Both before and after he moved on to the state Assembly in 1995, he was closely allied with Miguel Contreras, the legendary head of the L.A. County Federation of Labor, who forged low-wage Latino service workers into an organized political and economic force.

In fact, though, Villaraigosa's instinct for the center—or at least for conciliation—had been part of his earlier career as well. During two years as Democratic speaker of the Assembly in the late 1990s, he worked with Republicans on major legislation, including a gargantuan $9.2 billion school bond measure that was beset by some of the most aggressive constituencies in California politics. "As speaker, he had to moderate his own personal political views to move the state's agenda forward," says John Peréz, political director of one of the United Food and Commercial Workers' Los Angeles-area locals (and Villaraigosa's cousin). "It was an important lesson that he couldn't just be there as an advocate for his friends."

RACIAL SENSITIVITIES

In truth, no mayor of Los Angeles with ambitions for his own political future—which Villaraigosa clearly has—can afford to see the life of the city in zero-sum terms or even to let others cast it that way. Since the disappearance of its once-mighty aerospace and automobile manufacturing industries, the city's economy

"He's not a union leader anymore, he's the mayor. That means he's got to juggle a lot of issues and concerns."

—Maria Elena Durazo, head of the county Federation of Labor

has excelled at creating low-end and high-end jobs but hasn't done much for the middle class; the Los Angeles metro area now ranks last among 100 metropolitan areas in its percentage of middle-income neighborhoods, according to a 2006 Brookings Institution study.

So rebuilding L.A.'s middle class by raising the wages of the city's vast low-income workforce, as Villaraigosa's union and progressive allies want, makes sense; but then, so does the business community's argument that buttressing entertainment and trade-related industries and encouraging construction and development, which are fast becoming mainstays of the local economy, are vital to its future. At the same time, the city's complex and ever-changing demographic makeup means that its various racial and ethnic communities are acutely sensitive to how city government and the mayor treat them. A mayor who adopts a "my friends win, you lose" attitude is just asking for trouble.

Which is one reason Villaraigosa has made a strenuous effort to win support in the city's black community. This hasn't been an easy task. Blacks were deeply disturbed by Hahn's decision in 2004 to fire Bernard Parks, the city's first African-American police chief. It was in part because of Parks' firing that Hahn lost the mayoral election to Villaraigosa in 2005. But Villaraigosa, as a Latino, started out with problems of his own in the black neighborhoods. "The overwhelming fact of the city is the rise of Latinos," says Raphael Sonenshein, a political scientist at California State University, Fullerton. "And what's significant about Villaraigosa is that as the first Latino mayor, he could have been an ethnocentric politician." But, as Sonenshein says, that was not what the new mayor wanted to be.

Villaraigosa gave a perfect illustration of this in his handling of a lawsuit against the city brought by a black firefighter who alleged racial discrimination in a firehouse hazing incident. The city council initially agreed to a $2.7 million settlement, but Villaraigosa vetoed it, arguing that the settlement was financially irresponsible. With the council's black members refusing to go along and the NAACP labeling the veto "an outrage," the issue had the potential to spiral out of control: A black firefighter, in a department with a long history of racism, had been denied recompense by a Latino mayor.

But Villaraigosa quickly recast the matter, arguing that the real issue was a culture of harassment within the fire department, one that was costing the city millions in payouts to aggrieved firefighters. He dismissed the white fire chief and named a respected black fire department veteran in his place, giving him an explicit charge to instill a more respectful culture. The firefighter's lawsuit continues, but it has lost its explosive spark. "You see an outcry from black leadership on issues like this, but Antonio was very smart about how he handled everything," says state Assembly Majority Leader Karen Bass, a black Democrat who has known Villaraigosa for three decades.

There have been times, to be sure, when Villaraigosa's something-for-everyone approach has been criticized as little more than sharp deal-making. When the owner of downtown's premier existing hotel held up a new convention-center hotel project by threatening to sue to stop the city from subsidizing it, Villaraigosa settled the matter by agreeing that the owner could convert one-third of his hotel's rooms to lucrative condos in exchange for dropping his challenge. Then, when hotel workers complained that the move would cost them jobs, Villaraigosa agreed to promote the unionization of other downtown hotels. "New mayor, but same old L.A. business as usual," sniffed the *Los Angeles Daily News*.

Or, perhaps, it was just an ability to focus on larger goals. Villaraigosa has made a priority of redeveloping downtown Los Angeles, long a downscale shadow of its more robust counterparts in other cities. He has promoted and helped to shape two multibillion-dollar projects he hopes will inject new residential, entertainment and commercial life into the city's core. One central piece of these plans is to rejuvenate the city's convention center—"our convention center is a dog," admits one of the mayor's aides—and the convention-center hotel is a keystone of that effort. The three-way deal may have been business as usual, in other

> ## "In 25 years, I've never seen anybody function in the role of a municipal CEO as Villaraigosa has."
>
> —Business lobbyist Bruce Ackerman

words, but it removed a troublesome stumbling block to Villaraigosa's vision for his city.

"He is eager to show people he can represent other perspectives," says Eric Garcetti, president of the city council and a Villaraigosa ally. "He isn't easy to pin down as knee-jerk on anything."

HOUSING DILEMMAS

Villaraigosa has, in truth, been quite open about his goals. He wants to develop downtown. He wants a greener city, both literally and figuratively, one more densely built and less auto-dependent. He wants to change the cultures of the police and fire departments. He wants to reform the city bureaucracy, making it more efficient and responsive. And he wants to defuse the racial and ethnic tensions that have made Los Angeles a tinderbox in the past. This is hardly a radical agenda, although you wouldn't mistake it for a Chamber of Commerce wish list either.

As gentrification has become a top-tier issue in many neighborhoods, Villaraigosa has made affordable workforce housing a priority. "The fabric of our community is weakened," he says, "every time a fire-fighter or a nurse decides they can't afford to live here anymore." To keep those workers in town, the mayor pushed hard for a billion-dollar affordable-housing bond measure on last November's ballot; it drew majority support but narrowly failed to get the two-thirds vote it needed to pass. He worked with the city's public pension funds to have them invest in workforce housing; and has made the creation of affordable units a required part of any residential development using city subsidies. Villaraigosa also put $100 million into a housing trust fund for permanent supportive housing for the homeless. Those efforts all speak to Villaraigosa's progressive legacy and his desire to push the "center" toward the left.

But other choices on the same front point to the mayor's pragmatism about how far he can go. His old allies on the left have lobbied hard for a so-called "inclusionary zoning" measure, which would require residential projects—even if they're 100 percent privately funded—to include developer-subsidized affordable units. The idea is anathema to the city's business leadership, and Villaraigosa has shown no desire to see a showdown between the two sides. "I support inclusionary zoning," he says, "but I believe it's important that we craft an ordinance that has broad support, including support from the business community. I'm committed to working with the business community and the affordable-housing community to ensure that we come up with something that's balanced. There's no other way to do this."

Meanwhile, Villaraigosa has pushed city departments to think about ways to leverage private gain into public benefit. With immense pressure coming from developers to rezone industrial land for residential uses, the city has launched an effort to inventory the industrial land that is up for grabs, determine what impact rezoning it will have on well-paying industrial jobs, and then explore ways for residential developers to make up for the loss of those jobs should the land get rezoned. "Once a piece of industrial-zoned land converts to residential, it's gone forever," says Cecilia Estolano, director of the city's Community Redevelopment Authority. "Shouldn't we derive some small proportion of the increase in value the developers are getting for it?"

EVERYWHERE AT ONCE

Villaraigosa's tone and tactics may have turned moderate, but one thing about him remains extreme: his energy level. He seems to be everywhere at once: handing out toys to kids in Watts; speaking at a B'nai B'rith luncheon on the Westside; huddling with business executives downtown; appearing on Spanish- and English-language television stations; presiding over announcements of economic development projects large and small; presenting Section 8 housing vouchers to poor families; traveling to police and fire stations to meet with their officers; showing up at community parades and neighborhood tree-decorating parties in even the most far-flung corners of his immense city.

"His definition of a day has four, five, even six more hours to it than most people's," says Robin Kramer, his chief of staff. That might be seen as obligatory praise, except that more objective observers are saying the same thing. "His presence has been unparalleled," says Bruce Ackerman, whose San Fernando-based business group has lamented the lack of attention from previous admin-istrations. "I have never seen another mayor with the presence out here that he's had."

It isn't just energy that is making Villaraigosa a strong mayor; it's a rewritten city charter. The original charter was designed nearly a century ago to dilute central authority, parceling it out among the city council and a set of boards and commissions that have direct responsibility for city departments. In the late 1990s, however, the charter was changed to give the mayor the power to hire and fire the 44 department heads, called "general managers." Hahn never really used this newfound authority, but Villaraigosa has embraced it. "I can't overstate his impact on the department heads," says Bill Fujioka, Los Angeles' highly regarded and independent-minded chief administrative officer, who retired in December. "It's hard to say that he's asked people to leave, because that's confidential, but, well, a lot of people have left."

While Villaraigosa has put in place only a relative handful of his own general managers, he has brought wholesale change to the boards and commissions that oversee city departments. And he has used his appointments to internalize the careful balancing act that he is pursuing as mayor. The board of the Community Redevelopment Agency is a sterling example. It includes Peréz, the union political director, along with Madeline Janis, who spearheaded the unions' living-wage campaign for low-income workers during the 1990s; on the other hand, it is chaired by Bill Jackson, a high-profile commercial real estate lawyer, and includes business advocate Ackerman. The result is that while the CRA board has pushed developers to agree to contracts that create some "public benefit"—affordable-housing units, public space, training programs for construction workers—it has not gone as far as some of its more left-leaning members would like.

At the same time, Villaraigosa has set out to reform city operations. He has been holding monthly meetings with the 44 general managers—some of whom used to go for years, or entire administrations, without meeting the mayor—to make sure they're following his directions. He has demanded $15 million to $20 million per year from the city bureaucracy in new efficiencies, and put in place a cross-departmental team to develop performance and accountability measures on his priorities.

All of this, says City Controller Laura Chick, who is independently elected, is not just vital, but urgent. "My verdict on L.A. city government is we are anything but cutting-edge, state of the art, best-practices or a role-model city," she says. "We're stuck in the '70s and '80s in our use of technology, in management practices and in infrastructure—in the human infrastructure needed to run a role-model city." And while she acknowledges that there is a long way to go, she says that under Villaraigosa, "we're making progress across the board."

> *One thing about the mayor is still extreme: his energy level. He seems to be everywhere at once.*

The administrative reforms are important not only for reasons of efficiency but also as a signal to the business establishment that whatever the mayor's background may be, he knows how to run an organization. The signal seems to be coming through. "I've been playing in this arena now for 25 years," says Ackerman, "and I've never seen anybody function in the role of a municipal CEO as he has."

Still, there are limits to what any of these strategies can accomplish. If Villaraigosa has a single top priority, it is improving the city's public schools. Himself a high-school dropout who credits one teacher with picking him up and helping him get to college, he considers reforming public education the linchpin for everything else he is trying to do. "We will not compete in a global economy if our kids cannot read or write," he says. "We will not be able to grow and prosper together if half our kids drop out and can't read a bus schedule when they graduate." And so he spent a huge amount of time, energy and political capital during his first year in office trying to get control of the city's public schools, which are run by the board of the Los Angeles Unified School District.

Eventually, he was able to get the legislature to enact a law giving him limited control. But that measure was tossed out at the end of December by a state superior court judge—the first true setback of his tenure, although Villaraigosa has vowed to take advantage of upcoming school board elections to install a slate favorable to his goals.

In the next few months, Villaraigosa will be facing an even sterner test, as he negotiates with the two chief city employee unions on new contracts. Union members, sensing an opportunity, are pressing hard for better wages and changes in working conditions; they are determined to bring themselves on par with employees at the city's Department of Water and Power, a quasi-independent agency whose employees have one of the richest contracts in the country. Villaraigosa, who talks constantly about the city's $247 million structural deficit, is just as determined to keep a lid on the final contract.

It is, of course, an ironic position for a mayor who used to run a government employees' union. But it is one that places Villaraigosa in the center—where he feels he needs to be to maintain a coalition that can move his priorities. Maria Elena Durazo, the head of the county Federation of Labor and a friend of the mayor's for 30 years, believes that if both sides can avoid taking extreme positions, negotiations will succeed. "He's not a union leader anymore, he's the mayor," she says. "That means he's got to juggle a lot of issues and concerns."

31

Breaking the Density Deadlock

Alan Ehrenhalt

A local government that denounced density in blunt terms just six years ago is embracing it now.

Tysons Corner isn't much to look at. I don't mean simply that it's unattractive—although it is—but that when you pass through it, along the main commercial strip of Route 7, in Northern Virginia's Fairfax County, you don't even get the feeling that anything substantial is there. You see a long, loose string of office buildings built in the 1970s and '80s, scattered over a stretch of two or three miles, few of them close together or in any way congruent with each other. You pass two huge regional shopping malls, both tucked behind vast parking lots and barely visible from the high-way. You don't know for sure when you've reached the place, and there's no way to tell when you've left.

The utter placelessness of Tysons Corner is one important truth about it. But there's an even more important one: It is the 12th-largest business district in the United States. More than 100,000 people work there. Every morning and every evening, 40,000 cars inch down Route 7 and Route 123, overwhelmed arterial roads that lack the capacity to handle the traffic at anything more than a glacial pace.

In the four decades since the modern history of Tysons began, Fairfax County and its leaders have passed through several stages in trying to come to terms with what it is and what it means. First, there was sheer novelty—the presence of glass towers and upscale shopping on what had been farmland only a few years before. Then, in the 1980s, came an attitude of somewhat jaded acceptance: It's an eyesore, but it's a money machine, and besides, there's nothing we can do to change it now. Only with the start of the new century did planners and a few politicians dare to express a radical idea: A region that can produce the 12th-biggest

From *Governing,*
March 2007

168

business center in the country ought to be able to change it and civilize it.

It was five years ago, in the summer of 2001, that the New Urbanist architect Andres Duany came to Fairfax with slides of San Francisco and Paris, and told an audience of suburbanites that he could build something equally appealing for them right there in the Virginia suburbs. Genuine urbanism was within their grasp—if they were willing to go for it. "This is a fantastic opportunity," he exulted, "to create a truly wonderful place." It was like Pinocchio being told that if he shaped up, he might eventually become a real live boy.

But when Duany presented his dream of urbanizing Tysons, he wasn't simply talking about trees or parks or fashionable boulevards. He was talking about a dozen residential towers, tall enough to accommodate 12,000 people, big crowds on the streets, and heavy-duty public transportation. He was talking about density. He admitted it. "High density is not a punishment if it is built in true urbanism," Duany insisted that day. "High density is a true delight."

The audience was not swept away. "What Duany wants to do is put a city here," one resident complained. "We don't want a city here." One of the elected county supervisors, Gerald Connolly, was even more blunt. "I think he is being arrogant," Connolly said, "and frankly, ignorant. Any proposal that intense is dead on arrival." And Connolly was right: Duany's idea never went anywhere. Touchy as they might have been about the reputation of Tysons Corner, the citizens of Fairfax were not ready for density in 2001.

The question is, are they ready for it now?

If you work in local government anywhere, the odds are you have heard the joke that there are two things Americans can't stand: sprawl and density. I refer to it as a joke, but in fact it comes close to being a literal truth. Millions of Americans who live in places like Fairfax County visit places such as Boston and San Francisco and wish they could recreate some of that urbanity and elegance for themselves. But faced with the reality of what true urban sophistication requires—height, big crowds, and strangers from the city flocking in on trains, they back off. That's the deadlock of density.

It's quite plausible to argue that the deadlock will not be broken in our lifetimes: that if the price of containing sprawl is to turn suburbs into cities, it is a price American suburbanites simply will not pay.

But it is also plausible to argue that slowly and almost imperceptibly, the deadlock of density is being replaced by a willingness to take a few risks. It is even plausible to make that case in Fairfax County.

Fairfax didn't welcome Duany, but in the past year, the county board has given its approval to a stunning amount of dense high-rise development—more than Duany ever proposed. Two months ago, the board voted for a plan that will surround the original 1968 shopping mall with eight towers, some as tall as 30 stories, containing 1,350 condos and apartments, four office buildings and a 300-room hotel. And that's just on one side of the road. Across Route 7, where the second big mall is located, construction will begin this year on a cluster of eight more towers, most of them designed for offices.

It seems puzzling that a local government body that denounced density in such blunt terms just six years ago would embrace it now. But that's what's happening. The Fairfax County board voted 8-to-2 in favor of the main project at Tysons Corner Center. Gerald Connolly, the denouncer of Duany, is now the board chairman and was an enthusiastic supporter this time.

Connolly insists that he hasn't undergone a conversion—that the new plan is just better than Duany's. "It's more development on the ground," he says, "but it's mixed use, it's tied to transit, and it has lots of public spaces." He has a point. Even so, it seems clear that thinking in Fairfax has evolved quite a bit since 2001[,] that the county is buying something it wouldn't have bought in 2001 no matter who proposed it.

The developer of this project, the Macerich Co. of California, is pressing all the right New Urbanist buttons. Its computerized graphics envision spacious plazas, sculpture gardens, skating rinks and performance space. Macerich talks about making the Intersection of Routes 7 and 123 into a new "Central Park," a "100 percent downtown corner."

Most intriguing of all, Macerich is promising to take the blank acres of asphalt that dominate Tysons now and superimpose a grid that would provide 54 additional pedestrian-friendly streets for traffic to move in, generate a huge increase in sidewalk capacity, provide up to 14,000 curbside parking spaces, and in the end create something that doesn't just possess the density of a city but actually looks like a city.

All of this is to be timed to the extension of a Metro transit line, scheduled to reach Tysons Corner in 2012.

The Metro station will be right across from the redesigned mixed-use mall; all the residential towers are supposed to be within easy walking distance of the station—some literally in its shadow.

But there are some excellent reasons to be skeptical. The original transit plan, favored by Macerich as well as by local residents, was to place the subway line underground, leaving all the surface land around the station free for urban amenities. So far, that isn't happening: The U.S. Transportation Department and the Virginia congressional delegation say going underground would cost more money, and they don't want to pay for it. Barring a reversal, rail transit will come to Tysons in 2012 in the form of a 70-foot-high elevated track along Route 123, with disembarking passengers required to go down to the street and then climb back up a bridge to get to the plaza and the towers. It's not exactly the best way to signal the presence of an urban village.

But the really important part—and the hardest part— is the grid. Developers know how to build 30-story buildings; they know how to create plazas with skating rinks. But retrofitting 1,700 acres of suburban asphalt with a network of walkable streets will be an enormous challenge, one that will require huge investments of money and determination from both the developer and the government. The plain truth is that nobody has ever done this before—not on the scale that is being called for at Tysons Corner. And yet if the grid doesn't happen, Tysons may never be a vibrant city or any kind of city at all. It may just be a collection of tall buildings arranged a little more compactly than the ones that are there now.

My guess is that when all of this development is completed, 10 or 15 years from now, Andres Duany's vision won't be close to realization. Nor do I expect that Tysons Corner will much resemble the green pedestrian oasis pictured in the computerized Macerich sketches. But I think it will be quite a bit better than what is there now. I also think it will be a commercial success.

I'm convinced of that because I see all around me a generation of young, mainstream, middle-class adults— label them any way you want to—who are looking for some form of mid-level urban experience, not bohemian inner-city adventure but definitely not cul-de-sacs and long commutes. There are more of them coming into the residential market every year. They like the idea of having some space, but they aren't fleeing in terror at the mention of density. They aren't willing to sell their cars, but they appreciate the advantage of having another way to get around. If Tysons Corner is rebuilt on a reasonable human scale and with a modicum of physical appeal, they will go for it, imperfect as it may be.

And then we will begin to see experiments of this sort in suburbs all over the country, launched by developers and local governments that may still be a little nervous about density but will know one thing for sure: If Tysons Corner can be reborn, nothing in the suburbs is beyond hope. If the effort to rebuild Tysons Corner somehow succeeds, it will become a national model for reclaiming suburbia.

32

The 24-Hour Rush

Christopher Swope

In many metro areas, distinct periods of congestion have morphed into heavy traffic all day long.

Alan Pisarski has been studying Americans' commuting patterns for decades, so horrific tales of traffic tie-ups and three-hour drives to work don't faze him much. But even Pisarski was a bit shocked at one trend he spotted in his latest analysis of data from the U.S. Census Bureau: Fully one-quarter of the recent growth in commuting comes from people trundling off to work between 5 and 6:30 a.m. "People are leaving home earlier than ever," Pisarski says. "To me, leaving at 5 a.m. borders on insanity."

If more commuters are setting their alarm clocks to beat the morning rush, others seem to be sleeping in. Commuting between the hours of 9 and 11 a.m. also has increased significantly. Pisarski's findings, published recently in the book "Commuting in America III," are more evidence of a phenomenon that many drivers already know all too well: "Rush hour" as we know it is dead. That's not true everywhere. But in the most traffic-clogged regions, the notion of distinct periods of congestion in the morning and afternoon has morphed into heavy traffic from before sunrise until after sunset. Call it "rush day."

If that sounds awful, the consequences aren't entirely bad. Rush-day traffic means that additional capacity is being squeezed out of the existing transportation network. That's possible only because commuters are very adaptable and will sometimes go to amazing lengths to avoid getting stuck in traffic. Pisarski says he hears more and more stories of road warriors arriving at the office by 6 a.m., then catching an hour of winks in their parked cars before heading inside to work. "The genus 'Commuter Americanus' is a very resilient creature," Pisarski says, "but we're pushing them beyond the range of their flexibility."

From *Governing*, December 2006

There are other factors fueling the rush-day phenomenon. Beltways that were initially conceived as express routes for through traffic have become suburban arteries serving office parks and shopping centers. Homebuyers searching for sizable but affordable homes are pushing farther and farther into the exurbs. Technology and telecommuting are also starting to affect work and travel patterns. Pisarski found that more workers now telecommute than walk to work.

"In some cases, they will work at home in the morning, avoiding that long commute, but then get on the highway and drive to work at 10," says Tim Lomax, a congestion expert with the Texas Transportation Institute.

The emergence of rush day bends traditional ways of thinking about transportation infrastructure. Planners are trained to design road networks and transit schedules around peak-hour trips. As commuting patterns become more diffuse, however, that's becoming harder to do.

"It's not as tidy as it used to be," says Robert Cervero, a planning professor at the University of California, Berkeley. "It's getting more difficult to model commuting patterns and use that as a platform to predict the future."

Those patterns may become less predictable. The reason why planners weigh commuting data so heavily is because trips to work account for a large number of overall trips. But as baby boomers retire, a huge demographic bubble of nine-to-fivers will start moving around more in the middle of the day.

And the change is coming sooner, rather than later. In the Atlanta region, for example, one-third of the people over the age of 60 fall between the ages of 60 and 64. In other words, the retirement wave is upon us. "There's an enormous shift about to happen in standard circulation patterns," says Scott Ball, an Atlanta-based community design consultant. "But no one is doing well at surveying the transportation needs of seniors."

33

Pedal Pushers

Zach Patton

Fair- and foul-weather cities alike are gearing up to make it safer and easier for commuters to bicycle to work.

Chicago can be stiflingly hot during the summer and rain-chilled in the spring, and its wind-whipped winters are the stuff of legend. So when the subject is "bicycle commuting," Chicago is not the first city that springs to mind. But it's becoming a hot bike-to-work town. In the next decade, it plans to expand its network of bike trails to 500 miles, and has set a goal of putting a bike path of some sort within half a mile of every city resident.

Chicago is not the only place that is doing things like that. In fact, it's part of what's turning into a national movement. The motivation varies: Some cities see bike-friendliness as part of an economic development strategy, while others mainly want to fight traffic congestion. But the tactics are similar, from Los Angeles to Louisville, Phoenix to Minneapolis. Cities are adding bike lanes, building shower and storage facilities and spelling out pro-bicycling policies in resolutions and ordinances.

Given that a very small percentage of Americans rely on bicycles to commute to work—0.4 percent, or half a million people, according to the most recent Census data—the fuss over bicycle commuting may appear to be misplaced. But the Census numbers don't tell the whole story. They include only commuters who bike to work all the time. If bikers take the bus every other day or bike to a subway stop, they're not included in the count.

When you look at the trend lines—as opposed to just absolute numbers—you get a different picture. In Portland, Oregon, the number of cyclists has nearly quadrupled in the past 10 years. In San Francisco, bicycle commuting shot up 100 percent during the 1990s. Transportation officials in just about every big city are convinced that the momentum is building even faster now. There's no

From *Governing*,
November 2006.

shortage of explanations. "Over the past five years, we've heard a lot about health concerns and the obesity epidemic," says Andy Clarke, executive director of the League of American Bicyclists, a century-old advocacy group. "And then in the past year, higher gas prices have started to contribute, too."

All those developments have influenced decisions by individual commuters. Local governments have encouraged them for a variety of reasons. They see bike-friendliness as a way to bring downtowns and inner-city neighborhoods to life, and attract the "creative class" newcomers that nearly every city covets these days. In building the livable city that the creative class is thought to want, Clarke says, "bicycling and walking have got to be at the core."

Most bike promotion programs don't seem to have much trouble attracting money. In general, cities have been able to rely on corporate funding and federal transportation subsidies to build their systems. Chicago's new $3 million downtown bike station was paid for with federal funds and is now privately run. The transportation bill approved by Congress last year included about $4.5 billion for pedestrian and cycling projects—a 35 percent jump from previous spending levels. In many cases, bicycling improvement projects, particularly those that spruce up neighborhoods or provide safe routes to schools, qualify for Community Development Block Grants.

GETTING IN GEAR

American cities have gone in for bike-friendly fads in the past. Often they have fizzled out: Grand plans for miles of bike paths have fallen apart, and policies for protecting bicyclists and making more room for them on city streets have been imposed and then scrapped only a few years later. But recent efforts may have more staying power.

It certainly seems to be more than a fad in Chicago. One hundred miles of dedicated bike lanes circle the city, capped off by the popular 20-mile Lakefront Path that runs almost the entire length of the city's Lake Michigan shoreline. The new bike station downtown in Millennium Park, a multi-level, 12,000-square-foot facility, houses lockers, showers and a repair shop, plus 24-hour bike storage. Membership at the station costs $99 per year, but anyone can park bikes there for free. Last year,

the city's Parks Department established a "bike ambassadors" program. Its mission is to organize teams of teenage volunteers to educate commuters about bicycle safety.

Then, this summer, Chicago released its master bicycling plan, which it calls Bike 2015. The culmination of three years of study, the plan commits the city to a goal, less than a decade from now, of having 5 percent of all trips covering less than 5 miles made by bicycle. It pledges to cut the number of bike injuries in half. Thousands of new short- and long-term bike storage facilities are planned for locations all over the city. Many schools and transit stations would have dedicated bike lanes leading straight to the front door. "It's definitely a very ambitious plan," acknowledges Ben Gomberg, head of the city's bicycle program. But he insists it can be done.

One reason it might happen is that it has the powerful support of the city's longtime mayor, Richard M. Daley, a biker himself. Chicago is a city where the mayor usually gets what he wants, and bicycles, along with health and environmental improvements, have been a near-obsession for Daley over the past several years.

DIFFERENT STROKES

Chicago will have to go quite a distance to catch up with Portland, which has long prided itself on being the nation's most bike-friendly town, and has been awarded that distinction more than once by *Bicycling* Magazine. Portland already has 160 miles of bike lanes along its streets, another 70 miles in off-street bike paths, including a path to the airport, and 30 miles of what it calls "bike boulevards"—streets where auto traffic is limited and the layout is designed specifically to make bicycle travel convenient. There are bike-parking facilities throughout the city. All of these moves have had a direct impact on the numbers: Daily counts of commuting cyclists have gone from around 3,500 in the mid-1990s to more than 12,000 today.

Given its image as a tree-hugging coastal town, Portland might be expected to emphasize bicycle travel. So might Boulder, Colorado, where 95 percent of the city's roads have a bike lane. But similar things are happening in less likely places. Phoenix actually has 500 miles of dedicated bikeways—more even than Portland, albeit spread across a much bigger territory. Austin, Texas, is in the middle of a major bike-lane expansion project. New

York City, the national capital of subway-and-foot urbanism, recently announced a plan to increase bike lanes by 200 miles over the next three years. Seattle and Denver have new downtown storage stations. Cities in every region of the country now allow travelers to bring their bikes onto public transportation.

Lexington, Kentucky, hired a cycling chief three years ago expressly to balance out planning in a town built around cars. "We spent 50 years designing for the automobile," says Lexington cycling coordinator Kenzie Gleason. "But we're incorporating bike and pedestrian planning into every project we do now."

Not every city has successfully embraced bicycle commuting. Houston wanted to: It released a plan in 1994 to add 1,000 miles of bikeways, but never came close to completing it, and has had trouble even maintaining the lanes that already exist. Atlanta routinely gets singled out as the worst city in America for anybody who tries to commute to work on a bike. Earlier this year, *Bicycling* Magazine again ranked that city at the bottom of its list. Boston, which might appear to be friendly biking terri-

tory, never has been. Bike lanes there are scarce and not very well connected. Boston hired a bike-policy coordinator in 2001 but cut the position just two years later.

And there is pushback in some cities. In bike-friendly San Francisco, a five-year plan to create a network of bike routes, parking and racks all over the city has ended up in court. An opposition group is challenging the plan's scheduled reduction in parking and street space and has called for what it describes as a fairer balance in the use of public land.

The biggest lesson for cities, says Clarke, is that a successful bike-commuting policy is a combination of infrastructure, education and promotion. While cities must build the right facilities—bikeways, storage, parking—they also must help cyclists gain the skills and confidence to ride in traffic. Efforts in that direction may include bike route maps, for example, or the bike ambassadors that Chicago has been trying. Combining these elements, Clarke says, is key. "The places that have been successful at this have done much more than just add bike lanes."

34

Smart Decline

Christopher Swope

In 40 years, Youngstown has lost more than half its population. Those people aren't coming back. But shrinking doesn't have to mean dying.

Anthony Kobak has borrowed the mayor's Ford Taurus for a spin around Youngstown, but as he steers the sedan down a pitted asphalt road, he wishes he'd borrowed a Jeep instead. Driving comes pretty close to off-roading in this part of Youngstown's east side, where the surroundings are mostly fallow lots and a few scattered homes. Kobak stops at one street that is little more than a dirt path into the woods. But it is a city-maintained road all the same, with water, sewer and power lines. "We're just 10 minutes from downtown, but you can see it's very rural," says Kobak, who is Youngstown's chief planner. He points out the window toward a lone deteriorating house in a field. "Those are chicken coops over there. You can see the cages."

This part of Youngstown is called Sharon Line—the name, Kobak explains, came from a street car route that used to run through the area. Back in the 1950s, this place was expected to develop into a bustling urban neighborhood. The steel mills were still roaring, and with 170,000 residents, Youngstown was Ohio's seventh-largest city and the 57th most populous in the United States. Planners believed that the east side would soak up continuing growth and prosperity. What in fact happened was quite the opposite. Not only did suburbanization suck the life out of city neighborhoods, as happened in much of America, but in the 1970s, the steel mills closed and population went into a free-fall. Quite suddenly, Youngstown's growth problem had turned into an abandoned-property problem. In Sharon Line, new houses simply weren't needed anymore. The area remained an odd country enclave tucked inside a fast-declining city.

Now, Kobak and other Youngstown officials have come around to a drastically different vision for Sharon Line. No longer are they

From *Governing*, November 2006

176

holding out for a miracle growth spurt. Rather, they're embracing the radical idea of gradually turning this place back to nature. Roads and infrastructure may be taken out of service. Some properties could be converted to wetlands. Kobak calls this way of thinking "going from gray to green," and it's not just at work in Sharon Line. In Oak Hill, just south of downtown, and in Brier Hill, to the north, once-vibrant blocks now plagued by abandoned homes and weedy lots are candidates to become parkland, open space and greenways.

In Youngstown these days, an ambitious planning process has come to a haltingly honest conclusion: The city is shrinking. If that point seems obvious enough—population is now down to about 82,000—it's one that leaders of other declining cities stubbornly refuse to admit to themselves. Cincinnati, Detroit and St. Louis all have focused on reversing population losses in an attempt to reclaim bygone glory. By contrast, Youngstown's "2010 Plan" begins by acknowledging that Youngstown is a small city now, burdened by the overly ambitious infrastructure of its past. The plan likens Youngstown to "a size-40 man wearing a size-60 suit."

If Youngstown has made peace with its smaller self, however, its policy makers are still grappling with the key question: What does it mean to manage shrinkage in an intelligent way? Volumes have been written about how to implement "smart growth." But what about smart decline? Youngstown may emerge as something of a national laboratory for ideas on how to cope with urban contraction. It's not that the town's civic leaders want to be in that position—they simply see little choice. "We're on our way to accepting some obvious things about what the city is and isn't going to be," says Jay Williams, Youngstown's 35-year-old mayor. "It was unrealistic to think we'll be a 100,000 person city. But why not be an attractive city of 80,000 or 85,000 that offers a quality of life that competes with other cities across the state and across the country?"

Or, as Hunter Morrison puts it, "saying you're a shrinking city is not saying you're a dying city." Morrison was Cleveland's city planner for 20 years and now directs the urban and regional studies program at Youngstown State University. "Every city," Morrison says, "is looking back to when it used to be 200,000, 500,000, a million—whatever it was at its peak. As Marshall McLuhan put it, they're always looking to the future through the rearview mirror. And what we're saying in Youngstown is, the past is the past. It's time to turn granny's picture to the wall."

GLOBAL SHRINKAGE

Youngstown is coming to this self-assessment at a time when the fortunes of urban America are very much mixed. A decade ago, population in most industrial-era cities was continuing a downward glide path that had been well established since the 1950s. From New York to Seattle, the question wasn't whether big cities were losing people to the suburbs. It was how fast.

Then, in the late '90s, many cities began seeing an urban renaissance, fueled by immigration, dropping crime rates and favorable demographics. Population losses in New York and Chicago turned into gains. (New York, currently at 8.1 million people, has never been larger than it is now.) Other cities began experiencing a population paradox. Boston and San Francisco count fewer people than they did five years ago, yet they seem to be in better economic health. What they're essentially doing is losing families with school-age children and gaining singles, childless couples and empty nesters—smaller households with ample incomes that demand much less in the way of city services.

But that scenario is not playing out everywhere. In particular, smaller industrial cities, located mostly in the Northeast and around the Great Lakes, are finding it almost impossible to recover from the decline of their manufacturing employment base. San Francisco, Boston and Chicago can prosper in the 21st century as cultural and entertainment [c]enters with concentrated office and retail activity and strong downtown residential growth. Elmira, Flint and Youngstown can't realistically nurture any such hopes.

> "We're on our way to accepting some obvious things about what Youngstown is and isn't going to be."
>
> —Mayor Jay Williams

The problem of shrinking industrial cities is attracting fresh interest in academic circles and new attention abroad. Since the Berlin Wall came down, factory towns in eastern Germany and the former Soviet Union have been emptying out, forcing governments there to grapple with industrial and residential decay. Longer term, some European nations and Japan project national population declines of 20 to 40 percent over the next 50 years, owing to their low birth rates. German researchers recently published two volumes under the title *Shrinking Cities*, outlining strategies for managing urban decline around the world.

Closer to home, a shrinking cities exhibit currently on tour in Europe is set to arrive in New York next month and in Detroit in February. Also in February, the Institute of Urban and Regional Development at the University of California, Berkeley, is hosting a symposium on the topic. Meanwhile, the Shrinking Cities Institute at Kent State University is plotting provocative events in Cleveland, such as an urban campout. "We're trying to get people to recognize the change that's happened right under our feet," says Terry Schwarz, a Kent State planner. "It's a little surprising to see how much emptiness there is."

This isn't the sort of conversation most politicians are comfortable having. Instead of accepting decline and trying to manage it in a deliberate way, mayors tend to gravitate toward revitalization plans that involve building convention centers and sports arenas and subsidizing hotels and shopping malls. They also get into desperate fights with the Census Bureau over population estimates and counting methodology. "How many politicians in America will stand on a soapbox and say, 'I'm going to lead this city and we're going to shrink it?'" asks Joseph Schilling, a professor at Virginia Tech's Metropolitan Institute.

The urban planning profession is not well equipped to handle shrinkage, either. Planning literature is fundamentally oriented toward growth and how to manage it.

> "We're trying to get people to recognize the change that's happened right under our feet. It's a little surprising to see how much emptiness there is."
>
> —Terry Schwarz, Kent State planner

That's true of tools such as zoning regulations and pattern books, and it's true of planning creeds such as New Urbanism and "sustainable development." As Schilling says, "We have two predominant planning models in this country. One is growth, growth, growth. The other is redevelopment. That third approach—rightsizing cities—is not something that we've done a lot with."

There's one more force that has quietly but powerfully prevented cities from coming to terms with contraction. As cities lose people, they also lose federal and state aid, even as the woes of concentrated poverty and surplus infrastructure worsen. Meanwhile, federal, state and local policies continue subsidizing new development in the suburbs and exurbs. "When you go to an economically struggling city in Europe, they are more vital and vibrant than American cities, even though they've experienced the same economic shocks such as loss of the steel sector or the decline of coal," says Bruce Katz, director of the Metropolitan Policy program at the Brookings Institution. "That's because they don't sprawl as much."

NEW FACES

Youngstown's cycle of industrial boom and bust may sound familiar. But few cities that have gone through that cycle fell so far so fast. The Mahoning Valley was the nation's third-largest steel-producing center. Then on September 19, 1977—"Black Monday"—Youngstown Sheet & Tube announced it was shutting down. U.S. Steel and Republic Steel followed suit. Seemingly overnight, 40,000 jobs evaporated. Steelworkers abandoned homes by the thousands, crime reached epidemic levels and a plague of corruption settled in, symbolized most infamously by former U.S. Representative Jim Traficant, who eventually went to prison on bribery charges.

Lately, though, a new generation of civic leaders has come of age in Youngstown. Mayor Williams, a home-born banker who also worked as the city's community development director, was just five years old on Black

Monday. Several key positions are in the hands of outsiders whose thoughts aren't haunted by ghosts of the mills. Anthony Kobak, Youngstown's planner, arrived from Cleveland in 2000. So did David Sweet, the president of Youngstown State University, who had previously been dean of the urban affairs program at Cleveland State.

A year later, Sweet asked Hunter Morrison to join him. "Many of the politicians and the business leadership who were here when things collapsed either retired, moved or died," Morrison says. "One thing that happened in the 2010 planning process is people looked around and said, 'You know what? The boss is dead. We don't have to ask permission anymore.'"

The 2010 plan emerged from an unusual town-gown partnership. One of Sweet's first tasks at Youngstown State was to create a new campus plan. Meanwhile, the city was gearing up to re-write its comprehensive plan for the first time since 1951. Strategists on both sides saw the benefit of intertwining their efforts. The university, which sits on a bluff above downtown, is not only Youngstown's biggest employer but an obvious potential catalyst for new development. The city's deterioration, however, is a liability in recruiting students and faculty.

The city hired Toronto-based Urban Strategies to help with visioning and public engagement. City officials posted get-involved ads in newspapers and on billboards, screaming such provocations as, "Our kids go away and never come back!" It worked. Neighborhood input sessions averaged 75 attendees. More than 1,000 people twice packed the historic Stambaugh Auditorium, first to learn about the overall vision—including the idea of acknowledging Youngstown's smaller size—and then to see the plan in greater detail. By the time of last November's mayoral election, the 2010 plan had become an agenda setter. Williams, who as community development director had become the face of the 2010 process, won convincingly.

GREEN OPTION

But now comes the hard part: figuring out what it actually means to rightsize a city's neighborhoods and infrastructure. Unlike the industrialists who bolted from Youngstown 30 years ago, the mayor can't simply shut off sewers or stop plowing snow just because those services aren't economical. What he can do is target city investments where they will pay the greatest return to Youngstown's quality of life. Williams hopes to entice residents to relocate out of neighborhoods that are too far gone to save. At the same time, he wants to focus on stabilizing transitional neighborhoods and keeping healthy middle-class neighborhoods from wilting. "What it means is in many instances you have to start saying no," Williams says. "That's not easy as a public official, when it comes to people with all sorts of ideas that are well intended but not necessarily realistic."

One example is the city's program for helping low-income people fix up their homes. Until recently, that aid has been distributed on a first-come, first-served basis, going right down a waiting list, regardless of the condition of the neighborhood. Now, the Community Development Agency skips homes in far-gone areas. It's also looking at dangling rehab dollars as a carrot for people to move into more stable neighborhoods. "Does it make sense to invest $40,000 or $50,000 in a home that is on a street where more than half of the other homes have to be demolished?" Williams says. "Can we afford to keep investing that money on a randomly chosen basis and think that we're affecting sustainable positive change?"

Similarly, Williams has put a moratorium on the construction of homes financed with low-income housing tax credits. Over the past decade, nonprofits have built new homes in Oak Hill and other declining neighborhoods, using federal tax credits and other state and local subsidies. The new vinyl-sided homes are respectable enough, but Williams believes that they, too, represent a wasted investment. "We didn't have a plan and they popped up in areas that just didn't make sense," Williams says. "A brand-new house constructed between two houses that need to be demolished—we're not doing anybody a favor. It's not that we don't need decent quality housing for low-income individuals, but where we house them in the city has to be well thought out."

Many of Youngstown's shrinkage strategies are aimed at its massive abandoned-property problem. There are 14,000 vacant lots in Youngstown, and 1,000 derelict homes and commercial buildings sitting on them. Williams has quadrupled the funds available for demolition to $1.2 million—enough to take down about 350 homes this year. Another initiative, spearheaded by Mahoning County Treasurer John Reardon, is clearing a mountain of back taxes owed on those lots so that churches, businesses and residents can take ownership of them. His goal is to put 5,000 lots into productive

Rust-Belt Shrinkage
Population of selected cities, 1970–2005

CITY	1970	1990	2005	% CHANGE, 1970 TO 2005
Charleston, WV	71,505	57,287	51,176	−28.43%
Dayton, OH	243,023	182,044	158,873	−34.63
Erie, PA	129,265	108,718	102,612	−20.62
Evansville, IN	138,764	126,272	115,918	−16.46
Flint, MI	193,317	140,761	118,551	−38.68
Gary, IN	175,415	116,646	98,715	−43.72
Kalamazoo, MI	85,555	80,277	72,700	−15.03
Saginaw, MI	91,849	69,512	58,361	−36.46
Scranton, PA	102,696	81,805	73,120	−28.80
Syracuse, NY	197,297	163,860	141,683	−28.19
Utica, NY	91,373	68,637	59,336	−35.06
Youngstown, OH	140,909	95,732	82,837	−41.21

Source: U.S. Census Bureau

use within five years. Most of the time, "productive use" simply means allowing homeowners to triple the size of their yards by buying the empty lots next door.

If there is a guiding principle in all this, it is that Youngstown can afford to be generous with its land. That notion implies that stewardship is more important than the plat lines on Youngstown's maps. Looking at a row of empty lots tangled with vegetation, you don't have to squint too hard to see wild prairie or woodlands—or even a wetland. There's environmental value here, but there's also economic value—developers are under obligation to create a new wetland when they destroy one somewhere else. Youngstown has commissioned a survey of potential wetlands-in-waiting. Developers may come to value Youngstown land not because they want to build on it but because they don't want to build on it.

As Anthony Kobak sees it, the greening of Youngstown is also about enhancing quality of life. The city doesn't want to keep shrinking. It wants to make itself as attractive as it can be for the people who've stuck it out. If it succeeds, perhaps one day Youngstown can think about growing again. "You could call it declining gracefully," Kobak says, "but I like to think of it more as looking to be competitive and having the potential for growth in the future."

Back in the Ford Taurus, Kobak ends his tour of Youngstown at a conservatory that lies above the tip of Mill Creek Park. The leafy park, designed by associates of Frederick Law Olmsted, is one of those 19th-century gems, with boathouses and stone bridges, that even the wealthiest American suburbs are incapable of replicating today. If Youngstown is a size-60 suit on a size-40 frame, Mill Creek Park is its shiniest ivory button. There are others—a downtown with early 1900s skyscrapers, two solid art museums, a symphony, the university. They are vestiges, ironically, that a city of 82,000 could never possess unless it had once been twice that size.

Kobak leads a reporter though a trim and colorful rose garden to a shaded stone terrace. This is the spot, he says, where newlyweds come on Saturdays to take wedding pictures. It's obvious why. The picture-frame view opens up on a lake below, surrounded on all sides by a thick green canopy of trees. "Here's the pitch," Kobak says. "Look how easy it is to get out of the city and into the country. We're right off the interstate. Our housing stock is incredibly affordable. We're an hour from two international airports. Perfect for telecommuters, retirees, anyone trying to get out of the rat race. It's just amazing what's here.

"We know we're not going to be a city of 170,000 as we were in our heyday," he continues. "It will be a challenge. The city can decline more unless we do something about it. But I think we are trying to do that."

IX

Budgets and Taxes

There's a well-known piece of doggerel that sums up every government's dilemma concerning budgets and taxes:

Don't tax you,
Don't tax me,
Tax that feller behind the tree.

What these few lines succinctly sum up is that nobody likes taxes: not the taxpayers who have to foot the bill, and not the politicians who have to pay at the ballot box if they dip too far and too often into their constituents' pockets. Those lines also convey the harsh reality that somebody *has* to be taxed. It is just that everybody prefers it be somebody else. The paradox underpinning government finances is that while just about everyone likes at least some government expenditures, nobody likes paying for them.

True, many people say they are for cutting government spending, and just as many are for cutting taxes. But when it comes to specifics—exactly what programs should be cut, exactly who should pay how much for what remains—there is considerably less agreement. Who gets what and who pays for it are among the central questions of democratic politics, and they are at the heart of much of the political conflict in states and localities. As the readings in this section show, the reality of state and local government finances revolves around trying to find acceptable solutions to the difficult problems these issues present.

RAISING AND SPENDING MONEY

According to the most recent estimates, state and local government expenditures total more than $2 trillion—that's a 2 followed by 12 zeros.[1] By any measure, that is a lot of money. Where does it all come from?

State and local governments rely on six major sources of revenue: sales taxes, property taxes, income taxes, motor vehicle taxes, estate and gift taxes, and grants and transfers from the federal government. Of the taxes state and local governments levy, the biggest revenue producers are sales taxes (about $338 billion), property taxes ($297 billion), and individual income taxes ($200 billion). Grants from the federal government add another $390 billion to state and local coffers.[2] Other sources of revenue include everything from fees for licenses to hunt, fish, or marry to interest earned on bank deposits. There is enormous variation from state to state—and even locality to locality—in how governments raise their money. Some states (for example, Texas and Florida), have no individual income tax and rely more heavily on sales taxes.

There are pros and cons to employing different forms of taxation. Property taxes, for instance, are one of the most hated forms of taxation. They typically are levied as a portion of the assessed valuation of property. They most often are paid in a lump sum once or twice a year, and thus they tend to be stark reminders to taxpayers about how much the government takes from them. For most homeowners, property taxes work out to be about 1.55 percent of the house's value. So someone who owns a house worth, say, $2,000, will pay about $3,100 a year in property taxes. Writing a check that big can be painful (although maybe not as painful as owning a home valued at only $2,000 in this day and age).

While property owners are never going to be enthusiastic about them, property taxes have clear advantages for state and local governments. Most important of these, they are a relatively stable form of income. Income and sales taxes will rise and fall along with the ups and downs of the economy. Property values can fall too, of course, but they rarely fall by much.

Much of the controversy surrounding state and local taxes comes from the perennial issues of fairness and who pays. The advantage of a sales tax, proponents argue, is that it is a fair tax. Technically it is a flat tax, meaning everyone pays the same rate, regardless of their ability to pay. It doesn't matter whether Bill Gates or a cash-strapped college student buys a book or a television or a car; if they buy that product or service at the same place, then they pay exactly the same tax.

Critics of the sales tax say that equity is what makes it so unfair. To be fair, the tax should take into account ability to pay; taxes that do not do this are called regressive. In contrast, income taxes are typically progressive taxes, meaning how much you pay is dependent upon how wealthy you are. The tax rate increases progressively with income; in short, richer people supposedly get hit with a higher tax than poor people. Opponents of the income tax say that isn't fair—in effect a progressive tax punishes people for being successful. The arguments over sales versus income and regressive versus progressive taxes are neverending, and most states do not take an either-or approach. Most choose some mix of both, and generally speaking no one is happy with the result.

There is another prominent source of revenue governments can tap: borrowing. The federal government covers a significant chunk of its spending with deficient financing. In simple terms, the federal government covers the gap between revenue and expenditure with a credit card. State and local governments also borrow, primarily by issuing bonds. Bonds are nothing more than IOUs, certificates stating that the state or locality will pay the bearer of the bond a specified interest rate for a specified period of time and return the principle when the bond reaches maturity.

State and local governments, however, cannot engage in the same sort of "credit card" financing as the federal government. The vast majority of states are required by law to produce balanced budgets, that is, it is illegal for expenditures to exceed revenue. This is a major reason why state governments suffered so much a few years ago when a recession cut income and sales tax growth. States and localities simply have less wiggle room when times get fiscally tough—they are all but forced to raise taxes, cut spending, or do both. The only exception is Vermont, which alone among the states is free to run itself into debt in a similar fashion to the federal government.

What do states and localities spend their money on? Well, a big chunk goes to education, roughly $621 billion (about $428 billion is spent on elementary and secondary education, the rest goes to higher education). Other big-ticket items include social welfare programs (about $306 billion) and highways ($117 billion). Some government expenditures, however, are less visible to citizens than schools, roads, and a safety net for the needy. For example, state and local governments spend more than $127 billion annually on employee retirement benefits.[3]

RECENT TRENDS

The most notable recent trend in the budgets and taxes of state and local governments is uncertainty. For the past couple of years, states and localities enjoyed fairly flush coffers as the nation experienced a period of economic growth and a huge jump in property values. However, the property market started softening in late 2006, and the downturn in the housing market raised broader questions about the economic outlook for 2007 and 2008. And some spending obligations—especially those related to health care programs and public employee retirement benefits—are galloping ahead of state and local revenue growth. All of this has raised the question of how well state and local governments can withstand another economic downturn. The answer, at least in 2007, was nobody was really sure. In previous tough times, the federal government helped out with intergovernmental transfers. With two wars to fund and the federal coffers constrained by a series of tax cuts, it is not clear if the federal government can help out as much as in the past.

The readings that follow reflect some of this uncertainty and the issues underlying it. The essay by John Peterson takes a look at the recent history of state finances and tries to assess how state fiscal systems will stand up to economic turbulence. Jennifer Burnett examines the drive to cap property taxes. Property taxes, as already mentioned, are among the most hated of government levies, yet they remain a primary source of local government revenue. States are trying to put the lid on property tax growth, but doing so raises the question of how to replace lost revenue.

The essay by Jonathan Walters discusses how new accounting standards are clarifying just how much public employee retirement benefits cost state and local governments. The promises made to public employees in terms of retirement benefits are adding up to huge numbers, and it is not clear where the money is going to come from to cover those costs.

A second essay by John Peterson wraps up the section. Peterson predicts that the federal government is not likely to bail states out of a financial hole should budgets get tight in the next year or two.

Notes

1. Census Bureau, *Statistical Abstract of the United States,* 2007, Table 424. www.census.gov/compendia/statab/tables/07s0424.xls.

2. Ibid.

3. Ibid.

35

Seat-Belt Budgeting

John E. Petersen

There's economic turbulence ahead that state budget and fiscal systems may not weather well.

From *Governing,*
September 2006

The pilot intones the familiar phrase: "Put on your seat belts, we've got bumpy weather ahead." It's a good time for states to be thinking about that admonition. After a few years of smooth flying through the recovery in the national economy, states need to be asking whether their budgets and fiscal systems are prepared for an economic downturn.

The states are currently being kept aloft by revenue systems that have undergone restructuring during the past decade. They are now much more sensitive to changes in personal and corporate income. During good years, substantial corporate profits and capital gains bring in slugs of money. But this is followed by droughts when financial markets, business earnings and incomes turn down. Even the sales tax runs on a much more volatile mixture, with higher tax rates spitting out revenues on an ever-narrowing base. So, when incomes and expenditures change—up or down—the resulting bounce in state revenues is much greater. The shallow but prolonged recessionary conditions of 2001 through 2003 reflected this: State income tax collections in 2003 fell by about $24 billion from their peak in 2000.

State spending is also changing. Increasingly, it is driven by the needs of the very old, the very young and the less affluent. The major cost driver has been the Medicaid program, which has grown explosively and now accounts for one-quarter of state spending. The long-term prognosis is not good: State populations are aging, and the cost of health care continues to rise more rapidly than prices in general. Medicaid costs are projected to go up 8 percent a year over the next decade. In good years, state revenue systems meet that mark but not in bad years.

Furthermore, after a decade of subdued inflation, the prices that governments have to pay are growing. The overall price index for government spending, heavily influenced by the growth in the costs of medical care, is going up faster than the general price index. Thus, states in fiscal year 2006 increased spending by 7.6 percent, which appears pretty healthy until you crank in that the state and local price deflator has been rising by 6 percent recently.

What is happening on the inflation front is of critical importance in anticipating fiscal storms. Concern rotates around the impact of higher oil prices and interest rates on the state government sector. A few states—Alaska, Oklahoma, Wyoming—have benefited from higher prices with higher tax revenues, but most are burdened, both directly as the cost of fuel and energy rises and indirectly as increasing costs erode the buying power of consumers. The extra $10 to $20 per week constituents spend on filling up their car means less money to spend on other things. Since most gasoline is taxed per gallon, the higher prices don't help gas tax revenues; but the fewer dollars spent on other things does reduce state sales tax revenues.

Add to that the leveling off of real estate values. Housing starts are at their lowest levels in 15 years, and home listings are up by a factor of three in many markets. Local government finances, which held up well in the early part of the decade thanks to rising property values, may not do so this time around. The sagging real estate market may, in fact, trigger a downturn.

Adding to the uncertainties is the continuing malaise in pension finances. While better times and improved investment results brought some improvement to pension finances the past couple of years, the overhang of unfunded liabilities is unlikely to be dissolved by booming financial markets. And that doesn't even count in the latest fiscal joker—the unfunded employee retirement health benefits.

Nonetheless, state budgets for fiscal 2007 are calling for modest increases in spending and, after an assortment of tax cuts, a reduction in reserves. According to the National Association of State Budget Officers, state fund balances including rainy day funds, were rebuilt to 8.7 percent of expenditures by the end of 2005. Now, they are slated to drop to about 7.9 percent, with no growth foreseen in dollar reserves. Lest we forget, states ate a hole in their reserves in the recent recession—when those reserves were at 10.4 percent of expenditures. The windfalls from the tobacco settlement and the $20 billion in federal payments that were tied to the tax reduction act of 2003 are unlikely to be repeated. Thus, states approach future uncertainties with dwindling reserves, which is likely to mean quicker and deeper cutbacks as deficits emerge.

A downturn is not yet on the horizon, but a dose of fiscal prudence seems to be in order. Check those seat belts!

36

Capping the Burden

Jennifer Burnett

States look for a way to keep a lid on property taxes.

In 1927, Oliver Wendell Holmes said "taxes are what we pay for a civilized society."

Eighty years later, one form of tax—the property tax—is being scrutinized by state and local governments, due in part to the meteoric rise of property values in recent years.

A flood of legislation is being considered across the country to address concerns about property tax increases, how tax revenues are calculated and distributed, and local governments' reliance on those revenues.

Property taxes have often been the target of public discontent. In fact, the public considers the property tax to be the least fair among all state and local taxes, according to a recent poll conducted by the Tax Foundation. Gerald Prante, economist at the foundation and author of a new special report, postulates this is because "… taxpayers are more acutely aware of what property taxes cost them than they are of income, payroll, corporate or sales taxes. Sometimes, property taxes are paid into an escrow account without much personal attention from the taxpayer, but often property taxes involve the actual writing of a huge check to the local government."

This awareness means that property owners have become increasingly vocal about their rising tax burdens. In many states, grass roots organizations have sprung up to influence the property tax discourse. For example, Virginians Over-Taxed on Residences (VOTOR) has a single goal: to limit property value assessment increases and property tax rates. A New Jersey group called Citizens for Property Tax Reform reportedly had 500,000 participants in 2004. Dissatisfaction with property taxes is not a new phenomenon. Throughout the 1970s, states came under pressure from constituents to implement

From *State News,*
April 2007

property tax limits, culminating in the one of the most well-known of such measures—California's Proposition 13. Passed in 1978, Proposition 13 limited the property value assessment to the current value plus 2 percent per year. Many states followed California's lead and subsequently passed similar measures.

In 1980, Massachusetts voters went even further and passed Proposition 2½, which placed constraints on the amount of property taxes a city or town could levy, established two types of voter-approved increases in taxing authority, and allowed voters to mandate a reduction in taxing authority. In jurisdictions across the nation, property values—in particular, residential real estate prices—have skyrocketed in recent years and a renewed interest in limiting or reforming property taxes has followed. Figure 1 illustrates trends over the last 20 years in the S&P/Case-Shiller U.S. National Home Price Index.

While the index was relatively flat throughout the 1990s, steep increases can be seen beginning around 2000. There are, of course, variations across regions and even within states when it comes to how much residents have to pay. Of the top 10 counties (with populations greater than 65,000) that paid the highest median real estate taxes in 2005, six were in New Jersey and four were in New York. The residents of Westchester County, N.Y., made the highest median payment out of all these counties—$7,337. See table on page [188] for state property tax rankings.

Increased property taxes generally translates into larger revenue streams for local and state governments, but it can also result in huge tax burdens for property owners. The rise in property value and therefore property taxes has outpaced income growth, leaving property owners to pay out a growing proportion of their income to the government. From 2000 to 2004, property tax collections increased 27.7 percent, while over the same period personal income grew at little more than half that rate—15.9 percent.

This has led many states to consider revisions to existing property tax guidelines, often in order to provide relief for homeowners from steep tax bills or to limit how much those bills can grow in the future.

"Almost every state is looking at some form of property tax cap," said Myron Orfield, a property tax expert and law professor at the University of Minnesota in Minneapolis.

New York, with some of the heaviest property tax burdens in the nation, is considering a tax relief package aimed at middle class homeowners proposed by Gov. [Eliot] Spitzer.

"I believe those middle class New Yorkers, who bear the brunt of soaring property taxes and have the least ability to pay them, should be top priority," he has said.

Under the governor's proposal, the state would provide $6 billion in additional property tax relief over the next three years, with the majority of savings going to those homeowners with incomes at or below $60,000 ($80,000 in the New York City metropolitan area).

Alongside his relief package, Spitzer wants to shift some costs away from local governments—thereby reducing the

Figure 1 S&P/Case-Shiller U.S. National Home Price Index, 1Q 1987–4Q 2006

Note: The S&P/Case-Shiller® U.S. National Home Price Index is a composite of single-family home price indices for the nine U.S. Census divisions and is calculated quarterly.

property tax liabilities of homeowners—by increasing state aid to schools. Connecticut Gov. M. Jodi Rell is offering up a proposal with a similar intent. Though property taxes constitute a small portion of state tax revenue (usually less than 2 percent), local governments often derive a huge part of their budgets from these taxes and a large chunk of those revenues go to funding local schools. The Tax Foundation calculates that public schools are the greatest beneficiary of property taxes, receiving nearly 50 percent of all collected property taxes.

Given the aging of America, some legislative measures are aimed specifically at lessening the tax burden for older Americans on a fixed income. In 2006, for example, Nebraska Gov. Dave Heineman signed into law a revenue package that, according to AARP, "significantly expands tax relief to limited income older and disabled homeowners … and lessens the property tax burden on low-income seniors who might otherwise be forced out of their homes due to high taxes." As of March 2006, 25 states provided special property-tax exemptions or credits for

Another form of property tax reform known as property tax swaps—trading property taxes for an increase in another type of tax—has also made headlines over the last year. New Jersey, Idaho and South Carolina all chose to lower property taxes last year, and made up the lost revenue by increasing the sales tax. Texas, where property taxes rose almost 84 percent from 1996 to 2004, dropped property tax rates and picked up higher taxes on cigarettes and certain business activities. Proposals are in place in Florida, Indiana and Illinois to follow suit this year.

As previously discussed, increased property taxes were catalysts for many of these proposals. But, while home prices have been on the upswing the past few years, that trend has reversed in more recent months. (See Figure 1) According to the National Association of Realtors, the median price of an existing home sold in January 2007 was down 3.1 percent from last January—the sixth straight month prices have posted a year-over-year drop. Price drops could bring a reprieve from increasing property tax bills, but could also impact revenue streams for local governments and place pressure on policymakers to reconfigure newly conceived tax relief measures.

In the years to come, property taxes will likely continue to be a target of debate for property owners as well as an issue of concern for policymakers. As the real estate market cools off, the call for property tax reform may also cool off—for now.

State Rankings for Property Taxes

	Median Property Taxes Paid, 2005			Property Taxes as a Percentage of Income, 2005	
1	NJ	$5,352	1	NJ	6.75%
2	NH	$3,920	2	NH	5.86%
3	CT	$3,865	3	VT	5.07%
4	NY	$3,076	4	CT	5.00%
5	RI	$3,071	5	WI	4.79%
6	MA	$2,974	6	IL	4.68%
7	IL	$2,904	7	NY	4.59%
8	VT	$2,835	8	RI	4.45%
9	WI	$2,777	9	MA	3.95%
10	CA	$2,278	10	PA	3.57%
11	WA	$2,250	11	WA	3.55%
12	AK	$2,241	12	TX	3.53%
13	MD	$2,159	13	NE	3.48%
14	PA	$1,937	14	OR	3.44%
15	TX	$1,926	15	ME	3.37%
16	OR	$1,910	16	MI	3.29%
17	NE	$1,889	17	CA	3.17%
18	MI	$1,846	18	AK	3.13%
19	ME	$1,742	19	FL	2.95%
20	MN	$1,618	20	OH	2.93%
21	OH	$1,598	21	MD	2.70%
22	FL	$1,495	22	SD	2.79%
23	NV	$1,445	23	MT	2.79%
24	VA	$1,418	24	ND	2.64%
25	SD	$1,404	25	MN	2.60%
26	IA	$1,355	26	IA	2.59%
27	KS	$1,337	27	KS	2.49%
28	ND	$1,326	28	ID	2.47%
29	MT	$1,309	29	NV	2.37%
30	CO	$1,297	30	VA	2.13%
31	ID	$1,226	31	AZ	2.10%
32	AZ	$1,133	32	CO	2.03%
33	UT	$1,130	33	IN	2.02%
34	IN	$1,079	34	UT	1.96%
35	GA	$1,050	35	MO	1.96%
36	MO	$1,012	36	NC	1.91%
37	NC	$966	37	GA	1.82%
38	HI	$924	38	TN	1.63%
39	DE	$806	39	NM	1.56%
40	TN	$794	40	KY	1.49%
41	WY	$737	41	WY	1.40%
42	NM	$707	42	OK	1.37%
43	KY	$693	43	SC	1.33%
44	SC	$642	44	HI	1.28%
45	OK	$635	45	DE	1.27%
46	AK	$459	46	AK	1.05%
47	MS	$416	47	MS	1.02%
48	WV	$389	48	WV	0.97%
49	AL	$302	49	AL	0.66%
50	LA	$175	50	LA	0.37%

Source: Tax Foundation Calculations of U.S. Census Bureau data.
Note: All taxes are for owner-occupied housing.

37

Paying for Promises

Jonathan Walters

After the shock of the big numbers, states and localities are finding ways to deal with the costs of their retirees' health care.

C all it the six stages of GASB 45: anger, denial, sorrow, acceptance, study and action. That's been the general response to a new set of governmental accounting rules that ask state and local governments to spell out the costs of their promises to provide retired employees with health care as well as other post-employment benefits.

The new rules arrive courtesy of the Governmental Accounting Standards Board—the outfit in Norwalk, Connecticut, that sets all the accounting regulations for state and local governments—and are part of GASB's push to head these governments toward accounting for the long-range and cumulative consequences of financial obligations and promises made yesterday and today.

And when it comes to retiree health care, those promises carry quite a price tag. According to the 2006 Rockefeller Institute Report on State and Local Government Finances, aggregate state and local liabilities for retiree health care (as well as other non-pension post-employment benefits) come to around $1 trillion, with some individual eye-poppers such as the Los Angeles Unified School District's $5 billion and the state of California's $70 billion.

The new GASB rules don't require that states or localities actually do anything to close the liability gap. However, the gap will, over the next few years, become part of a jurisdiction's comprehensive annual financial report, and rating agencies will be watching to see how various governments deal with the new red ink being splashed across governmental ledgers.

According to Parry Young, head of public finance for the rating agency Standard & Poor's, his company is not expecting miracle fixes for what he acknowledges is a large and vexing new hole in public ledgers. "What we're looking for," Young says, "is a thoughtful plan on how they're going to manage this liability."

Figuring out how to react to GASB 45 has certainly been a sobering experience, says David Manning, chief financial officer for Nashville's metro government. Back-of-the-envelope calculations there indicate that Nashville is on the hook for about $1.5 billion. The city can tack on another half-billion or so if it includes teachers in the equation.

Nashville is currently where most states and localities are: They've done the quick and dirty calculation, and now they're trying to home in on a more exact number and figure out what to do about it. "Right now, we're updating our actuarial estimates to try and get a handle on what the implications are for us," says Manning. The city has a GASB 45 task force that was created by Mayor Bill Purcell to consider alternatives for dealing with the new directive. That task force has yet to report.

What's clear though, is that most states and localities are past the anger, denial and sorrow phase of GASB 45, and are developing concrete ways to deal with the new rule. Those responses have ranged from paying down the liability by digging directly into general funds to floating more debt. Governments are also taking a hard look at what, exactly, has been promised to retirees by way of benefits, with an eye toward cutting back and thereby reducing long-range liability. Some jurisdictions, meanwhile, have decided to try to slide some of their liability onto the feds.

TRUST FUNDING

Those public entities that have decided to begin pre-funding the liability are turning to the same vehicle they now use for pension obligations. In California, for example, the Public Employees' Retirement System (CalPERS) has created investment funds for governments that already participate in the CalPERS health care system, allowing localities to start putting money away for down-the-road health care payouts. Where necessary, states have passed or are in the process of developing legislation authorizing localities to create their own liability trust funds for "other post-employment benefits"—known as "OPEBs" in the accounting world.

Numerous states and localities have either begun to pay into such accounts or are in the final stages of working out how much to set aside. One of the first items of business for the new Massachusetts governor and legislature, for instance, is passing legislation to set up and begin funding an OPEB liability trust to cover that state's $7.6 billion obligation, says Eric Berman, who is part of a network of state officials who have been looking at the new rule. South Carolina Governor Mark Sanford has recommended that this year's budget include around $250 million to go into a dedicated OPEB trust fund to begin paying up his state's estimated $23.5 billion liability. Wisconsin, meanwhile, was prescient: Two years ago, it floated a bond to begin covering its post-retirement liabilities.

Localities, likewise, are facing facts. In New York City, Mayor Michael Bloomberg has said the city is ready to commit $2.2 billion of its current budget surplus to a down payment on its estimated $53.5 billion in OPEB liabilities. Plano, Texas, is already setting aside $7.6 million per year from its general fund to cover that city's $150 million OPEB hole. "We opted for advanced funding," says Plano CFO John McGrain. "We felt that it was fiscally sound reasoning for Plano to go ahead and do that." The city has set up an irrevocable trust in which to collect the OPEB's cash. McGrain acknowledges that Plano is lucky in one respect: It's not that generous when it comes to OPEBs and so isn't facing the same level of liability as many other jurisdictions.

SETTING LIMITS

The other widespread response to GASB 45 is to look at a range of options related to the benefits themselves—from scaling back, to boosting co-pays, to lengthening vesting periods or even to sloughing some of the long-term liability off onto someone else. The San Diego County Board of Supervisors, for instance, is trying to cut $50 million in annual health care subsidies for all post-March 2002 retirees. North Carolina has extended from five to 20 years the time it will take for state employees to become fully vested for health care benefits. In Chicago, the city is trying to negotiate both higher employee health care contributions and benefit cuts with its transit workers.

The heightened profile of the cost of retiree benefits—a fallout from the accounting rule—is very much on the minds of those who represent public employees. "We're very concerned," says Bill Cunningham, a lobbyist for the

American Federation of Teachers. "We have members who've retired or who are about to retire who believe they had a commitment from their employer. This is clearly a problem that is going to have substantive fiscal and political ramifications."

It's not only the rank and file who find themselves in a hot seat over benefits, though. For example, a few years back, the Nashville Metro Council promised that any of its members who serve at least two terms would be granted a lifetime's worth of health care benefits after they leave office. That's a commitment that CFO David Manning bets would have been of interest to voters had reporting on the long-range cost associated with the promise been required.

Meanwhile, some jurisdictions are considering strategies that have nothing to do with cutting benefits. In West Virginia, the state pension board recently approved a plan to shift prescription drug coverage for state retirees to Medicare Part D, which the board says will carve $3 billion off the state's estimated $8 billion OPEB liability.

Critics of that strategy argue that the fiscal and administrative complexity of such a switch may make it less attractive than it first appears and suggest caution in trying to push OPEB costs onto the feds. Underlying such notes of caution, of course, is the stark fact that Medicare itself is amassing trillions of dollars in unfunded liabilities, which could put its long-range fiscal viability in doubt.

BREAKING AWAY

Despite the flurry of action in the field, there are still those jurisdictions that seem stuck in the "denial" phase of GASB 45. In Travis County, Texas, the chief auditor, Susan Spataro, has taken a defiant position on 45. In the first place, she argues, OPEBs in Travis County have always been handled on a pay-as-you-go basis, delivered year to year at the discretion of the county commission. For that reason, Spataro contends, they don't represent any long-range fiscal liability at all.

Furthermore, in trying to calculate the county's OPEB liability, her office—in concert with a variety of outside actuaries—has come up with numbers that are all over

Best Guesses

Estimated OPEB liabilities in selected states, as of September 2006

State	Amount (billions)
Alabama	$19.8
Alaska	7.9 or more
California	40 to 70
Illinois	43 to 53
Maryland	20
Massachusetts	13.2
Nevada	1.62 to 4.1
New York	47 to 54

Source: Associated Press

the map, ranging from $89 million to $380 million. Therefore, she thinks any number the county were to settle on and report in its comprehensive annual financial report would for all intents and purposes be false. "And it's a criminal offense to falsify a government record," says Spataro. So she's not planning on entering any number at all. Rather, she hopes to persuade the Texas legislature to pass a law pulling Texas out from under GASB rules and placing it under a system of generally accepted accounting rules developed and administered by the state.

It's a novel argument and strategy for sure, says Massachusetts' Eric Berman. But Berman, like many who are in the throes of responding to the new rule, doesn't think such a "head in the sand" approach serves government or citizens very well.

According to Steven Gauthier, point man on GASB 45 for the Government Finance Officers Association, most jurisdictions are, like Berman's shop, stepping up and dealing with the future cost of OPEBs. "Most of my colleagues understand and agree with the fundamental notion that a financial statement should show you that you've incurred these obligations."

38

The Check Is in the Mail

John E. Petersen

If the economy turns down this year, will the feds rescue the states the way they did in 2003?

From *Governing*, January 2007

As state budgeteers plan for the next fiscal year, they are faced with remembrances of times gone by. When there is an economic downturn, state finances are less than stable, and recent figures show such a slowing is visible in several areas. Housing construction, in particular, comes to mind.

While the slowing may be just a "pause that refreshes," the fiscal bottom may again fall out, leaving state finances vulnerable. In part that's because their tax systems are leveraged so highly on bases that are sensitive to economic changes. For example, the general sales tax base is riddled with exceptions and exclusions that tend to make revenue from the tax hyperventilate with changes in discretionary spending. So, when home buying slows, people spend less on furniture, fixtures and the types of big-ticket items that weigh heavy in the shrunken tax base. Similarly, state income tax systems tend to rely on the biggest earners when they are earning the big bucks. But those revenues wither when capital losses replace gains. Also, states over the years have turned to lesser charges that are cyclically sensitive, such as levies on deeds and property transfers.

But the other vulnerability is on the spending side—Medicaid in particular. This health insurance program for the poor has been the fastest growing segment in state budgets for several years. Recent reports suggest a slowdown this past year—Medicaid spending fell by 1.4 percent in the first nine months of 2006, the first decrease in spending since the program began in 1965. But that change doesn't alter the basic working premise behind Medicaid: When recessions hit and the unemployment rate goes up, the number of eligible persons increases. Between 2001 and 2002, Medicaid enrollments nationally went up by 8.6 percent at the same time that state tax revenues were falling by 7 percent. It is estimated that each newly unemployed person led to an added $300 or so in Medicaid expenditures, on average, during the 2001–02 slowdown.

So, what to do if cyclical economic pressures come calling again? In 2003, the federal government took unprecedented steps to lessen the recession's fiscal blow to the states by passing, as part of a tax cut package—the Jobs Growth and Tax Relief Reconciliation Act—some $20 billion in grants for the states. The assistance was apportioned at $10 billion for Medicaid and $10 billion for general assistance. That $20 billion went a long way in closing the roughly $50 billion in estimated state budget deficits.

Will this benevolence be repeated the next time around? With the long-term declining condition of federal finances, state folks are not holding their breath. Besides, arguments against federal counter-cyclical aid to states are well understood. First, the single-shot appropriation process leads to both delays (which have the assistance arriving after the recession) and divergences. For example, the $10 billion in general fiscal assistance that was adopted in 2003 was allocated on a per-capita basis with the small states getting a floor payment. As a result, states that had high unemployment and weak revenues often got less on a per-capita basis than states that were doing better. A second argument suggests that once the states come to expect a federal handout, they will save less in balances and rainy-day funds.

There are good arguments on the positive side. If the criteria are set right, states can avoid cutbacks in spending—cuts that hit the poor the hardest—or tax increases that stifle recovery. There is a glimmer of interest in counter-cyclical financial aid and much to be said for reviewing the role of counter-cyclical assistance to soften the impacts of a decline.

One thing that has changed over the past 20 years is the states' role in providing health care to dependent populations. Changing demographics and a riskier economy intensify this role, and the costs of delaying or denying basic health care can be both socially dispiriting and personally deadly. With the steady retreat of private health insurance coverage and the slippery footing of lower-income workers, the next slowdown could be worse.

Voters, sensitized to the vagaries of an economy that seems beyond their individual reach and understanding, may support more affirmative actions by governments to address their insecurities. That attitude might be good news for states, which are stuck in the middle of an intergovernmental system where they pick up the tab for costs over which they have little control, using revenue systems designed to rely on continuing growth.

Policy Challenges

If the readings in this book make any one overall point, it is that state and local governments are expected to do a lot. Better schools and health care, more ethical government, more qualified public employees, management of growth and decline ... the list is endless. There is no aspect of social, political, and economic life in the United States that is not touched in some way by state and local government policy.

Given that they do so much, it is hard to boil down their expansive agendas into a comprehensive list of "most important" or "major" policy challenges. Fact is, state and local governments face a countless number of major (and minor) policy challenges. You name it—from potholes to pot, from illegal immigration to white flight, from test scores to tax rates—it's on the agenda in some form or another at a council meeting, a legislative committee, a governor's policy team, or before a state judge.

Governments, though, have limited amounts of attention, time, and money. So while state and local governments in a broad sense deal with just about everything, there is a much smaller spectrum of issues that attracts a disproportionate share of government's interest and resources. What are those issues likely to be?

TRENDS

A good way to figure out what state and local governments consider most important is to follow the money—who is getting it and who isn't. By that yardstick, education and health care rank up there as two of the most important issues on the public agenda. They consume the most state and local tax dollars and are considered primary responsibilities of these two levels of government. Conflicts over education policy and health care policy are central components of state and local politics.

Yet more and more, state and local governments are dealing with issues fundamentally different from those typically thought of as state and local issues. Global warming, illegal immigration, the war on terror, and minimum wage laws are all examples of policy arenas traditionally considered more the province of the federal government than of state and local governments.

One of the most notable policy trends of late is a mounting frustration among states and localities about federal government action—or, more accurately, inaction—on such issues. State and local governments increasingly are taking matters into their own hands, stepping into the policy vacuum left by the federal government and giving literal meaning to the old saying "think globally, act locally." The theme of states and localities aggressively wading onto the traditional policy turf of the federal government has cropped up in other readings in this book (notably in William Pound's essay on the evolving role of states in the federal system in Part I and Mary Branham Dusenberry's essay on gubernatorial state of the state speeches in Part V). The readings in this final section focus specifically on a series of nontraditional policy efforts that represent, by any definition, important and major challenges for state and local governments.

The first essay, by Zach Patton, gives an overview of the current policy landscape at the state level. Many of the issues described in this piece are state government perennials: education and health care, of course, but also taxes and such big-ticket infrastructure items as roads and bridges. Also noted are policy challenges related to the perennial power struggle between state governments and the national government that is the inevitable byproduct of our federal political system. Fights over gay rights and federally mandated standards for state identification cards, for example, are often struggles about which level of government has the power to decide what to do and which level of government has to foot the bill.

The issues periodically may reshuffle themselves, but the underlying tension over questions of authority and power is as old as the political system itself. What is most notable about Patton's overview are the issues that states are tackling that traditionally have been considered the province of the federal government.

Other essays pick up on just these sorts of issues and provide more in-depth examinations of them. Larry Morandi takes a look at how states are attacking the problem of global warming. While the federal government has gridlocked on how to control greenhouse gases, a number states have begun pursuing their own solutions. A notable example is California, which has been among the most aggressive in rallying behind legislation that seeks to reduce the carbon emissions that contribute to global warming.

In a related vein, Judith Crosson's article looks at renewable energy projects at the state and local level. A key obstacle to developing cleaner, renewable energy sources is demand thresholds. To help overcome this obstacle, states are starting to mandate that certain percentages of power generation come from renewable sources. For example, New York is ambitiously looking to have 25 percent of its future energy needs come from renewable sources. Energy policy has become an increasingly important policy arena for state governments not just for its global environmental implications, but also for hard-nosed economic reasons. As Crosson details, renewable energy is not just a boon for the environment—it is a windfall for rural economic development.

Tom Arrandale's essay ends the section with a highlight of how states and localities are on the front lines of the war on terror simply because of what they do. Drinking water is a primary responsibility of local governments, and these community water systems are all potential terrorist targets. Most people don't give a thought to their water systems—just turn a faucet and safe, drinkable water comes out. Keeping that mundane fact of life a, well, mundane fact of life, means thinking like a terrorist and taking a clear-eyed look at vulnerabilities in the water system.

39

Issues to Watch

Zach Patton

While states will be watching to see if new congressional leadership will result in action on major issues at the federal level, they won't be waiting around to find out.

M uch of the Democrats' success in state elections last year was due to dissatisfaction with the way things were going in Washington, D.C. Voters felt Congress was stymied by partisan bickering and the federal government had failed to address some of the nation's most pressing issues.

That's a feeling shared by many state officials, regardless of party. And much of the legislative action in state capitols this year will be fueled by lawmakers' frustration with inaction by the feds. State-house Democratic wins will certainly bolster issues such as climate change, minimum wage increases and universal health insurance coverage. But even on more conventionally Republican issues, such as immigration reform and business taxes, states will be leading the way.

Although much of the focus in the states will be on subjects that have fallen victim to Washington gridlock, legislators will also be tackling some of the perennial state-level issues. Relatively healthy budgets will allow states to consider plans to expand early education programs and deal with backlogs of highway maintenance needs.

It's possible that new leadership in the U.S. House and Senate will result in congressional action on some of these issues. And states, of course, will be watching. But they won't be waiting.

ILLEGAL IMMIGRATION

Georgia threw down the gauntlet on illegal immigration last year, enacting one of the nation's toughest laws against undocumented residents. The measure requires people seeking state social welfare benefits to prove they are legal residents, and police officers to check

From *Governing,*
January 2007

the legal status of anyone they arrest and report any violations to federal officials. It also imposes sanctions on employers who hire undocumented workers, requires companies that do business with the state to run background checks on their employees and withholds a portion of state income tax for individuals who fail to provide proper documentation.

Expect more of the same this year. In fact, legislators in Texas could be considering a bevy of bills that would make Georgia's statutes look relatively permissive. Before their session even started, Texas lawmakers had filed several tough anti-illegal-immigration proposals. One would prohibit the children of undocumented immigrants from receiving state employment, professional licenses or public assistance. Others would impose a hefty fee on money that's wired to Central or South America and empower Texas to sue the feds to recover money the state has spent on illegal immigration.

In Arizona, debate on immigration reforms stymied last year's session, and legislative leaders have promised to make immigration measures a prominent feature of the 2007 docket. House Speaker Jim Weiers has called illegal immigration "the most important issue in Arizona."

It's not just border states that will tackle illegal immigration. An Oklahoma lawmaker has vowed to refile a bill to punish employers that hire illegal laborers, a measure he says will be "the toughest bill in the nation." And South Carolina legislators will debate a bill that most likely will be modeled after Georgia's.

UNIVERSAL HEALTH COVERAGE

Since Massachusetts passed a sweeping plan last year requiring everyone in the state to have health insurance—and offering help to those who can't afford it—the issue of universal coverage has risen to the top of the policy agenda in many other states.

Following his reelection in November, Governor Tim Pawlenty announced a plan to move Minnesota toward universal coverage, with an initial focus on children. Democratic leaders in the state legislature are on board. California Governor Arnold Schwarzenegger has said that health care reform is his top priority and that his goal is to cover all of his state's uninsured residents. His administration has said that all options are on the table—including mandates that employers cover the costs for their workers.

In Maryland, a state health panel recently outlined a plan for universal health insurance. The draft plan, released in November by the Maryland Health Care Commission, would require residents to have coverage. It also would create an insurance exchange where individuals could choose a plan regardless of their employer. Similarly, a legislative task force in Illinois last month endorsed a plan that would require every resident in the state to obtain insurance. And New Jersey lawmakers are working on universal insurance legislation.

Other states may not be looking at universal coverage, but the Massachusetts plan will serve as an impetus to examine other health care reforms, notes Alan Weil, executive director for the National Academy for State Health Policy. "We can expect health insurance to be a major issue in states this year," he says. "States are realizing they can't just copy Massachusetts' program. It's still early to see what angle they're going to take on it and adapt for themselves." But Weil expects universal health insurance for children to be discussed in more than a dozen states.

MINIMUM WAGE

Few state issues have more momentum this year than increasing the minimum wage. The federal wage standard has not been raised in a decade, and states are no longer waiting for Congress to act. Twenty-nine states now have a minimum wage higher than the federal hourly standard of $5.15, and 11 states have set wages in excess of $7 an hour.

Last year marked a watershed for the issue, with 12 states voting to raise wages. More than half of those increases were approved by voter initiatives that tied future wage rates to inflation. In a special legislative session last month, Illinois became the latest state to hike wages. That state's new minimum hourly pay rate of $7.50, which takes effect in July, will be among the highest in the country.

Lawmakers in New Mexico plan to take up the issue this year, after failing to agree on a wage proposal in 2006. Governor Bill Richardson has pledged to increase the minimum pay in his state, and one bill would raise hourly wages to $7.50 over two years. Legislators in Kentucky and Texas also plan to debate minimum wage increases this year.

In Iowa, lawmakers stalemated over minimum wage last year, with political parties split evenly in both houses. But the November elections brought Democratic control to both chambers and the governor's seat for the first time in four decades. Incoming House Speaker Pat Murphy has made a minimum wage increase a top priority, promising action early in the legislative session.

Some of these state actions could be eclipsed at the national level if Congress approves an increase to the federal minimum wage. Incoming Democratic leaders have pledged to raise the wage during the first few weeks of the new congressional session this month. That action would likely set a new national wage floor at $7.25 an hour.

CLIMATE CHANGE

Frustrated by inaction on environmental issues at the federal level, states have increasingly taken the helm on the issue of climate change. Thus far, 22 states have adopted policies to require or encourage utilities to increase their use of alternative energy sources, such as wind or solar power, in an effort to curb the greenhouse gases that contribute to global warming.

Voters in Washington State approved an initiative in November requiring that 15 percent of the state's electricity come from renewable sources by 2020. Earlier last fall, California became the first state in the nation to enact a cap on greenhouse-gas emissions, with a plan to reduce emissions to 1990 levels by 2020.

More states could follow suit this year. New Mexico Governor Bill Richardson last month endorsed an ambitious new plan released by a state climate-advisory group, which lays out nearly 70 recommendations for cutting New Mexico's greenhouse-gas emissions, including increased mileage standards, greater use of renewable energy sources and stricter building codes.

Similar measures could be on the table this year in New Jersey, where Governor Jon Corzine has identified global warming as a top priority, and in Colorado, where incoming Governor Bill Ritter stressed alternative energy in his election-night acceptance speech. In Alaska, a climate-change study panel appointed by the legislature last year will present its preliminary findings in March.

States also have been trying to encourage federal caps on greenhouse gases. Last month, a coalition of a dozen states, led by Massachusetts and California, argued before the U.S. Supreme Court that the federal government has the right and responsibility to regulate carbon dioxide, a leading greenhouse gas, under the Clean Air Act. If the court rules that the feds don't have the right to regulate CO2, it could stymie state efforts to do so. The court could also determine, however, that while the Clean Air Act does empower the U.S. EPA to regulate carbon dioxide, it doesn't require such regulation. Under those circumstances, states would be freer to pass greenhouse-gas regulations on their own.

REAL ID

While states are leading the way in many policy areas because of gridlock at the federal level, there's one major issue facing states that's been driven by Congress: The REAL ID Act, passed in 2005, sets strict new standards for state identification cards, such as driver's licenses.

The act doesn't actually require states to make changes, but residents of states that don't comply with the standards won't be able to use their driver's licenses as a valid form of ID to board planes, enter federal buildings or receive federal services such as Social Security. Thus, many states are viewing REAL ID as an unfunded mandate. And with a looming May 2008 deadline and a staggering price tag—some have estimated states' costs at more than $11 billion—this is an issue that demands legislators' attention.

The act will require individuals to provide a host of documentation—a photo ID as well as proof of date of birth, Social Security number, address and citizenship—in order to get a driver's license. States will then be required to authenticate that data, make digital copies of the documents, archive them in a database and then make that database available—securely—to other states.

It's no small order, and it requires resources beyond the means of most states' current DMVs. But the most frustrating aspect for many states is that they have been waiting more than a year for the Homeland Security Department to release detailed requirements of the act's provisions.

The anticipated magnitude of these requirements and the relatively short deadline has led many experts to assume the federal government will ultimately have to push back the deadline or scrap certain aspects of the act. But that doesn't mean REAL ID won't be an important issue for states this year.

Governor Phil Bredesen recently told reporters he wants to set aside money so Tennessee can become compliant with the new regulations. "This is going to be one of those things where half of the states are never going to comply remotely with some schedule, and they're going to end up pushing it back," he said. "But I'd like not to be one of those causing that pushing it back."

EARLY EDUCATION

Several states will be focusing on early childhood education initiatives this year. Twenty states don't have comprehensive full-day kindergarten, but lawmakers in many of those places will be exploring that option. Nevada, New Jersey, Oregon and Washington will debate expanding their kindergarten programs to include every public school in the state.

Many states start by offering full-day kindergarten programs at at-risk schools. Last month, Indiana Governor Mitch Daniels announced a plan to start a full-day kindergarten program for the state's neediest children. If legislators approve his proposal, every Indiana child who qualifies for free or reduced-priced lunches could begin attending all-day kindergarten this August.

Lawmakers in other states will be discussing even earlier education opportunities. Pre-kindergarten programs have become increasingly popular in recent years. Forty states now have some form of publicly funded Pre-K program, and that number is likely to increase this year, according to Libby Doggett, executive director of Pre-K Now, an advocacy group. State-level spending on Pre-K has increased by $1 billion in the past two years alone, with states in the South providing the most funding and access. Most of the 10 states without Pre-K programs are in the Upper Midwest.

Existing programs are likely to be expanded. Leaders in Illinois, Kansas, Massachusetts, Oregon and Tennessee have identified early education as a priority. Last year was the first time in at least five years that no state decreased funding for its Pre-K program. The vast majority increased funding. That dedication represents a turning point, advocates say: States are increasingly viewing Pre-K as a part of the mainstream education system.

ROADS AND BRIDGES

Infrastructure maintenance is a perennial issue for states, but this year could mark a redoubled effort to improve their roads and bridges. With hefty budget surpluses in many places, states will be working to chip away at their backlog of maintenance needs. "Because of budgetary shortfalls, particularly during the recession in the early part of this decade, there was a certain amount of raiding of highway trust funds," says Jennifer Gavin, of the American Association of State Highway and Transportation Officials. "Now, though, with more cash on hand, states are returning to their maintenance needs."

In many states, those maintenance needs are daunting. Colorado's proposed transportation spending next year, for example, falls $1.5 billion short of what it estimates is required to maintain and improve its roads and bridges. The state's outgoing transportation director, Tom Norton, met with legislative budget leaders last month and told them they must begin to consider new ways to increase the amount of money available for transportation.

Massachusetts faces an equally serious maintenance backlog, according to one budget analyst, who says the state's focus on Boston's Big Dig project has led to deferred maintenance issues elsewhere in the state. Louisiana, still grappling with post-[Hurricane] Katrina repairs and a labor shortage, has a staggering $13 billion backlog of maintenance needs. Governor Kathleen Blanco has asked the legislature for $400 million to begin addressing the backlog, most of which predates Katrina.

In Pennsylvania, the amount needed to fix the state's transportation infrastructure exceeds $1.6 billion, according to a state transportation commission report released in November. It recommended new revenue from increases in the state gasoline tax and motor vehicle registration fees. But the commonwealth may turn to a more novel approach: privatization. Illinois and Indiana made headlines last year by leasing toll roads to private companies.... Last month, Pennsylvania Governor Ed Rendell announced interest in a similar solution for the Pennsylvania Turnpike. "The first job on roads, bridges and highways is to repair and properly maintain what we have," Rendell said. "That's not being done."

BUSINESS TAX REFORM

Some states will be debating whether to restructure the way they tax corporations. In Michigan, though, the question won't be whether, but how. Lawmakers there voted last August to repeal the Single Business Tax, which they criticized as too complex and inequitable—one-third of the tax was paid by just .02 percent of businesses in the state. But the tax provided the state with $1.9 billion per year. The legislature scrapped it without a plan for filling that revenue gap, so replacing the lost funding will be a top priority this year. Governor Jennifer Granholm submitted a replacement tax plan in late November, but legislators said they would wait until the new session to discuss their options.

"They're definitely going to be spending a lot of time on this in Michigan," says Joseph Crosby, legislative director of the Council On State Taxation. Other states won't be focusing on the issue quite as specifically, he predicts. "But we'll see business taxes being a larger or smaller component of tax reform discussions in general, depending on the state."

In North Carolina, a newly formed State and Local Fiscal Modernization Study Commission will be examining ways to completely restructure the state's revenue system, including business taxes. A similar panel was created in Georgia last year. Kansas, Kentucky and Louisiana are likely to look at modest changes aimed at business-tax relief. Ohio and Texas, which both passed sweeping changes to their tax structures in the past two years, will probably be "tweaking" their plans this year, Crosby says.

Pennsylvania lawmakers could take up the issue, especially if Governor Ed Rendell reintroduces a business-tax reform plan he pushed unsuccessfully in 2005. In Oregon, there's been talk of altering the state's corporate-income tax Kicker Law, which returns unanticipated business-tax revenue, and instead keeping it for the state's rainy-day fund.

GAY RIGHTS

Gay marriage is not a live issue this year in most states: Forty-five of them have taken legislative action to prevent same-sex marriage. And 27 of those have passed constitutional amendments limiting marriage to one man and one woman—seven of them in the most recent elections. Court challenges against gay-marriage bans failed last year in several places, including more liberal states such as Washington and New York.

Instead, legislative wrangling will revolve around other rights and benefits for same-sex couples. A New Jersey Supreme Court ruling last fall gave legislators six months to determine how exactly to define gay spousal benefits. That decision mandated equal rights for gay and straight couples but charged the legislature with delineating the specifics. In other states this year, legislators may find themselves forced to act on similar court orders. Legal challenges are pending in California, Connecticut, Iowa, Maryland and Oklahoma.

Alaska legislators have so far defied a court order to establish health benefits for same-sex partners of state employees—despite meeting in a special session in November to discuss the issue. The deadline for implementing the benefits was January 1, so this will certainly be a hot-button issue for legislators this year. Elsewhere, states may consider bans on adoption by gay couples. At least 16 states discussed constitutional amendments to ban such adoptions last year, but none made it to the ballot. In Arkansas, incoming Governor Mike Beebe has called for reinstating the state's ban on same-sex adoptions, which was struck down by a federal court in 2004.

HOME FORECLOSURES

There's one issue that might not yet be on legislators' radar but that they may soon find themselves forced to confront. Home foreclosure rates across the country have skyrocketed over the past year, as housing markets have cooled and buyers who only barely qualified for mortgages have defaulted on home loans.

Nevada's foreclosure rate in last year's third quarter jumped nearly 240 percent from the year before. Minnesota's rate increased 212 percent; California and Kansas each saw jumps of about 170 percent. In Colorado, which has the nation's highest rate, the state reported one new foreclosure for every 127 households. Nationally, foreclosure rates are up over 40 percent.

Predatory lending practices are partially to blame. About half the states have passed laws targeting the practice, in which lenders impose unfair or abusive loan terms on borrowers. More states will be looking at these laws this year. Minnesota's incoming attorney general, for example, has said that targeting lending abuses will be her No. 1 priority.

Much of the current rash of foreclosures, however, can be attributed to the booming popularity of so-called "exotic" or nontraditional mortgages. These include no-money-down loans, interest-only loans and adjustable-rate mortgages.

To combat foreclosure rates, then, consumer-protection advocates will be pushing for broader laws that incorporate the concept of "suitability" or "fiduciary duty." These types of laws hold lenders responsible for providing a loan that's in a borrower's best interest. States will be looking to Rhode Island and Ohio, where lending laws that just took effect this month include provisions that approach suitability standards. Ohio's new law, for example, prohibits state-licensed mortgage brokers from issuing "unfair" or "unconscionable" loans.

40

Tough Act to Follow

Larry Morandi

As the federal government wrestles with its role in controlling greenhouse gases, states attack global warming.

Massachusetts is suing the Environmental Protection Agency to force regulation of greenhouse gas emissions in a case that is before the U.S. Supreme Court. At issue is whether the Clean Air Act requires EPA to control these gases, which contribute to global warming. States are split on either side of the issue in *Massachusetts v. EPA,* with 11 states siding with Massachusetts and 10 with the federal government.

The Clean Air Act requires EPA to "prescribe...standards applicable to the emission of any air pollutant from...new motor vehicles or new motor vehicle engines, which in [EPA's] judgment cause, or contribute to, air pollution which may reasonably be anticipated to endanger public health or welfare." EPA contends that this language does not require it to regulate greenhouse gas emissions because any standards "will not meaningfully address an air quality issue like global climate change, which is caused primarily by... emissions from outside of the United States."

EPA also argues that the petitioners lack legal standing to sue because they have not suffered a particular injury that can be remedied by the court. The petitioners counter that left unchecked, greenhouse gas emissions will cause global warming that will trigger rising sea levels, reducing states' coastlines and increasing flooding. If the high court determines that there is no standing, it need not consider any other arguments. But if it concludes that the petitioners have standing, it can decide whether or not EPA has the authority to regulate emissions. The final decision is expected in June.

Regardless what the Court decides, several states have taken the initiative and adopted policies aimed at curbing greenhouse gas emissions (see April 2006 issue of *State Legislatures*). The most

From *State Legislatures,*
March 2007

sweeping new legislation passed in California last session. Sponsored by Assembly Speaker Fabian Núñez, the California Global Warming Solutions Act is the first enforceable statewide program to cap all emissions from major industries and penalize those that do not comply.

The act cuts carbon emissions to 1990 levels by the year 2020—a 25 percent reduction. The California Air Resources Board is to develop a program for greenhouse gas emissions reporting and to monitor and enforce compliance. The board is to adopt measures for reducing emissions that are cost-effective and technologically feasible, which may include a cap-and-trade program.

The potential impacts of global warming on California—vulnerability of the coastline to rising sea levels, reductions in snowpack essential to the state's water supply, and public health threats from intense heat waves—

are severe, Núñez says. As someone who grew up in a poor urban neighborhood, he is pleased with the economic opportunities available in the new law. "We are sending a clear market sign to employ clean technology," he says, emphasizing technology that can create jobs and generate economic benefits for the state. Noting Governor Arnold Schwarzenegger's enthusiastic support for the bill, Núñez says, "there is no partisan divide on global warming."

Critics of state actions to combat global warming argue that only a national approach can have any real impact. But if California were a country, it would be the 12th largest emitter of greenhouse gases. Ten other states have adopted California's tough air pollution standards for motor vehicles. Will they follow California on climate change? Perhaps the better question is, will the federal government?

41

Gung Ho for Green

Judith Crosson

Renewable energy helps states be environmentally friendly and boosts rural economic development.

J im Magagna is a Wyoming sheep farmer—one used to the rigors of living off the land. In this topsy-turvy world of high-energy prices, however, he thinks it may be time to "go green" and get his power on the ranch from an alternative source, say wind for instance.

"Never did we think we could use the wind this way. We've been putting up with it for so long," Magagna, who is also executive director of the Wyoming Stockgrowers Association, joked. But what Magagna realizes is the serious effort farmers, ranchers and others in rural communities are making to find innovative ways to cut energy costs.

"I think high energy costs have really hit home. People have a general understanding that the reason we have these high energy costs is that we are at the whim of unstable regimes, hurricanes and other factors, some out of our control. It makes people believe very strongly in the idea of energy independence," says Minnesota Senator Ellen Anderson.

It doesn't stop there. Renewable energy, struggling to find its way in the marketplace for three decades as proponents argue its benefits to the environment, may have another asset—job creation in rural areas.

"Economic development was the real driver," says Washington Senator Erik Poulsen about a bipartisan effort in 2005 that is touted as the most progressive renewable energy legislation in the country. "This is not just about clean energy," says Poulsen, chair of the Water, Energy and Environment Committee. "It is about bringing new jobs and new industries to Washington state."

From *State Legislatures*, May 2006

Washington's new laws established incentives for homeowners and small businesses who generate power with solar, wind or anaerobic digesters. Manufactures of renewable energy systems get tax breaks—bigger ones if they locate in economically depressed areas of the state.

Anderson says that if just 20 percent of the energy consumed in Minnesota were to come from renewable sources by 2020, an estimated 14,000 jobs could be created—especially in rural areas.

Renewable energy from biomass, wind, geothermal sources, solar and even ocean power, while representing a tiny share of energy capacity today, is expected to make a greater contribution to the mix in the future.

According to the federal government, renewable energy demand is expected to grow as a result of state programs such as renewable portfolio standards, technological advances and higher petroleum prices. By 2025, marketed renewable fuels are expected to grow to 9.6 quadrillion Btu's, up from 6 billion in 2004. The United States currently consumes about 100 quadrililion Btu's.

A BIG CHANGE

To make incremental changes in how America produces the energy to keep the lights on in homes, power factories and operate colossal transportation system, lawmakers, businesses, utilities and voters are going to have to stand back and look at the big picture.

It is such a major undertaking that no one should be surprised if the transition takes time.

"The system that we have works really well right now. It's not like when we changed from the horse to the auto and it was possible to see the benefits," says George Douglas, spokesman for the National Renewable Energy Laboratory. Such an undertaking requires a big change in the way the energy business is conducted and that's where state lawmakers come in.

Renewable Portfolio Standards that require a certain percentage of power to come from renewable sources may be the force needed to get the job done. Today 21 states plus the District of Columbia have some type of standard in place ranging from 1.1 percent in Arizona by 2012 to 25 percent in New York by 2013.

The biggest stumbling blocks to renewables such as wind or solar are often the electric utilities. Their highest priority is to make sure that electricity keeps flowing to residences and homes at a reasonable price.

"Utilities are looking at all sources of energy to meet their demand," says Edison Electric Institute spokesman Keith Voight. "But it has to make economic sense. The point is to provide a reliable and affordable supply. Utilities want to have the power there when the customer wants it."

THE DEMAND SIDE

And utilities had better keep their eye on the ball. The Energy Department's Energy Information Administration estimates American demand for energy to rise about 34 percent by 2030.

With televisions, VCRs, computers, microwave ovens and even electric toothbrushes sucking electricity—even when they aren't being used—energy demand outstrips increases in population.

Utilities can face penalties if they fall short of the amount of power that is required to keep on the grid, according to Richard Halvey, project manager for the clean and diversified energy initiative for the Western Governors' Association.

Governors from the western states passed a resolution calling for about 10 percent of current capacity—or about 30,000 megawatts—to come from renewable energy by 2015.

"If you look at projections for between 2005 and 2015, we will need between 50,000 and 60,000 megawatts of new capacity," Halvey says. "The governors would like about half of that to come from renewable energy."

WIND

2005 was a banner year for the wind industry, with a record 2,431 megawatts of capacity installed in 22 states at a cost of nearly $3 billion, according to the American Wind Energy Association, a trade group.

Commercial wind turbines now operate in 30 states, able to generate 9,149 megawatts of power—enough energy to power the lights, laptops, TVs, dishwashers and other appliances used by 2.3 million American homes annually.

Four new wind projects were recently completed in the Northwest, one each in Washington, Oregon, Idaho and Montana, bringing the region's production to 1,000 megawatts of new renewable energy annually, enough to power 250,000 average homes in the region, according to the Renewable Northwest Project in Portland, Ore.

Riding the Wave of Ocean Energy

Oceans cover more than 70 percent of the Earth's surface, making them both the world's largest solar collector and the world's largest machine. Not surprisingly, these are the two characteristics harnessed to produce ocean power. Ocean thermal power generates electricity using the thermal gradient between warm surface water and the colder deep ocean water. In contrast, ocean mechanical power utilizes the energy locked in the movement of waves and tides.

It is no wonder that Hawaii has become the nation's proving ground for these new technologies. "We have a constant and reliable source of energy and because we have one of the highest prices for electricity in the nation we are the perfect location for siting wave projects," says Hawaii Representative Cynthia Thielen.

The United States Navy is building a 40 kilowatt wave power station off the Marine Corps base on Oahu. Located approximately one kilometer off the coast in 30 meters of water, the data gathered from this system will support the continuing evolution of these technologies.

It is not just the U.S. military moving forward with ocean energy projects, New Jersey has a PowerBuoy™ off the coast that is already producing power. States are supporting the development of ocean energy technologies primarily through renewable portfolio standards. Coastal states and those situated in the Great Lakes region allow ocean, tidal and wave resources to qualify.

This year is shaping up to be another record breaker. "We're actually just about fully committed for '06 and '07. We are taking orders into '08," according to George Krakat, marketing communications manager for General Electric Corporation's GE Energy, the leading [manufacturer] of wind turbines in the United States.

GE Energy sold about $2 billion worth of turbines last year—a healthy share of the $16.5 billion GE's energy subsidiary garnered last year.

"Before, people thought the only control they had was turning off the lights. But now they're connecting the dots," Lisa Daniels, executive director and founder of Windustry, a nonprofit organization in Minnesota that encourages community-owned wind energy programs.

Although lease payments to farmers who allow a turbine on their land typically amount to $3,000 a year, the payoff can be better for the area if the farmer or someone else in the community owns the turbines.

The Role of Renewable Energy Consumption in the Nation's Energy Supply

Renewable energy made up 6 percent of total U.S. energy consumption, which was 97.6 quadrillion Btu in 2002. Hydroelectric energy provided 45 percent of renewable energy consumption, while nonhydroelectric energy sources collectively provided the remaining 55 percent.

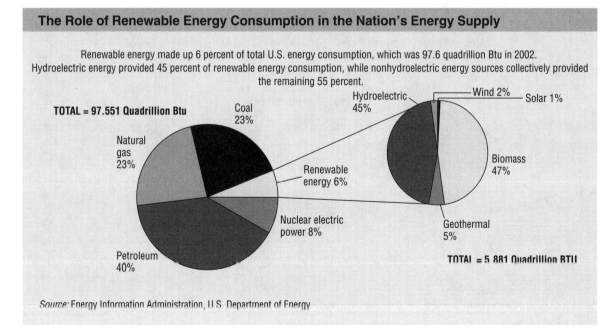

TOTAL = 97.551 Quadrillion Btu

Coal 23%
Natural gas 23%
Renewable energy 6%
Nuclear electric power 8%
Petroleum 40%

Hydroelectric 45%
Wind 2%
Solar 1%
Biomass 47%
Geothermal 5%

TOTAL = 5.881 Quadrillion BTU

Source: Energy Information Administration, U.S. Department of Energy

Renewables Depend on Federal Tax Credit

If there is one thing business people want from government rules and regulations, it's consistency and predictability. Developers need to know the true cost of a new technology. Bankers deciding on a loan application need to know if a tax credit will be around for the term of the loan. Manufacturers who plan to increase capacity for a cutting-edge technology want to know how long a tax credit will run.

But the history of the U.S. Production Tax Credit has been an up and down adventure full of extensions and uncertainty, resulting in a boom and bust industry, especially for wind power.

The federal production tax credit rewards electricity renewable energy production rather than investment. The program started with the Energy Policy Act of 1992 with a 1.8 cent per kilowatt-hour credit for the first 10 years of production for a wind project, but has since been widened to include other forms of renewable energy.

The act was originally scheduled to end on June 30, 1999; it was later extended to the end of 2001, the end of 2003, 2005, and now 2007.

"The federal production tax credit comes and goes," says Senator Ellen Anderson of Minnesota. Such uncertainty is not the way to ensure a consistent stable market for new technologies, she contends. "There are so many federal laws that pick winners and losers. Fossil fuels and nuclear have been the winners for decades," she says.

Now it is time for the renewables to get that leg up.

And business agrees. "It would sure be helpful for all those involved to have a more stable policy on that," George Krakat, marketing communications manager for GE Energy, says.

The Iowa Policy Project estimates that for every 1,000 megawatt wind generation facility, about $17,300 stays in a community or state annually when the project is owned by out-of-state interests. But the figure jumps to $167,200 when the wind project is owned by a local community member, research associate Terry Galluzzo says.

The biggest challenge to installation of renewable energy systems is the upfront costs, which are higher than for traditional forms of energy. "But states as well as the federal government can help with these programs," Galluzzo says. Iowa provides interest-free loans for up to 50 percent of the project with a 20-year repayment

States with Renewable Portfolio Standards

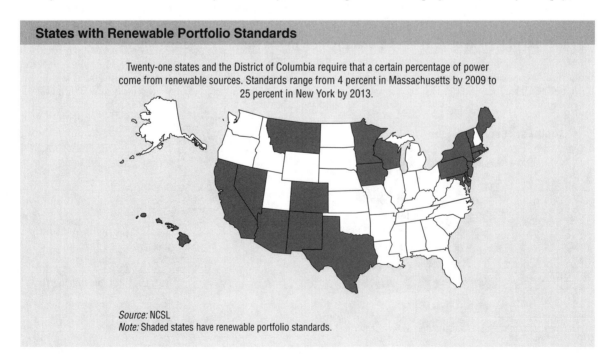

Twenty-one states and the District of Columbia require that a certain percentage of power come from renewable sources. Standards range from 4 percent in Massachusetts by 2009 to 25 percent in New York by 2013.

Source: NCSL
Note: Shaded states have renewable portfolio standards.

plan. And once wind, solar or hydro systems are up and running, there are no fuel costs to operate them.

Payments to local landowners, which then add to a county's tax revenues, begin to tell the story. The Klondike Wind Farm in Sherman County, Ore., added $321,205 in the 2002–2003 tax year—for a 10 percent increase over the previous year, according to the Renewable Northwest Project. The added tax revenue meant an extra $113,000 for schools, nearly $70,000 for roads and $115,000 for the general fund.

Although wind energy is making progress around the globe, a problem continues with getting approval for siting turbines.

Troy Gagliano, senior policy analyst with the Renewable Northwest Project, says the state of Washington has come up with a plan that answers many of the problems with siting. An area considered for a wind project must first undergo an environmental assessment and action can then be planned to avoid problems. If an area is special, a developer can proceed with an offset program, setting aside an equal or sometimes even greater acreage at another location. A post-construction technical advisory committee with representatives from the community, the developer, the utility and wildlife officials is also created.

"What makes Washington unique is that environmental protection is a major consideration and it gives the developers consistency," Gagliano says.

GEOTHERMAL

One of the most intriguing renewable energy sources is geothermal—the heat from the earth's core.

Geothermal projects operate in four western states, California, Hawaii, Nevada and Utah, producing 2,700 megawatts of power. But a study conducted by the Western Governors' Association figures that as many as 11 western states could line up for similar projects.

"The earth is very hot. There is a lot of resource, if we could capture it, with a lot less risk up front," says Karl Gawell, executive director of the Geothermal Energy Association.

If geothermal projects were expanded in the Western United States, 100,000 jobs, including 23,949 full-time, would be created, Gawell's group estimates.

There is scope for both large and small projects. Geothermal sources with lesser heat potential can still power small projects such as heating a farm building to house livestock or the capitol complex in Boise, Idaho, Gawell says.

SOLAR

Solar may be one of the best-known forms of renewable energy, but it lags far behind other forms because of the high costs to install it. That is unfortunate, because the immense power of the sun could take care of all the world's energy needs.

"The payoff is a much longer period of time. Electricity remains an extremely cheap commodity," says NREL's Douglas. The reason people talk so excitedly about solar power is its "potential," he says. There are important forces behind solar. Earlier this year the California Public Utilities Commission approved the California Solar Initiative to install 3,000 megawatts panels to power homes and businesses over the next 11 years.

Proponents of solar energy contend that a portion must be set aside for it within renewable portfolio standards. Of the 21 states plus the District of Columbia that have standards, five require that a share of the renewable energy created come from solar.

Because solar is more expensive than other renewables, especially wind, it could be tossed out of the equation if set-asides were not implemented, says Jon Miller, executive director of the Oregon Solar Energy Industries Association, whose members are installers, small business contractors, manufacturers and distributors. "Whenever you do a renewable portfolio standard you're entering into the market place. Lawmakers have to be extremely careful. You could do harm to solar by shifting the focus of utilities to meet their requirements. You end up messing around with the marketplace," he says.

In Colorado, voters approved a ballot measure in 2004 that requires 10 percent of the electric energy in the state to come from renewable energy by 2015. Solar has to account for 4 percent of the renewable figure and large utilities must give a $2 per kilowatt—up to 100 kilowatts—rebate to residents who install solar power in their homes. Installing solar in the home generally costs between $8 and $9 a kilowatt.

Homeowners interested in installing a solar system first determine how much of their electric power they want from solar. "Someone could install a very small system or a very large system. In the Northwest, people offset 30 to 40 percent of their electric use," Miller says.

Colin Murchie, director of government affairs at Solar Energy Industries Association, says solar will cost consumers about as much as their cars: "Figure the cost of a car. If you have a $15,000 car, it would cost about $15,000 to install solar in your home. If you have a $25,000 car, figure $25,000," he says. Residents with fancier cars probably have bigger homes and more appliances in their homes.

With the participation of renewable energy still a tiny share of America's energy pie, proponents can get discouraged. But there may be hope on the horizon.

42

Hydro Defense

Tom Arrandale

Despite spending millions on security upgrades, drinking-water systems are still vulnerable to sabotage.

For a few hours last spring, Blackstone, Massachusetts, thought it might be dealing with many communities' most dreaded post-9/11 nightmare: In the dead of night, intruders scaled a 14-foot security fence topped with barbed wire, demolished an electrical panel and smashed their way through a 2-inch-thick steel door. Then they scrambled atop the town's year-old, 1.3-million-gallon water tower in a remote wooded area and kicked in its protective fiberglass cover. When the break-in was discovered, local officials had no choice but to assume the worst: Terrorists had poisoned the drinking water that supplies 9,000 businesses and homes in this community 50 miles southwest of Boston.

As it turned out, the perpetrators were three Blackstone teenagers bent on mischief. At the worst, it's suspected that two 15-year-old boys urinated into the tank during the caper; the *Boston Herald* couldn't resist running a headline about Blackstone's water tank "whiz kids." But state and local officials didn't find the situation so amusing. By the time the teens were heard bragging about their exploits the next day, Massachusetts environmental regulators had issued a "do-not-drink" order shutting down the town's water system. Schools and local businesses closed for two days, and Blackstone officials spent more than $40,000 to flush and backwash the tank, repair the facility, and buy bottled water for students. "Our system was not contaminated, but it was compromised," Raymond W. Houle Jr., Blackstone's town manager at the time, remarked after the incident.

The Blackstone episode made clear that the nation's drinking-water systems remain at risk for more malevolent assaults that could truly threaten the lives of thousands, if not millions, of Americans. But after spending millions of dollars to build security fences, install

From *Governing*, April 2007

tougher locks, hire armed guards and foil intrusion by computer hackers, water utility operators acknowledge they can't completely protect all their water sources, reservoirs, storage tanks, pumping stations, treatment plants and thousands of miles of pipes against sabotage.

In the federal Bioterrorism Act of 2002, Congress ordered 8,600 community water systems that supply 3,330 or more people apiece to conduct formal assessments of weaknesses that could expose their facilities to deliberate attack. Federal law doesn't mandate that water systems actually take steps to improve security; Congress last year exempted treatment plants from a new law regulating how chemical facilities safeguard dangerous chemicals such as the chlorine that utilities stockpile to disinfect drinking water.

To help New England's numerous small community systems, the U.S. Environmental Protection Agency's Boston office circulates a "Top 10" list of steps to protect drinking water supplies. Those measures advise local utility operators to draft emergency response plans, identify alternative water supplies, stay in touch with local police and sheriff deputies, post emergency numbers at pump houses, install lights around treatment plants, fence and lock wellheads and manholes and "do not leave keys in equipment or vehicles at any time."

RAISING THE ALARM

Those may reflect only common sense, but in major cities that are the most likely targets, big metropolitan water agencies have been forced to take more elaborate precautions to protect their extensive and technologically vulnerable facilities. Since 2001, for instance, the Los Angeles Department of Water and Power has nearly doubled its security force, increased water testing 50 percent, bought two new helicopters to patrol aqueducts and pipelines, and begun fingerprinting and investigating the backgrounds of all its employees. New York City's Department of Environmental Protection spent $100 million on fencing, security cameras and five new precinct stations as the city tripled a special police force that guards 19 upstate reservoirs and three protected lakes in a 1,900-square-mile watershed that supplies water to 9 million people.

This February, New York City beefed up its patrols after a pipe bomb was discovered 3,000 miles away in the California Aqueduct, which carries water to Southern California. Officials concluded a fisherman attempting to illegally stun fish probably had placed the bomb, reports Pete Weisser, an information officer for the Department of Water Resources. "DWR does not discuss security issues in detail," Weisser adds. "Along with many other utilities and water agencies, DWR has increased security and today regulates access and monitors activities at its facilities."

As Blackstone and other small rural communities have discovered, that's not an easy task. In the past few years, vandals have also broken into the Volusia County, Florida, water treatment plant, and a storage tank serving 400 customers in two Washington State subdivisions. Water was shut off to Vermont's Lyndon State College and 200 nearby homes after five rugby players pried the cover off the town's water tank. "It's not that difficult to get up on top of a water tower. Every high school kid in the country has done that during his senior year, usually to write his girlfriend's name on it," says Ralph Mullinix, the water and power director for Loveland, Colorado. "You can harden your perimeter around your key facilities, but the fact is that water systems are very vulnerable. All you have to do is go upstream and put something in the river just above the intake." Mullinix says.

Municipal drinking water is delivered through such an extensive array of natural watercourses and manmade facilities—from the headwaters to household taps, and then back to rivers and lakes through sewage and stormwater systems—that securing supplies against every intruder will never be practical. That leaves government officials exploring ways to detect contaminants that saboteurs might pour into the system and immediately set off alarms to keep people from drinking them. For years, Loveland's treatment plant has kept a tankfull of trout swimming in its supply that are susceptible to damage from chemical substances. Three times, Mullinix says, the trout began dying right after farmers upstream dumped copper sulfate to kill algae in irrigation canals draining into the Big Thompson River that supplies domestic water for the city's 60,000 residents. That may be a primitive alarm, "like the canary in the mine," he says, "but it does tell you something."

Along these same lines, New York City, San Francisco and Washington, D.C., now monitor water supplies with more sophisticated technology developed 20 years ago by the U.S. military. Water agencies keep common bluegill fish swimming in aquariums filled with city water—with the chlorine removed—and continuously monitor their respiratory behavior through electrodes and complex computer software. The system calls an alert if six of the eight fish start showing signs of stress that might stem from toxic materials like cyanide, pesticides or solvents. The bluegills have proven sensitive enough to detect reservoir sediments that divers kicked up 40 miles away, and the fish are regarded as more reliable than currently available man-made sensors.

Government and private researchers are working on more sophisticated sensors, but the prospects are hard to judge. Loveland agreed to try out a monitoring system designed by Colorado State University engineers and a California-based company, but Congress has yet to fund the project. While keeping the details hush-hush, EPA's water security research program recently confirmed that the Greater Cincinnati Water Works has begun testing a computerized detection system that Sandia National Laboratories in New Mexico developed. Whether those fixes pan out or not, "that's a Band-Aid solution," contends Kevin Morley, a security expert for the American Water Works Association. "At the end of the day, whether bluegills or a black box tells you there's something in the water, the question is 'What do I do now?'"

ALL-HAZARDS RESPONSE

Water-utility operators are now concluding they'd better start planning to deal with the consequences when their facilities unexpectedly get taken out. The threat of terrorism created public fear that has spurred Congress to fund homeland security programs, but local utilities have recognized that natural disasters are likely to pose more devastating threats to both drinking water and sewage disposal.

A decade ago, California's water agencies formed a mutual aid pact to help each other cope with damaged systems. Florida utilities forged their own agreement after the 2004 hurricane season; Texas adopted a plan after Hurricanes Katrina and Rita two years ago, and Morley says utilities in at least six more states are circulating their own plans to come to the aid of stricken community water systems, regardless of how the damage is caused. "In the water sector," Morley says, "there's been a recognition that there should be much more planning for resiliency: How do you take a hit and keep on ticking?" Planning for such "all hazards" response is catching on, and federal and state regulatory agencies continue working with AWWA and other industry organizations to devise security benchmarks to determine "how do we know we are better off than we were five years ago?" notes Bridget O'Grady, the policy and regulatory affairs director for the Association of State Drinking Water Administrators. While natural calamities may be more likely than terrorism, there's a resignation among regulators and utility managers alike that a terrorist group or a disgruntled individual could be capable of deliberately contaminating somebody's water supply—and that no community can afford to let its guard down. As Elizabeth Hunt, Vermont's drinking water planning chief, points out, "after 9/11, we can't just assume that it's only some kids goofing off."

Text Credits

Page	Credit
5	From *State Legislatures* magazine, copyrighted by National Conference of State Legislatures 2006–07.
9	From *State Legislatures* magazine, copyrighted by National Conference of State Legislatures 2006–07.
12	From *State Legislatures* magazine, copyrighted by National Conference of State Legislatures 2006–07.
15	Copyright 2006 by Oxford University Press—Journals. Reproduced with permission of Oxford University Press—Journals in the format Textbook via Copyright Clearance Center.
30	From *State Legislatures* magazine, copyrighted by National Conference of State Legislatures 2006–07.
35	From *State Legislatures* magazine, copyrighted by National Conference of State Legislatures 2006–07.
38	From *State Legislatures* magazine, copyrighted by National Conference of State Legislatures 2006–07.
41	Reprinted with permission of *Campaigns & Elections.*
43	From *State Legislatures* magazine, copyrighted by National Conference of State Legislatures 2006–07.
56	Reprinted with permission of *Campaigns & Elections.*
62	Reprinted with permission of *Campaigns & Elections.*
64	Reprinted with author's permission.
71	From *State Legislatures* magazine, copyrighted by National Conference of State Legislatures 2006–07.
75	From *State Legislatures* magazine, copyrighted by National Conference of State Legislatures 2006–07.